I0605472

# IT'S NO WONDER

**Also by Dr. Margena A. Christian**

*Empire: The House That John H. Johnson Built*
*(The Life & Legacy of Pioneering Publishing Magnate)*

# IT'S NO WONDER

## The Life and Times of Motown's Legendary Songwriter Sylvia Moy

MARGENA A. CHRISTIAN

DA CAPO

NEW YORK BOSTON

Copyright © 2026 by Margena Christian

Cover design by Elizabeth McConaughy-Oliver. Cover photo by Gilles Petard/Getty Images. Cover copyright © 2026 by Hachette Book Group, Inc.

Hachette Book Group supports the right to free expression and the value of copyright. The purpose of copyright is to encourage writers and artists to produce the creative works that enrich our culture.

The scanning, uploading, and distribution of this book without permission is a theft of the author's intellectual property. If you would like permission to use material from the book (other than for review purposes), please contact permissions@hbgusa.com. Thank you for your support of the author's rights.

Da Capo Press
Hachette Book Group
1290 Avenue of the Americas
New York, NY 10104
grandcentralpublishing.com
@grandcentralpub

First Edition: February 2026

Da Capo Press is an imprint of Grand Central Publishing. The Da Capo Press name and logo are registered trademarks of Hachette Book Group, Inc.

The publisher is not responsible for websites (or their content) that are not owned by the publisher.

The Hachette Speakers Bureau provides a wide range of authors for speaking events. To find out more, go to hachettespeakersbureau.com or email HachetteSpeakers@hbgusa.com.

Da Capo Press books may be purchased in bulk for business, educational, or promotional use. For information, please contact your local bookseller or the Hachette Book Group Special Markets Department at special.markets@hbgusa.com.

Library of Congress Cataloging-in-Publication Data

Names: Christian, Margena A. author
Title: It's no wonder : the life and times of Motown's legendary songwriter Sylvia Moy / Margena A. Christian.
Description: First edition. | New York : Da Capo, 2026. | Includes bibliographical references and index.
Identifiers: LCCN 2025038646 | ISBN 9780306833632 hardcover | ISBN 9780306833656 ebook
Subjects: LCSH: Moy, Sylvia | Sound recording executives and producers—United States—Biography | Wonder, Stevie | Motown Record Corporation
Classification: LCC ML429.M815 C47 2026 | DDC 781.49/092—dc23/eng/20250912
LC record available at https://lccn.loc.gov/2025038646

ISBNs: 978-0-306-83363-2 (hardcover); 978-0-306-83365-6 (ebook)

Printed in Canada

MRQ-T

10 9 8 7 6 5 4 3 2 1

*Dedicated to my father, Edward Christian Sr., and my mother, Marion Christian*

# Contents

# IT'S NO WONDER

# INTRODUCTION

During the nineties, dozens of television talk shows heated up the airwaves, but none seemed to put the sizzle in the steak more than *Geraldo*. Hosted by award-winning reporter and former attorney Geraldo Rivera, the New York–based weekly syndicated show's tabloid structure quickly established a reputation for itself as must-see TV. Viewers were constantly left wanting more, because it always hit the bull's-eye: delivering a hearty daily dose of high drama, jaw-dropping revelations, and controversial guests.

The Friday, October 19, 1990, episode does not disappoint. It's titled "The Women of Motown," and on it legendary singers and songwriters who worked at the African American, Detroit-based record label when it first began share their memories about their time at the trailblazing company founded by Berry Gordy Jr. in 1959.[1]

Filmed in front of a live studio audience, the show features viewers witnessing a panel that includes a plethora of key players, including: Mable John, older sister of singer Little Willie John and the first female artist signed to Gordy's Tamla record label (which later became Motown); Raynoma "Ray" Gordy Singleton, Gordy's second wife, who cofounded the label with him and authored the then newly released book *The Untold Story: Berry, Me, and Motown*; Janie Bradford, one of Motown's early female songwriters, who cowrote Tamla's first hit, "Money (That's What I Want)," with Gordy; Kim Weston, a singer best known for "It Takes Two," the feel-good duet with Marvin Gaye; Gladys Horton, a member of the Marvelettes, who recorded "Please Mr. Postman," which was Motown's first #1 song to top the pop and R&B charts; and Syreeta Wright, a songwriter and singer with a whistle register who was once married to Stevie Wonder.

Martha Reeves, lead singer of the Vandellas and known for the songs "Jimmy Mack" and "Dancing in the Street," is introduced by Rivera last. She makes a grand entrance to applause by gracefully sauntering out as her group's classic "Heat Wave" plays in the background. Reeves takes her seat on the far left end of the row, where she is seated next to Sylvia Moy, the lone in-house songwriter and producer featured on the panel. Though she's best known for her work with Stevie Wonder, Sylvia also wrote the biggest hit of Kim Weston's career, "It Takes Two," and penned several songs for Reeves, including "My Baby Loves Me" and "Honey Chile."

Conservatively dressed in business attire, Sylvia sports a royal blue blazer, black slacks, and two-toned flat shoes. The long hair she had when she first came to Motown in 1964 continues to cascade down her shoulders and back. During this appearance, however, Sylvia's luxurious locks, featuring feathered bangs, are now colored auburn.

Reeves explains how she got her start at Motown as the secretary of Weston's ex-husband, William Stevenson, aka "Mickey," the label's first A&R head. Reeves goes on to talk about how she was part of a wonderful movement with Gordy as a true visionary leader, one who possessed a one-of-a-kind knack for gathering the most talented people in Detroit. Sylvia looks at Reeves and nods her head in agreement.

When asked about Ray's book and her take on Gordy, Reeves clarifies to Rivera that she knew Gordy personally but not intimately, so there's a lot that she can't really speak about. Rivera, the audience, and the panelists alike clap while laughing at the shrewdness of Reeves's response. Sylvia, with clasped hands around her left knee, tells Reeves with a slight smile, "Very well put." Reeves continues going on about how Gordy is one of the most talented geniuses she's ever met and how much everyone loved him.

Gladys Horton, the Marvelettes' lead singer, echoes Reeves's sentiments about Gordy and feels compelled to remind everyone that women are to be recognized, because "behind every great man, there is a lady." The panelists and audience members clap in agreement before Rivera asks Horton if that statement is intended to acknowledge Ray's role in building Motown's history, which Horton confirms. Horton then adds that Gordy had a lot of good energy coming from all the ladies.

Be that as it may, *Geraldo* didn't come to be a top-rated talk show by playing it safe. So, Rivera does what he does best—he plays devil's advocate. Upon spotting a crack in the foundation, he flat-out questions whether it was tough for a female writer or producer and deliberately addresses Sylvia by name to respond. Before she can get a word out, songwriter Janie Bradford interjects, "No! Not at Motown."

Without hesitation or missing a beat, Sylvia becomes feisty. She quickly snaps back and puts Bradford in her place. "Now wait, Janie," Sylvia says firmly, all while maintaining eye contact with Bradford. Caught off guard by Sylvia's spontaneous response, the panelists and audience members erupt into laughter and clap again. Steadfast and intentional, Bradford does not seem to care. She goes on about how everyone was given an equal chance at Motown. Bradford, it should be noted, is a member of "the first five," a group of musicians and songwriters who were there at Motown since its inception. She also is the only woman—along with Gordy, singer and songwriter Smokey Robinson, songwriter Brian Holland, and singer Robert Bateman—to hold that distinction.

Rivera allows Bradford to finish her thought before saying, "I want to hear Sylvia's side of the story." Sylvia obliges. She reveals how, when she arrived at Motown in 1964, "it was hard for women producers at that time" and admits that "there was some sexism there." She quickly adds, "But it was worse at other companies," before immediately expressing how much she appreciated Ray's book, which brought renewed attention to the fact that Motown was a family with Berry Gordy as the father figure. Sylvia also points out that there were others at the company who "helped to make it what it was," which Ray's book affirms.

In fact, Sylvia herself was one of those quiet forces who helped drive the machine at Hitsville U.S.A. with her lyrical mastery. As an independent thinker, Sylvia felt that unless a person walked in her shoes, *no one* had the right to try to derail or detract from her opinions, especially not on a national TV show.

Ever collected and poised, Sylvia stresses how proud and thankful she is for her Motown experience. She continues, "It was great but there were also some other—" before once again being abruptly cut off, this time mid-sentence by Bradford, who talks over Sylvia, shedding light on how the year of Sylvia's arrival marked a moment of great change at Motown. Super producers like Holland-Dozier-Holland had come into their own along with A&R head Mickey Stevenson, clarifies Bradford. Chuckling and pointing her finger to Stevenson's ex-wife, singer Kim Weston, Bradford concludes, "You had her husband, who is still a male chauvinist pig."

Weston, laughing and interjecting, says, "Now, wait a minute. What everybody *else* was." Bradford goes on to say that the fellas were still developing and strengthening their skills when Sylvia came along, "wanting to equal the guys." Bradford admits that "had some women in the beginning progressed with the guys, it would have been different." Weston, steady in her defense of her ex-husband, adds, "But this same guy that was a chauvinist pig was the one that brought Sylvia there and gave her the opportunity."

Most of the panelists continue to laugh and clap at this remark. Martha Reeves isn't in the camera's view, but everyone responds favorably to the assessment except for Ray, Horton, and Sylvia. Appearing to simply go with the flow, Sylvia nods her head once again in agreement. Ray, who details in her book some of the problems that plagued Sylvia in her attempts to be a producer, sits at the opposite end of the row but leans forward to glance at Sylvia.

A subtle look of disdain covers Sylvia's face like a mask. Luckily, she is adept at possessing a type of grace under fire, but she's never had to carry out this delicate balancing act for all the world to see. As such, Sylvia plays her role patiently and sits stoically as she peers straight ahead into the audience as they clap robustly. Then, Rivera signals for the show to cut to a commercial break.

Just like that, it is over. The curtain closes on Sylvia Moy's first and last national television appearance where she discusses Motown. Afterward, she goes through her usual routine for calming herself down when nervous. She walks out of the studio and promptly lights up a cigarette.

At this point in her life, nothing came as a surprise to Sylvia anymore. There had long been gender barrier aspects of the recording industry that echoed societal norms and restricted women from certain parts of the studio. As a result, women were not conditioned to see themselves as songwriters or producers because they were deemed as merely consumers and not creators. Black women did not even *factor* into the equation in a world that limited and defined their scope of possibilities, solely because of the color of their skin.

Accordingly, writing songs, playing an instrument, or producing records was not deemed acceptable or even imaginable for women, so to do all three—as well as to be a singer *and* to be a person of color—well, that was unprecedented.

Fortunately, Sylvia wasn't very concerned about those societal norms.

Sylvia Moy laid the groundwork for the generations of women that followed in her footsteps. Though she intentionally flew under the radar, she was ultimately a unicorn who shaped and intervened through a male-controlled society and music business while challenging stereotypes and prevailing beliefs about a woman's ability to become a multi-hyphenate success.

Despite her importance as one of the preeminent songwriters at the height of Motown's golden age and in music history, Sylvia's contributions and cultural impact have long been diminished by narratives of primarily White men and White women. In the pantheon of great songwriters during the sixties, Sylvia is never mentioned, among other reasons because Black women were severely underrepresented. Due to barriers from racial discrimination, opportunities as songwriters—and producers—were not presented to Black women, because they were not considered intellectually capable or competent enough to excel in these positions.

Her often ignored and overlooked story illustrates how dominant views of race, gender, and genre affected the classically trained vocalist personally and professionally during her life—and the legacy she left behind. Today, White female songwriters noted for shaping rock and roll like Carole King, Cynthia Weil, and Ellie Greenwich (all based in

New York, on the East Coast) have been credited in music history—at least, along with their songwriting husbands as partners—as pioneering women who opened doors for others in the sixties. Sylvia, however, made history of her *own* in Detroit, in the Midwest. And unlike King, Weil, and Greenwich, Sylvia did not cowrite with a spouse or a partner. As such, she was forced to fend for herself in the shark-infested, patriarchal waters of the entertainment industry.

When thinking about a female songwriter and producer at Motown who experienced commercial success, Valerie Simpson is often the first to cross one's mind. Notably, Sylvia actually arrived at Motown two years before Simpson, the award-winning songwriter and producer who, like King, Weil, and Greenwich, worked alongside her husband, Nickolas Ashford. As a songwriting duo, Ashford and Simpson took home the 1968 Broadcast Music Inc. (BMI) Rhythm and Blues Songwriter of the Year Award during a 1969 ceremony; they also won three additional R&B honors for songs they wrote together, including "Ain't No Mountain High Enough," "Ain't Nothing Like the Real Thing," and "Your Precious Love."

That same year, however, it was a three-way tie. Sylvia tied with them for BMI's Songwriter of the Year Award and won three honors in the R&B category for songs she'd written, including "Honey Chile," "I Was Made to Love Her," and "Shoo-Be-Doo-Be-Doo-Da-Day." Motown producer and songwriter Norman Whitfield also tied that year for BMI's Songwriter of the Year, and he, too, earned three additional awards in the R&B category for his songs, including "I Heard It Through the Grapevine," "I Wish It Would Rain," and "You're My Everything." At BMI's first-ever R&B ceremony, Motown ended up sweeping the event.

Though listeners often associate songs with their singers or the bands behind them, there are many people behind the scenes who help bring those pieces to life, often even before a voice comes into the picture. Songwriters work on music and provide the force behind the pen, the power behind the lyrics, the catchy progression of notes that weave into and out of the melody; their job is to establish the heartbeat, soul, and bloodline of a tune. A producer, on the other hand, pulls it all together and is considered to hold the thinking person's position akin to the quarterback in football. The producer is the leader, the one who assembles the right musicians and sounds to generate the perfect track while staying on budget. Not only did Sylvia write many of Motown's greatest hits, but she pulled double duty as a producer, persevering as a courageous army of one alongside seventeen male peers who were also producing. In the face of all this pressure, she held her own and did so with dignity, integrity, and grace, even when her male colleagues refused to recognize her as a producer and denied her credit for her efforts.

Ultimately, this was not just a Motown thing. This was a man thing and a music industry thing at large. Up to this point in the entertainment world, women had been mostly relegated to roles behind the microphone as singers. If a woman was permitted to become a songwriter, she was forced to choose between pursuing a career as a singer or behind the scenes as a writer. Though men were allowed to do both, few women were given the chance to consider this option. What's more, they were often partnered with men if they were even considered for opportunities as songwriters at all. With men in charge of every aspect of the process, women didn't have creative control of their careers; therefore, an inkling of thought toward becoming a producer was a formidable notion to most women.

A January 2024 report on inclusion in the recording studio found that even today, only 19.5 percent of songwriters are women, and the numbers were significantly lower for women producers, at just

6.5 percent.[2] Factor in race for both instances, and those figures are even lower. As a matter of fact, the report found that out of 1,972 producing credits, only nineteen went to women of color.[3] Imagine how dismally deficient rates were in the sixties—virtually nonexistent. Sylvia not only dared and dreamed to do both, but she turned these ambitions into a reality, and she effectively made her mark on Motown during the height of its notoriety as one of the country's greatest recording companies.

Sylvia's challenges weren't just limited to competition at Motown, however—or even the industry at large. Sylvia also fought tooth and nail for public recognition because her name was never listed on records as a producer. Though Motown greatly profited from her contributions, the company failed to accurately and truthfully document her accomplishments; consequently, she has long been overlooked within the annals of music history. History is only as accurate as the historical record; if information is inaccurate or incomplete, fallacies prevail, which is one of the main reasons why so few listeners today know Sylvia's name, even if they know all the words to the songs she wrote.

Ultimately, Sylvia's contribution to music was bigger than the songs she wrote, the singers she worked with, or even the company that employed her and then assumed credit for her work. Sylvia's prolific catalog represented a historical achievement for women and African Americans at a time when both groups were fighting painstaking battles for basic rights, autonomy, and respect. The women's liberation movement of the late 1960s sounded the alarm about issues such as equal pay, acceptance of women in the workplace (especially in gender nonconforming roles), and sexual harassment. Simultaneously, the civil rights movement was marked by a period of segregation and discrimination in which Black people faced significant danger in their quest for justice and equality alongside their White peers. Considering that

Sylvia and many of the people in her life risked their lives in pursuit of these basic human rights, her accomplishments—in retrospect—are all the more extraordinary.

At the end of the day, Sylvia's story serves to remind us all of the power we hold in our own lives to be agents of change—no matter what obstacles lie before us. In learning how to maneuver through oppressive systems and find her own way, Sylvia proved that adaptation—and achievement—were possible, even in the face of adversity. With unwavering faith and courage, Sylvia sacrificed for her craft and paid the price so that perhaps the next generation of women songwriters and producers to follow, such as Mariah Carey, Missy Elliott, Beyoncé, Alicia Keys, Rihanna, Kandi Burruss, H.E.R., Ester Dean, Nettie Wood, WondaGurl, Starrah, Victoria Monét, Muni Long, Nija Charles, Tayla Parx, Nova Wav, Makeba Riddick-Woods, and Tiffany Red, would not have to shoulder those same burdens.

Had Sylvia not been so determined to sound the alarm by standing up for herself and the credit she was due, over the years her existence and legacy might have been not only diminished but completely erased. Thankfully, for as much as some tried to disregard and minimize the truth surrounding her contributions, she tried even harder, determined to make them hear her and never forget that she was here. Forever patient, she waited for the time when she would be allowed to bask in the glow of the spotlight on her efforts; my hope is that this book will serve as that spotlight **now**.

You've heard the history, but this is *her* story.

## CHAPTER 1

# "I Was Made to Love Her"

Sylvia Rose Moy was born into a life of music on September 15, 1938, in Detroit, Michigan. It was the third Thursday of the month, which would hold a special meaning for her later in life. But for now, this time held another significance, because it was around this same period when jazz jumped to the forefront of modern music as a bona fide national sensation.

Just three months earlier, Chick Webb and His Orchestra had featured singer Ella Fitzgerald on their rendition of "A-Tisket, A-Tasket." Fitzgerald's new twist on the old nursery rhyme gave way to a truly innovative sound, and the song quickly became the breakthrough tune of her career, one that launched the powerhouse vocalist into superstardom. Appropriately so, this moment would align with Sylvia's arrival in the world. She entered a realm where Lady Ella would go on to become the gold standard for vocal excellence, earning the titles "Queen of

Jazz" and the "First Lady of Song." Fitzgerald's growing catalog of hits would end up having a huge impact on Sylvia throughout her childhood, inspiring her to venture into music herself as she got older.

Sylvia was the second-oldest of nine children born into a musical family headed by a gospel-loving mom, Hazel Vernice Moy (née Ridgell), and a jazz-loving dad, Melvin Bell Moy. Hazel was born in Monticello, one of the largest towns in southeast Arkansas, though she'd often claim Little Rock as her hometown. Hazel's mother, Rosalie Ridgell (née Goodwin), was a tailor and an outstanding seamstress, and she was well known throughout Arkansas for her work. Hazel's parents were from two different Native American tribes, Choctaw and Chickasaw. Rosalie herself was considered an "Indian" with no African American blood, and there was much mystery surrounding the background of Hazel's half Irish and Choctaw father, Alfred Ridgell, an acclaimed businessman who owned a cleaners and a farm in Arkansas. When Rosalie and Alfred divorced, Hazel and her daughter left Monticello and went to stay with Rosalie's sister in Monroe. That's how Hazel eventually landed in Louisiana, where Sylvia's parents first met in 1933.

Sylvia's father, Melvin, came from a large family, one of seven boys and a girl born to Elberton Moy and the former Sylvia Wade. The origins of the surname Moy are usually assumed to be Chinese, and Sylvia said that the name was inherited from her Chinese grandfather.[1] However, the name has also been said to have originated among the French and Native Americans. And Louisiana is well known for its population of Creoles, people of mixed European and Black descent.

The Moys resided in Wall Lake, a rural neighborhood and city in Ouachita Parish, located in West Monroe, Louisiana. Most of the Black people who lived around Wall Lake were related. Described as feisty, Melvin was only about five foot seven in height but very strong. In the departments of personality and inner strength, Melvin was a titan.

"Our father was almost like a philosopher," said one of Sylvia's sisters, Ronnie. "He's the one we would go to with problems and issues."

Above all else, eighteen-year-old Melvin was a man who went after what he wanted—and he had his eyes set on Hazel from day one. He wooed her with his conversation and charisma. Melvin's tenor vocals were the cherry on top. He serenaded her with love songs he made up off the top of his head. Music colored their world, and it would be a vital foundation upon which the Moy partnership—and their future family—was built.

Just as Sylvia would later take an instant liking to music as a kid, so did her father, who found ways to immerse himself in the business of music from a young age. After leaving high school early, Melvin figured out new and innovative ways to make ends meet and support himself financially. Since music had always been a passion, he decided to do something with the arts. His high-pitched singing voice, which was mostly tenor but could easily hit second bass, replicated that of a classic crooner. As a teenager, he also took some piano lessons. "He could do a couple jazz or blues runs," said Sylvia's youngest brother, Christopher. "He was a very sociable person and he loved music. He loved jazz and the blues."

Whenever the beat dropped on the radio or on a record, Melvin, who could tap-dance, whipped out one of his fancy moves. Sylvia's uncles on her dad's side played the trumpet and others in the family played the guitar and banjo. As with everything else, her dad had his own way of standing out from the rest when the music played and when it stopped. In an effort to provide entertainment in West Monroe, a teenage Melvin teamed up with two older friends to start a new venture. "My daddy and some other guys in Louisiana formed a social club and started booking big band acts in Monroe," recalled Sylvia's sister Ronnie. "Daddy started being a booking agent down there in the 1930s. They dealt with folks like Cab Calloway."

The singer and bandleader, nicknamed Mr. Hi-de-ho and known for his hit 1931 song "Minnie the Moocher," was among one of the top performers Melvin managed to book, along with other jazz greats like Duke Ellington and Count Basie. The social club was modeled after Harlem nightclubs during the thirties with a vibrant community of well-dressed, elegant Black people socializing, dancing, and enjoying the latest big band tunes. Though Melvin did not finish high school, he deeply valued education. He made certain that a portion of the proceeds raised were used to benefit the underprivileged with scholarships so they could attend HBCUs (historically Black colleges and universities) such as Xavier University, Dillard University, or Southern University.

After a few years of courtship, Melvin and Hazel tied the knot in December 1935 and welcomed their oldest daughter, Lazoe, a year later. Though Sylvia's father had found his niche as a music promoter in Louisiana as a young man, he longed for steadier work that could help support his growing family. He was looking to the future and earned certifications to repair appliances. This skill would come in handy when he relocated to Detroit.

Though Melvin was the first of his brothers to leave Louisiana, money wasn't the only reason he left. Growing up in Louisiana, he had been forced to bear witness to racial segregation and be subjected to the Jim Crow laws that institutionalized White supremacy and Black inferiority throughout the South. Like his daughter Sylvia, Melvin resented others telling him what he could do and what he could not do. The more he was told to stay in his place and accept the terms of marginalization and inferiority, the more desperate he was to find a way to go against the system—even though he faced the threat of danger, violence, or even death.

Ultimately, as racial tensions bubbled around him, the decision to move north was made in a moment of necessity—a pure survival instinct. "Daddy's life was threatened. Many of the racist white men in Louisiana felt that Mother should not be with a Black man," explained Angel, one of Sylvia's sisters. "Pretty women like Mother belonged to them and so they turned on Daddy. They wanted to eliminate her from being with him, so Daddy had to get out of town in the middle of the night and leave. He left Mother and my sister Lazoe in Louisiana until he could get work and get settled wherever he was going."

And so, Melvin left Louisiana with only $5 and a pair of baseball shoes. "Dad's goal was to go as far north as possible, away from the Jim Crow South," explained Celeste, one of Sylvia's sisters. He made it to Toledo, Ohio, but Melvin didn't stay there long; there was much more going on in Detroit. Sylvia once recounted how her dad "hobo'ed. He rode the trains. He made his way north. My dad, in his efforts to look for a better way for his family...had practiced going without food and water, so that he could come in here and find work. And that's how my family got here."[2] Sylvia's father finally settled down in Detroit in 1937.

Melvin's departure turned out to be a blessing in disguise, and he and his wife joined the more than six million African American people who left the South and moved to the North in order to enjoy economic opportunities and social advancement during the Great Migration, a mass movement that took place between 1916 and 1970. While racism was still prevalent in the North, segregation was not enforced like it was in the South with Jim Crow laws. Consequently, the Black population in places such as New York, Chicago, and Detroit—the largest and most populous city in Michigan—increased by more than 60 percent.

Melvin chose to take up residence in Detroit because he knew he'd be able to provide a better standard of living for his family. After completing trade school to become a boiler, he settled into a career as an appliance repairman and secured employment at Crowley's Department Store. It was one of Detroit's Big Three downtown retailers and Hudson's fiercest rival in the department store business. In addition to later having his own business, Melvin also did service repair for appliances at the Good Housekeeping stores in Detroit. He had friends of all nationalities and professions, many of whom were clients. They were Italian, Polish, and Greek. The fruits of his labor allowed his family to reside in the Conant Gardens Historic District, located on the northeast side of Detroit. "It was a nice neighborhood of Black people," recalled Sylvia's sister Ronnie. "There were doctors and lawyers in our neighborhood."

During the 1930s, this was also one of the few areas where African American people could live because there were no deed restrictions for Black people who wanted to purchase property. The land on which the district was located once belonged to abolitionist Shubael Conant, who worked throughout his life to end slavery. In fact, he was the first president of the Detroit Anti-Slavery Society, organized in 1837. Prior to his death, he left instructions in his will to allow Black people to purchase or build new homes on his property.

Detroit was originally nicknamed the Motor City because of its booming auto industry, which dated back to 1908 when Henry Ford made his first Model T. In fact, the Moys' neighborhood had initially been developed to house White autoworkers, and though the section was segregated, federally backed loans were approved in the area in 1934 by the Federal Housing Administration. However, by the 1940s and 1950s, its residents were largely well-educated Black people. It was later considered one of Detroit's most prosperous Black neighborhoods, with the highest median income of all of Detroit's Black neighborhoods. This place would have a profound impact on Sylvia's childhood and the importance of musicality in her upbringing, as she later explained: "Blacks began to migrate [to Detroit] and formed, at the bottom of the city, Black Bottom...They brought with them their music, which was gospel, jazz—our music. Because of the factories, our music got a little louder."[3]

Transitioning from the South to the Midwest was an adjustment, but the Moy family welcomed the change—and their new community.

After settling down in Detroit, the Moys welcomed their second child, Sylvia, to the family, and seven more children followed her: sister Merril Baronica (aka Ronnie); brother Melvin Pernell; sisters Angelica (aka Angel) and Celeste; brother Christopher; and sisters Francetta and Anita. Though Sylvia was born Sylvia Rose Moy, it took some of Sylvia's younger siblings a while to figure out the truth about her birth name. For years, they assumed it was "Baby Sis," not realizing this was simply a nickname given to her after her parents brought her home from the hospital and introduced her to big sister Lazoe as "your baby sis." As the family grew in size, the catchy moniker stuck—and even Sylvia's younger siblings kept calling her "Baby Sis."

Sylvia was actually named after her paternal grandmother, Sylvia Wade, and her maternal grandmother, Rosalie Ridgell. In addition to her name, Sylvia's paternal grandmother gave her another special trait: an extrasensory ability that some called "the gift," where she could read a person's energy and thoughts. It was also said that Wade could see into the future, which wasn't unusual for those coming from Louisiana. And this "second sight," which supposedly provided Wade with perception beyond ordinary vision, didn't just come from Sylvia's father's side of the family. Hazel, Sylvia's mother, was also said to be gifted, but because she grew up in a household where privacy and secrecy were a way of life, she never discussed it much. As children, Sylvia and some of her other siblings discovered that they, too, had inherited this ability, with the power to "see into the future," as Ronnie, one of Sylvia's sisters, later reflected, before adding that "people knew we were different." Despite their gifts, the children followed their mother's example and did not talk about it. As Celeste, another one of Sylvia's sisters, explained, their mother had always been "very reluctant to talk about what she knew about her family. A lot of people from the South have a lot of secrets, and my mother was no exception."

Though the Moys were now firmly established in their new home on Fleming Street, they never forgot about the rest of their family. After Melvin was settled, he eventually sent for his mother, father, and all of his brothers to come to Motor City and stay with him until they got set up, too.

Despite the migration, the family's ties to their Southern heritage remained strong, even after years spent adjusting to the Detroit cold. Sylvia grew up loving the Cajun and Creole cuisine her dad prepared, as he was an excellent cook. Melvin was particularly known for his barbecuing; his low and slow method of cooking ribs helped tenderize the meat and enhance the flavor. When he barbecued, it was usually the talk of the town.

As a small child, Sylvia noticed how her family stood out from others in the neighborhood—and it wasn't just their approach to cooking. There were often many people living in the Moy house and money was tight, though Sylvia later remembered their resourcefulness with pride. Toys were made for her and her siblings. The family also grew their own food, including peanuts, in a field next to their house. Everything they ate was either grown in that field or kept in the basement, like their chickens, ducks, and geese.

The family was willing to do whatever they could to survive, and though they weren't rich, there was always a wealth of love in the Moy home. "My grandfather used to tell my grandmother, 'I was made to love you.' That's where I remember hearing that all the time," said Jackie, Sylvia's firstborn nephew, from her oldest sister, Lazoe.

Sylvia's parents made sure to share their love through consistent actions and terms of endearment, so that even if money and other resources were tight, Sylvia never felt without.

## CHAPTER 2

# Banging on Pots and Pans

In addition to love and affection, the Moy house was always filled with music. Everybody sang at home, in church, and on holidays, just like the generations before them had. Most everyone in Sylvia's immediate household eventually learned how to play an instrument or was musically inclined, and they'd showcase these skills during impromptu jam sessions around the house.

During the early days, when there were only three Moy kids, young Sylvia quickly learned to be resourceful, converting makeshift items around the house into instruments. The family didn't have the money to buy a piano until years later, so any instruments she had access to as a small child were ones that she made herself. Thanks to her vivid imagination, it was rather easy for her to build her own musical toys and gizmos. Anything and everything she could get her hands on that was around the house was fair game. She'd fill empty oatmeal boxes with rice or beans. Dishes also became percussion instruments, along with sticks, pots, and pans. Not much was off-limits to the crafty creator. Even the radiator served a major role in Sylvia's make-do band.

"She made drums and even a guitar. She found some wires and rubber bands. She took cigar boxes and made a guitar. She used to sing with her guitar. And she'd say, 'Ronnie, you get over there on the piano.' I'd go to the heat register and pretend to play," recalled Sylvia's sister Ronnie later on.

Mostly self-taught as an instrumentalist who played by ear, Sylvia soon learned how to play the piano and bongos. "She taught herself at church and at school, because she was always in the choirs and in the choir rooms. Anywhere she could find and use a piano or any other instrument, she spent time on it," said Ronnie. Sylvia also had a basic knowledge of drums and bass, though her formal training was focused on the guitar. After recognizing Sylvia's vocal talent, her parents signed her up for classical voice lessons. Rosalie Ridgell, her maternal grandmother, had been a singer, too. She'd earned herself a reputation as "the little singing lady" at church, said Ronnie, who remembered how enamored her granny was with Sylvia's abilities. "She was amazed over Sylvia being so young and being into music. She would teach her different songs."

Like a mother who can distinguish her child's cry from others in a nursery, Sylvia's ear was naturally attuned to the elements of sound and tone. She even differentiated her siblings' voices based on how they spoke in certain keys. There was something mystical, magical, and special about music for her, and even as a child, she knew she was different.

"I've always heard things, seen things other people didn't," Sylvia later noted. "When I was a little girl, I'd say to Mama, 'Do you see what I see?' 'No, honey, I don't see anything,' she'd say. But I still do. I see colors, pictures. I'm caught up in time and rhythm. I sense movement. I hear rhythms when people talk. I hear sounds in the street—horns, strings. I feel the rhythm of the seasons. I love nature. Even tulip bulbs say something to me."[1]

Considered shy and usually quiet in most social settings, once Sylvia finally felt comfortable in a given environment, she would say whatever was on her mind and call things as she saw them. Ronnie, a couple years her sister's junior, described her big sister as "a tattletale as a child." She recalled an incident when a family friend visited the Moy residence. The gentleman asked their father for a drink, to which Mr. Moy responded that he didn't have any alcohol. "Sylvia said, 'Yes you do. Right over there. You put it in there.' My parents were *so* outdone," Ronnie said with a laugh.

Her bold, unflinching honesty was a trait that only intensified as time went on. However, as she got older, she also learned that not everyone was ready to be confronted with the truth or wanted to hear anything other than what they already believed. As Sylvia would later discern through tough lessons, some things were better left unsaid. Still, being highly intuitive, it was *hard*. She could always feel negative energy or when something was off.

Fortunately, music remained a consistent positive for her. Singing and playing music were as natural as breathing to Sylvia—and performing in church made her feel right at home. "She'd have ears ringing," said Sylvia's youngest brother, Christopher. "You could tell she was a little tight and then she would eventually break through. She'd have everybody into her singing. She commanded the stage once she got into the song. She used her hands and arms to express the emotion...she could sing the mess out of [the Mahalia Jackson gospel classic 'If I Can Help Somebody']." According to Christopher, by the end of the song, she would have the entire church clapping and crying.

And Sylvia wasn't the only Moy child who sang at church; her sister Ronnie joined in, too. The congregation came to expect the duo to bring down the house. Known by everyone as "the sweet little Moy sisters," they were often requested throughout their childhoods to perform in various church programs because of their amazing two-part harmony. And while their vocal abilities were attention-worthy, so were some of their public antics. An incident on Easter at First Community Baptist Church was one neither could easily forget.

On this particular bright, sunny Sunday morning, the church was adorned with lilies and filled with people in their best attire. Sylvia, about six at the time, and Ronnie were prepared to perform a duet of the gospel classic "In the Garden." Sylvia wanted everything just right, and so she directed Ronnie closely. Dressed beautifully with ribbons in their long, flowing hair styled into pigtails, the adorable pair delighted the congregation when they were introduced. "Sylvia was kind of the lead singer between us," explained Ronnie. "When the piano player came in with the accompaniment for us to start singing, she figured I wasn't going to know when to come in so she nudged me. I thought to myself, 'How *dare* you!'"

Ronnie immediately nudged Sylvia back with her tiny elbow. The Moy sisters kept singing and nudging each other back and forth while maintaining their vocal harmony, never missing a beat. However, by the time the song ended, it was an all-out mini brawl between the sisters. Needless to say, their mother was fairly embarrassed by the little girls' behavior on full display in front of the congregation on such a special day.

When they weren't performing at home or in church, the kids were providing entertainment for the neighborhood children. Sylvia, Ronnie, and Lazoe frequently put on talent shows in their basement. Each sister played her position well. As chief instrument maker, Sylvia was in charge of music. Since Lazoe was into drama and liked acting, she handled that arena. But Lazoe also loved money, according to Ronnie, so Lazoe decided the audience should be charged a nickel for each performance, and she waited at the door eagerly for everyone to pay up. Younger brother Melvin was also permitted to help his sisters build a stage.

All the neighborhood kids were invited to these shows and many of them—at least twenty—attended. "We got some old sheets and made curtains in front of the stage. Mama was looking for her sheets. She hollered down the stairs, 'Have y'all seen my flower sheets?' We did not respond. Sylvia had her music ready and we wrote some scenes. We had old couches and chairs in the basement. The kids were in awe," said Ronnie.

Melodies and harmonies were constantly swarming in Sylvia's mind even in her earliest memories. As a preschooler, the only way she learned the alphabet was when her mother taught the letters to her as a song. Without a rhythm and beat, she had little interest. As a small child, she loved learning and always knew she wanted to pursue a career in music. Teaching seemed like a natural fit, so at first, she thought that perhaps the classroom would be her calling. She said she never realized back then that music would provide another path for her later on.

Sylvia's innate talent was further nurtured at Courville Elementary School, located on the northeast side of the city. Widely recognized for its music program, the school's concert choir was a highly regarded performance ensemble with a repertoire that included everything from eighteenth-century classics to gospel and urban pop. At that level, Sylvia didn't have any Black teachers, but she did have ones who were Jewish, English, and Polish, so she heard and was introduced to a lot of other types of music.

Around the same time, she also brought her love of music outside the classroom and taught her own songs to four friends who liked to sing. It was as if she was already producing music at a young age without even realizing it. When the singing group she put together was ready, Sylvia christened them the Calypso Ettes. After hosting a few small gatherings and parties to raise money, they could finally afford matching attire: sweaters with the group name stitched in white right across the front. And since blue was Sylvia's favorite color, she made certain the pullovers were some variation of this hue before settling on royal blue.

Upon graduating from Courville, Sylvia continued pursuing music at Pershing High School, where she studied under the guidance of legendary choral music director and conductor Kenneth Jewell. An accomplished composer of organ music, Jewell's chorale performances were acclaimed locally and nationally. He was a member of the American Society of Composers, Authors and Publishers (ASCAP) as well as the American Guild of Organists. To get his stamp of approval was major—and Sylvia stood out enough to do just that. He quickly noticed her talent as a singer and her ability to play drums, keyboard, and guitar mostly by ear. Even as a high schooler, Sylvia was so impressive that she was accepted into Wayne State University's college music group, along with other community groups. She was also invited to perform guest solo performances with the Detroit Symphony Orchestra.

One of Sylvia's high school classmates was a student named Louvain Demps, who also attended Courville Elementary School with her, where they'd sung in the choir and shared the same teacher, Stephanie Reisner. Demps would later become one of the three Motown in-house background singers collectively known as the Andantes. In some instances, the Andantes even replaced band members who theoretically should've been present on the track, like doing background vocals on "My Baby Loves Me" with Martha Reeves *instead* of the Vandellas. Andantes member Marlene Barrow, a second soprano, recalled the day that "Holland-Dozier-Holland took me aside quietly and asked me to come into the studio...That is me and Mary [Wilson] on [the Supremes'] 'You Can't Hurry Love.'"[2]

Demps was a first soprano and recognized that Sylvia had an expansive range, even though it didn't reach quite as high as her own. "She could get up there. When we auditioned for choir A, the best choir at Pershing, Sylvia auditioned for second soprano," recalled Demps. The two friends would sit together in music class and dote on the regular about their musical inspirations. For Sylvia, jazz greats were always her favorites; Sarah Vaughan and Ella Fitzgerald topped the list, hands down.

At home, Sylvia and Ronnie would have it out when it came to listening to their preferred kinds of music. Sylvia usually wanted to unwind with the smooth sounds of jazz because her personality was similarly mellow. Little sister Ronnie, on the other hand, loved dancing and preferred R&B music, such as Little Willie John's "Fever" or Little Richard's "Long Tall Sally." Whenever Sylvia tried to play her calmer music, Ronnie would boldly turn down or turn off whatever Sylvia was playing in favor of her own up-tempo tunes—often disrupting the peace of the household.

Though everyone in the family loved and appreciated music, no one else expressed their thoughts about music quite like Sylvia did, and she carried this passion with her everywhere she went. As a child, Sylvia adopted the belief that to be the best, a person must learn *from* the best. Her music idol Sarah Vaughan was well regarded as one of the greatest jazz singers of all time with her distinctly unique three-octave contralto range. The things that she could do with her voice intrigued Sylvia.

The "Divine One," or "Sassy," as Vaughan came to be known, was also sometimes called the "Queen of Bebop," because she could do bop phrases while singing. "Tenderly," a song that came out in 1947 when Sylvia was just nine years old, was among her favorites, because the lovely jazz standard showed off the singer's wide range. Vaughan was an audacious vocalist and Sylvia challenged herself by learning to imitate her. "It's Magic," another 1947 song that was originally written for singer and actress Doris Day, became another favorite only when Vaughan's rendition gave the standard pop classic ballad a jazz feel that touched Sylvia's soul. Vaughan's influence on her wasn't limited to music, however. Smoking was encouraged and considered "cool" and "stylish" during the fifties, and with her singing idol constantly puffing on cigarettes, it wasn't long before Sylvia picked up the habit herself in high school.

Another jazz master that heavily influenced Sylvia's musicality was Ella Fitzgerald. Known as the "First Lady of Song" and the "Queen of Jazz," Fitzgerald had a voice that could imitate actual instruments with her scats, which captivated Sylvia. Like Vaughan, Fitzgerald did things vocally that Sylvia never could've imagined or anticipated. Sylvia recognized Fitzgerald's pure timing and flawless pitch as a mezzo-soprano jazz singer, with a vocal range that could hit both the highest high notes and the lowest low notes. "A-Tisket, A-Tasket" might have started out as a nursery rhyme, but when Fitzgerald's rendition was released, the song took on new meaning, empowered by her broad range and sweet voice. Like Sylvia, Fitzgerald was always fairly shy and reserved, though no one would ever guess that was so once she hit the stage.

Sylvia's idolization carried over to her musical performance, as well. Demps said that one time, she and Sylvia were having "girl talk" in class when Sylvia announced, "'Guess what? I bet you can't guess who I can imitate. I can imitate Sarah Vaughan. You want to hear?' She sounded *just* like Sarah Vaughan. She hit it right on the mark."

A fan of Gregorian chants, Demps would often take the long route to choir practice at the church, along with her sister, just so they could walk through Sylvia's neighborhood to visit, meet up, and talk. In high school, Sylvia was always poised and took the business of learning seriously, Demps observed. But attending school in the fifties wasn't always easy, especially as a young Black woman.

Despite a large and thriving Black population, racism was everywhere, with prevalent residue from blatant and cruel discrimination at every corner. The first great race riot in Detroit took place in June 1943; White citizens were resisting attempts at desegregation as Black people moved into neighboring communities and worked alongside them in factories. When the whole episode was finally over, thirty-four people had died; twenty-five of those were Black people, of whom seventeen were killed at the hands of police. More than four hundred others were injured and eighteen hundred were arrested following three days of unrest that ended when federal troops in armored cars came wielding automatic weapons.[3]

Over a decade later, fair treatment remained an issue for African Americans in the Motor City. Sylvia's sister Ronnie recalled Pershing High School being "rather racist," with the vice principal being widely regarded as a "redneck." She added that some teachers were not so nice to Black kids, either. "They encouraged the White kids to do well. They did not push us. They were harder on Black children."

One particular White female music teacher, whom Demps described as a "spinster," made life particularly hard for Sylvia. This woman had earned a reputation for punching music students in the stomach to drive home the point that singing must come from the diaphragm. Demps said Sylvia was a great singer and already properly trained. She already knew that power came from the diaphragm, so Sylvia was not fond of this teacher's training technique, especially since the teacher took special delight in performing it on Black students.

Apparently, as Demps put it, word spread like a raging fire one day in the school's hallway that this same teacher did not punch Sylvia, but she supposedly took it a step further and actually slapped her. Demps said that Sylvia must have had "a knee-jerk reaction" and supposedly slapped the teacher back so hard that the woman fell to the floor. "Everyone at Pershing talked about that day," remembered Demps. "People knew not to underestimate Sylvia, and the running joke was that she beat the teacher to the punch."

As Sylvia's family members later explained the same incident, the choir director had asked Sylvia to come in early before classes started. There was a program taking place, and he apparently wanted her to rehearse with him. Another teacher, presumably this same person mentioned by Demps, saw Sylvia in the hallway before classes, which wasn't allowed per school policies. A confrontation ensued when the teacher insisted that she leave. Sylvia refused. She said that she was not going anywhere, because she needed to attend her rehearsal as requested. The teacher put hands on Sylvia first by grabbing her beautiful sweater before Sylvia abruptly pulled away.

While the accounts from that fateful day differ, one thing is for certain: Sylvia's life was never the same. After that day, Demps said she never saw her dear friend Sylvia at Pershing High School again. One of Sylvia's younger sisters, Angelica, known by the nickname Angel, remembered with great disappointment how "that teacher caused her to be expelled in her senior year. She was graduating with honors."

The unexpected setback forced Sylvia to alter her course and rethink her direction. In her final year of school, she ended up transferring to Northern High School, located on the east side of Detroit. There, she studied and performed jazz and classical music at the high school along with her friend and fellow singer Erma Franklin, the older sister of soul singer Aretha Franklin, who also attended but left to pursue music. And that wasn't all. Singers Obie Benson and Lawrence Payton, who later became members of the Motown soul group the Four Tops, attended

Northern, too, along with singer Smokey Robinson, who led the Motown group the Miracles, and his bass singer, Warren "Pete" Moore.

After such an unexpected change, Sylvia was keeping good company.

---

After graduating from high school, Sylvia initially decided to pursue a career as a music teacher, and by singing in public, she gained not just exposure but also earned money to help her pay for college. She cast a wide net when seeking opportunities to sing, especially after leaving Pershing, since Northern did not offer the same caliber of music program. Eventually, Sylvia became a member of Michigan congressman Charles Diggs Jr.'s choir and performed on a regular basis with the group on his Saturday night radio show broadcast. "Sylvia was asked to join as a teenager," said her sister Angel. "Our father would gather all of us around the radio at home to listen. He had us convinced we could pick out her voice from that huge choir. 'There she is! I hear Sylvia,' we would say."

When it came to musical genre and even language, even though she liked jazz best, Sylvia was fluid. It wasn't unusual for family members to hear her singing opera; she could even sing in French. When cleaning around the house, though, she'd mostly play jazz records, especially while vacuuming the floor or doing the dishes. Sylvia's youngest brother, Christopher, loved hearing her sing and wasn't afraid to let her know it. "There was a fourteen-year age difference between us. I watched what she did. She sang gospel and opera. Whenever she played jazz music, I would come in the room with her. She noticed this."

In addition to music, Sylvia was creative in other ways, too; she made things out of wood and clay, and she also wrote poetry, drew, and painted. She'd been a multifaceted creative since she was young. Around the age of seven, she'd decided to test out her artistry by painting on the walls at her home. When she saw the expression on Grandmother Rosalie's face, Sylvia knew she was in big trouble. She immediately denied being the culprit until her grandmother turned the tables and used reverse psychology on the little charmer. "'This sure is a beautiful picture. I sure would like to hug and kiss the person who did this,'" recalled Ronnie, chuckling at the memory of her grandmother's setup. "So Sylvia said, 'Oh, that was me! I did the beautiful painting!' *Then* she found out she was in trouble."

Teachers recognized Sylvia's drawing abilities as clearly as they recognized her vocal abilities. Display windows at school showcased her paintings, and whenever different holidays came up, she would create special artwork for the school.

Another reason that Sylvia aspired to become a teacher after high school was because a teacher had been so pivotal in her own life. Her visual artistry was elevated because of her friendship with Dr. Elma Barbara Wilson, whom everyone called Barbara. Ten years Sylvia's senior, Wilson was a graduate of Wayne State University, where she'd majored in art education and minored in social studies and science as an undergrad. Barbara went on to earn a master's degree in art education from Wayne State and also became a member of Pi Lambda Theta, one of the nation's most prestigious education honor societies. Later, Sylvia encouraged her to return to school and earn a doctorate, where her research was conducted in general supervision and administration with a focus on radio, television, and film.

The whole family grew to love Barbara as one of their own. As Sylvia's sister Angel recalled, "Barbara was a sweetheart. She lost her mother and father. My parents stepped up to the plate and became surrogate parents to her. We called her 'Sister Barbara.'"

"I loved her just like a sister," added another of Sylvia's younger sisters, Celeste, who went to see her first play, *The Little Match Girl*, thanks to an opportunity presented by Barbara. "She was an art teacher in the Detroit Public School system. She was also a vocalist herself. Barbara really encouraged, inspired, and trained Sylvia to expand her artistic side. There's one abstract painting Sylvia did. It's of a singer in motion. It's just moving. You can't look at it and not be captivated by it."

Sylvia's love of art also rubbed off on her little brother. She observed youngest brother Christopher's talents for drawing and painting. He had long been enamored with his big sister's abilities, and she'd inspired his own interest in drawing. She often drew with pencils or charcoal, and he recalled her drawing with what he called "a very loose hand. She liked drawing horses, sometimes plants, but mostly animals and sometimes the bust of a person."

It was always family first in the Moy household. Sylvia doted on her little brother, who, in addition to artistic sensibilities, had an immense fascination with taking things apart and putting them together again—just to see how they worked. Christopher loved anything mechanical or engineering-related, and he used to save up his money to buy model car kits and model airplane kits. He was also just as invested in reading and learning as she was. He went to the library a lot so that he could learn how to design airplanes and make them fly better. "She saw I was different from my siblings. She noticed things and would take me to museums. She always found time to spend with her younger siblings," said Christopher, who pointed out that his sister's early nurturing was a big reason that he grew up to become a design engineer at Chrysler.

The younger siblings were all inspired by their big sister Sylvia. But for Sylvia, the family's oldest sister, Lazoe, was the true role model. Lazoe didn't have much of an interest in music vocally, but she was quite a writer. She had a real way with words and could listen to a song and interpret lyrics with ease. Academically gifted though she might have been, Lazoe was fairly disinterested in school; fortunately, she managed to graduate from high school by the age of seventeen, even receiving a double—where she was promoted a class ahead—in elementary school.

Like Sylvia and the rest of the Moy girls, Lazoe was stunningly attractive, and she wanted to become a fashion model. That dream became a reality as she landed some print work, but it was nearly dashed, or at least delayed. Before moving to New York to pursue her career full-time, Lazoe and her steady boyfriend encountered an unexpected situation. "The man that she loved, my father, convinced her to make love and on the first time, there *I* was," said Jackie Vernon Boyd, Lazoe's son and only child.

After her big sister got pregnant at seventeen, Sylvia witnessed Lazoe give birth in 1954 at the young age of eighteen. Lazoe was a free spirit, but her liberation was threatened by motherhood. And during the fifties, at least for the Moys, once a person got pregnant, marriage was sort of expected. But with no real interest in strolling down the aisle (even though she truly loved her son's father), Sylvia knew that the only reason her sister reluctantly wed Jackie's dad was because she had no other choice. According to Ronnie, their father insisted that the child's father marry Lazoe, and the baby grew up adored by his young aunts and uncles. "Jackie grew up as another brother to us. It was more like a brother-aunt relationship for me," said Ronnie.

In the blink of an eye, Sylvia saw her sister's life change forever. Being a mother and a wife were not in her greater life plans, and Lazoe wasted no time making that known, quickly leaving the baby with her parents and running back to model in New York. Sylvia's parents then raised Baby Jackie and he grew up calling them Mama and Daddy. With such a profound age gap between them, Sylvia took a special interest in raising him. "When Lazoe took off and went to New York to be a model, Sylvia took that position like my mom," said nephew Jackie. "They always treated me special because I was their first grandson for ten years. My mother was so close with Sylvia and Ronnie when I was born. It was like I was all their baby."

After sharing such a close bond with her oldest sister, Sylvia had no idea that her own life was about to be upended—and she never could've guessed how closely her path would mirror Lazoe's.

## CHAPTER 3

# "I Ain't Too Proud to Beg"

Though many women wore wigs and other hair accessories throughout the fifties, Sylvia never had to do this—thanks to her inherited good looks and lush locks. She had long, thick, luxurious hair that cascaded down her back—just like her mom's hair had when she was younger—and a smooth, caramel brown complexion, all set atop a svelte frame that stood at five foot seven.

Sylvia was a head-turner, no matter where she went. Whenever she entered a room, she stood tall and "had a quite elegant walk, especially when she wore gowns," remembered Christopher, her youngest brother. Young and old men alike vied for her attention, but Sylvia did not entertain any of her hopeful suitors—except for one.

Alexander "Al" Wright was Sylvia's steady beau. He lived in her neighborhood and even attended the same church as the Moy family. He also attended Pershing High School with Sylvia, though he was two years her senior. "They were in love with each other. They were always together," recalled Sylvia's sister Ronnie.

Al was considered by many to be extremely handsome—a brown-skinned fella who wore an Afro. At six feet tall, Al was also quite muscular and had an athletic build, and he dressed well, to boot. But it wasn't just his looks that drew Sylvia to him. Al's intellect was the real turn-on for Sylvia; she was equally impressed that he was a track star. Because he spent so much time with the Moy family, they became fond of him as well. "He was really smart and played chess," added Ronnie. "He got Mama into playing chess. They played together all the time."

Another thing he and Sylvia had in common was music. He took to the sounds of Sarah Vaughan just like she did. But, unlike Sylvia and the Moy clan, Al was not much into the singing or playing instruments. Instead, he preferred dancing with his sweetheart, which worked out well for Sylvia, who liked dancing as much as singing. Ballroom dancing was popular at the time, and that's what the twosome did most often. On the dance floor, anyone observing would be hard-pressed to take their eyes off the electrifying couple. "People in the neighborhood were in awe over the way they danced all over our parents' basement floor," recalled Ronnie. "It was so smooth. She could jump up and he would swing her out and bring her back. It was so beautiful. She would lift up her little leg. They were so in love."

From an early age, Al had realized that he was the type of man who needed to be married. He yearned for a wife—and Sylvia was *the* woman he wanted to spend the rest of his life with. There was only one problem: Sylvia had no interest in exchanging vows, although she cared a great deal for him. To her, getting married meant being tied down, committed to a life at home where she'd be expected to mind the children. For some men during this time, the woman's place was at home and in the kitchen—and those limitations stifled Sylvia's ambitions, more and more so as time progressed.

"Sylvia kept getting into music. They weren't together as much," explained Ronnie. "He wanted to marry her. She was in love with him, but she was afraid to marry. During that time, husbands weren't open to their wives working outside the house. She didn't want that. Marriage would interfere with her God-given gift, which was music."

At her core, Sylvia was a free spirit, committed only to living in the moment and going with the flow. As much as she loved Al, she did not want to hold him back because she knew they had two different life goals. And there was one other big factor that made Sylvia wary of committing herself to Al forever.

As intelligent and charming as he was, Al also had a dark side: He was extremely controlling. He was so in love with Sylvia that he became obsessed with her and, on some levels, acted like he owned her. His insecurities also led to extreme jealousy and instances where he became aggressive with her. On at least one occasion, even their intimacy wasn't consensual. After nearly a year together, Sylvia realized that the darkness far outweighed the light in their bond, and she decided to eventually end the relationship. However, as she worked to distance herself from Al, Sylvia's world was turned upside down by a shocking new development: She was pregnant.

For Al, the pregnancy was further proof that getting married would be the best thing for them both. But Sylvia was adamant about remaining single, even though she knew that her child would be considered illegitimate, something that was, more often than not, frowned upon at that time. The circumstances surrounding the pregnancy were shrouded in secrecy—even from many of her family members—and

Sylvia struggled with feelings of shame. "She was crying because Mother always told us to 'keep your dresses on. Don't come up with no babies and not be married. You've got to be married first,'" said Ronnie. "That's what our parents taught us. She thought she really disappointed my mother."

Around the age of twenty-two, after some complications, Sylvia's water broke during her sixth month of pregnancy. She gave birth to a son, who was born alive and appeared to be healthy. Hazel, Sylvia's mother, was right beside her, marveling at the baby. Yet, as quickly as they were overcome with joy, they were enveloped by the brisk and unpredictable winds of grief. A short while after the delivery, Sylvia was blindsided to learn that her son had died. Overcome with sadness, the pain was unbearable.

"We all knew about her child, and she would talk about her child," said Anita, Sylvia's youngest sister. "For some reason, there was something there that she did not believe that her child died. She felt like her child was taken, and that she was told that the child died."

So, what really happened? At the time of the baby's birth, some hospitals considered babies that lived for only a few hours as stillborn, yet the term is typically used only when the baby dies before or during birth. "She was told that the baby was born too soon. This is why she did not think this was true. During those times, they did do stuff like take babies," explained Ronnie.

Sylvia wasn't the only one to believe that the baby was stolen. According to Ronnie, Sylvia's mother believed the same thing—because she'd seen the baby, too. "She said he was beautiful and seemed fine. If [our father] believed that the baby was stolen, he never talked about it to anyone, so I never knew his feelings. Sylvia saw the baby. He was strong. He was crying loud and kicking. He was alive."

The child's father, Al, wanted to be there for Sylvia and to comfort her, yet he kept applying pressure for a reconciliation—regardless of whether or not the baby was in the picture. Still, Sylvia's mind was made up. With the loss of their son, she wanted to be alone. She needed time to process just as much as she could and try to clear her head. After a few months, he decided to come around once more with a final demand.

It was all or nothing.

During a Moy summer family gathering, Sylvia's dad fired up the grill. Mr. Moy had earned himself a strong reputation for world-famous barbecue over the years. His homemade sauce was so delicious that folks weren't ashamed to lick their fingers and come back for more. A few friends, but mostly family, were at this particular gathering, which took place in the Moys' backyard. People were laughing, talking, and having a good time—when word came that Al was at the front door.

Al showed up with one intention in mind: He wanted to let Sylvia know how much he still loved her, but he also wanted her to know that there was another woman who had an interest in him. This woman apparently wanted to marry Al, but Al wanted only Sylvia. Al also reminded Sylvia of their connection and brought up the baby, telling her that she would always be a part of him because they shared a child. Al was hoping the pressure would jolt Sylvia into changing her mind, as *this* was her last opportunity to reconcile.

"'If I got to give you up, I'm going to go. I'm at the age now where I need to be married. I'm begging you. I ain't too proud to beg,'" Ronnie recalled hearing Al tell Sylvia.

Unsurprisingly to everyone but Al, Sylvia was not moved in the least. She knew that aggressive men often begged and pleaded for sympathy, promising to change, because they wanted to stay in control. Inevitably, though, once they'd been forgiven, they often returned to the same destructive behavior. Sylvia refused to live in fear or to live in dysfunction. She let Al know that it was never going to happen. Beside himself with anger, Al lost control and slapped Sylvia straight across the face with his open hand.

Just as Mr. Moy turned his attention from the smoky pit in the backyard, he heard the commotion coming from the front of the house. Mr. Moy was beside himself when he saw Sylvia crying. Al hadn't even been invited to the family gathering and then to not only crash the party, but do something like this? It was unacceptable. It was disrespectful. And Al was already on borrowed time after impregnating his beautiful daughter Sylvia. A small-framed man, Mr. Moy was no physical match for Al's athletic build. He also wasn't a violent man; he didn't even believe in using profanity.

But this was different.

Mr. Moy's first inclination was to run into the house and grab his shotgun from the closet. Fortunately, he opted to not do so; it just wasn't worth it. Instead, a confrontation ensued.

"Daddy told Al, 'I never asked for you to do this before, but you need to leave my yard. You're doing her wrong. You get out of here.' And he left," Ronnie later remembered.

And just like that, Al was gone forever. Never to be missed. And just several years later, after moving on with his life and getting married, Al died of cirrhosis of the liver.

Even after Al's death, the couple's son was never far from Sylvia's mind—or her mother's. Ronnie said Hazel didn't talk about it much, but she was someone who, like Sylvia, believed the baby boy had been stolen. But not all family members were so sure. "I can understand the possibility," said Jackie, the son of Sylvia's oldest sister, Lazoe. "I can understand Sylvia not ever understanding what really happened to her child and believing that her child is [still] out there. I've seen studies on this and I know that that kind of stuff happens. She talked about it. She wondered whatever happened, but would never go much more into that with me about it."

Sylvia never ignored her feelings, and in this case, her intuition and even motherly instincts kicked in that something was way off-kilter. Was it possible that the doctor had lied, and she had become a part of a black-market baby adoption cover-up?

From the end of World War II in 1945 to 1972, the United States was marked by an increase in premarital pregnancies. Accordingly, there was also an increase in the rate of newborn adoptions, leading some to call this period the "Baby Scoop Era." Over this three-decade span, some four million women in the United States allegedly gave up their newborn babies to adoption. At least two million of these took place during the sixties alone. Sylvia had been taken to a small hospital on Detroit's east side, and in terms of black-market baby adoption schemes, unmarried women—especially young ones whose children had been conceived through questionable circumstances—were most often targeted.

Though those numbers do include voluntary adoptions where the mother willingly surrendered her child, it was also common for hospitals at this time to force adoption upon unwed mothers. In 2012, the *National Post* conducted an investigation about this period in American history, where dozens of mothers admitted that they had been forced to give up their babies because they were young and unwed.[1] Some of these women, however, said they did not give up their child of their own accord. They were told their baby was stillborn or had died shortly after birth, when the reality was that their baby was adopted or given to a married couple without the mother's knowledge or consent.[2] If the birth mother was told that her child died, this information was accepted without pushback—and neither the mothers, the babies, nor the adoptive parents would be any the wiser.

How can a person know that he was adopted if he was never told? What might happen if he ever learned the truth? Assuming that this child was alive, unless he took a DNA test later on, the truth might forever remain a mystery. But each day of her life, Sylvia held on to the belief that her allegedly dead son was actually alive somewhere in the world—and that one day, they'd be reunited.

Most of Sylvia's siblings were too young to understand the magnitude of her trauma. Because Hazel grew up believing that private matters should be kept private, there wasn't much room for discussion. Some of Sylvia's siblings recalled how after the baby was born, their sister returned home from the hospital and cried a lot. As they got older, some believed in retrospect that perhaps Sylvia had been suffering from post-traumatic stress and was not thinking rationally. Others thought she was stuck in intense denial, a way of coping with "the death."

Over the years, Ronnie had many private conversations with her older sister about the loss of her son. "[Sylvia] never got over this. She never believed what she was told. She never did and that hurt her all her life. She talked to me about it all the time. She would say, 'I wonder where my child is.'"

Despite the fact that this traumatic, life-altering event would haunt her entire adult life, Sylvia made an earnest effort to carry on, according to her family—though her energy definitely shifted. The setback had been difficult, but it also forced her to reevaluate the previous plans she'd made regarding college and her eventual goal of becoming a music teacher. In lieu of her own flesh and blood, songs and music became her children.

She learned to embrace life again, slowly but surely, and decided that in order to really start fresh, she needed to step out on her own. Since she had so many younger siblings still living at home, Sylvia felt the time had come for her to move out. During this time, Barbara—Sylvia's older friend, who was also a singer and a teacher—took Sylvia in and gave her a place to stay.

"[Around this time,] Sylvia was down on her luck. She was kind of struggling. She did some odd jobs working the night shift as a desk clerk in a hotel and taking classes during the day," explained Angel, one of Sylvia's younger sisters. "She was trying to make her way and pay her way because our parents had the younger kids they were trying to raise."

The women developed an even closer bond as Barbara offered Sylvia encouragement and companionship in her darkest hour. The darkness, Barbara assured her, would eventually give way to light. And music would become Sylvia's muse, holding her hand as they walked forward together.

# CHAPTER 4

# Coming to the Stage

By 1963, Sylvia was firmly focused on healing and achieving her goal of becoming a music teacher. In many ways, the aspiration was attainable and within reach, but there was one major obstacle that still stood in her way: Sylvia didn't have enough money to attend college.

After gigging as a guest soloist performing opera with the Detroit Symphony Orchestra, Sylvia hoped that she might be able to receive a scholarship to help foot some of the bill. The conductor of the orchestra took notice of Sylvia's talent and sent a letter to Wayne State University to recommend her admittance into its music department. Sylvia was hopeful that this might be just the thing she needed to help her get her foot in the door.

This budding momentum stopped, however, after she was thrown a cruel curveball. Despite recommendations from conductors and other prevalent members in the music community, Sylvia was bluntly rejected by the Wayne State University Music Department. During this time, it was hard for many of the Black kids who wanted to join the university's music program because they had to audition, meaning that they had to keep up with those youngsters who had been playing instruments since the age of two or three. Because of Sylvia's lack of formal training and the fact that she did not know how to read music (only how to play instruments by ear), the head of the department felt that she would have a difficult time keeping up with others who had been taking piano lessons from childhood.

Though she initially felt discouraged after being declined by her dream school, Sylvia did not let this one no hold her back. As would become a running theme in her life, she simply figured out another way to get where she felt she needed to go.

Taking a leap of faith, she enrolled as a student at two institutions. "All I wanted to do was music and art," Sylvia later said. "I took academic classes at a junior college [Highland Park], and I took music classes at [the] Detroit Institute of Musical Arts."[1] Because she was a self-taught pianist, Sylvia managed to learn how to play after only a month of receiving formal training. But when it came to figuring out how to pay the tuition, the answers didn't come quite so quickly.

Luckily, her friend Barbara had a suggestion: Why not sing professionally for cash? This was exactly how Barbara had financed her own education. When it was all over, she'd obtained a bachelor's degree with a major in art education and minors in social studies and science at Wayne State University. If she could do it, so could Sylvia.

This plan made total sense to Sylvia. Anytime she was offered a chance to sing for money, be it a club or a funeral, Sylvia accepted.

Much like Sylvia herself, Sylvia's voice was incredibly adaptable and could perform in whatever way was needed for the space she was in. Over years of listening to her musical heroes, Sylvia had learned to use her voice as various instruments like Ella Fitzgerald and learned to bebop like Sarah Vaughan. "One of the most fascinating things I used to love to see her do was use her voice like different instruments," said her younger sister Celeste. "She could hear what the strings should do, what the horns should do, what the drums should do. She used her voice to teach the drummer or the guitar player, whatever instrument she wanted them to play."

Barbara and her sister, Janice Foster, who was also a teacher, told Sylvia that she had something special and that she should own it. Right away, Barbara went to work helping Sylvia find jobs as a vocalist. Before long, Sylvia built a base for herself as a songstress and developed a solid reputation. She even started traveling the country as the lead singer with the Premiers, a supper-club band. Based in Detroit, these were musicians who performed at dining restaurants that also functioned as social clubs with nightclub-like live entertainment.

Though she'd been singing in front of audiences in church since childhood, the thought of performing at nightclubs made Sylvia nervous in a way she'd never experienced, because now she was in the midst of so many people unfamiliar to her. It wasn't exactly getting onstage that was the problem. It was getting her *to* the stage that was the real stumbling block. Recognizing her struggles, her father accompanied her to shows just to encourage her to walk out in front of the audience, and then sat himself amid the crowd so she could steady herself by looking directly at him while singing.

"Dad would tell her, 'Your audience is waiting. You don't want to disappoint the people.' I knew because he took me with him to her shows," recalled Celeste. Unfortunately, the time Sylvia spent filled with anxiety and stress came with a price—she ended up with an ulcer that would distress her later in life. But eventually, she figured out a way to move beyond the fear: She consciously created an alter ego for herself up onstage. She walked out from the curtains onto the stage and picked up her mic. Once she hit the stage, Sylvia commanded it and the audience.

"She was 'Sylvia Moy,' a totally, completely different person. She had an incredible range," added Celeste. "She could sing soprano, alto, and tenor. She could even go really low, like a baritone almost. And, boy, was she a good performer!"

Billed as "Detroit's newest singing discovery" in a 1963 *Detroit Free Press* newspaper ad, Sylvia was well on her way to making enough cash to pay for college. She performed with a vocal instrument group—noted for its members having vocal and instrumental prowess—where she sang and played cocktail drums. She also landed major gigs at the London Chop House and at the historic Baker's Keyboard Lounge (known as the "world's oldest jazz club"). Founded in 1933 and considered Detroit's jazz mecca, Baker's was particularly renowned for performances by greats such as Louis Armstrong, Ella Fitzgerald, Sarah Vaughan, Miles Davis, Cab Calloway, Nat King Cole, John Coltrane, Oscar Peterson, Art Tatum, and Joe Williams, to name a few.

For her performance at Baker's in November 1963, Sylvia joined a trio that featured front man Johnny Griffith, an acclaimed pianist. Griffith was a member of the Funk Brothers, the in-house studio band of Motown, which was the hottest record company in town. Sylvia had heard of Motown at this point but hadn't worked with them directly, though she had been advised to cut a record with them—or any other record label—if she could swing it, since she'd be able to make more money doing that than by singing at gigs alone.

It turned out that Sylvia also had a bit of a Motown connection. Barbara was good friends with songwriter Gwen Gordy Fuqua, whose brother, Berry Gordy, was the owner of Motown. Barbara suggested that Sylvia consider trying out, and together, Sylvia and Barbara called to try to get an appointment for an audition. Unfortunately, despite their connection and for unknown reasons, they did not receive a response.

Undeterred, Sylvia immediately started calling up other record companies to find out how she could cut her own record. Sadly, they all gave her the same response. Everyone wanted to deal with only well-established artists in the studio. On top of that, she was also told that she needed an original song. She met with further resistance after reaching out to local songwriters, who said they, in turn, wrote only for known performers. She'd come up against a brick wall, but she wasn't going to let this block her from figuring out a way to move forward.

Sylvia knew she couldn't afford to wait around for an opportunity that might never arise, so she sat at a table, turned on the radio, and intently studied the songs and lyrics she heard. She quickly caught on to the importance of telling a story through lyrics with a well-constructed beginning, middle, and end. She also understood the need for a catchy melody and a solid hook. She pulled from her own experiences to tell stories about love and the difficulty of letting go once a relationship ended. For one song, "I'm Still Loving You," she reminisced about her relationship with Al and what she might say to him in her secret thoughts. She couldn't stop thinking about the tense showdown at her parents' house, where he told her that he wasn't too proud to beg for her to take him back—and ultimately those memories wound up in the lyrics of the sixth verse. "I've given up all my pride.

I got to let it go." With her second song, "A Little More Love," she chose a different sentiment, focusing on feeling safe in one's relationship while requiring extra reassurance. She started it by writing, "Just squeeze my hand instead of a mere hello. Kiss my cheek while we sit in the show." After a couple of weeks, she convinced herself that she, too, could write marketable tunes about love, which would later become part of her signature style.

Eager to record, Sylvia also needed to produce her own track beats since she could not afford to hire a backing band. To accomplish this, Sylvia relied on the skills she'd learned as a child when making her own instruments out of wood and hinges. She also got some shakers and beat on the table. For background rhythms, she had her younger siblings bang sticks and spoons while she sang.

With a finished cassette tape finally in hand, the only thing left was for Sylvia to find a way to get her music heard. Thanks to support from friends Barbara and Janice, Sylvia gathered up enough money to travel to New York in the hopes of snagging a recording deal. She was already anticipating auditions with some of the major record labels, such as Columbia and Atlantic.

The future looked bright.

In the 1960s, New York was considered the epicenter of rock and roll music along with American popular music. This was largely attributed to one of the most prestigious addresses there: the Brill Building at 1619 Broadway. It was an eleven-story building, noted for its "vertical integration," because it housed a hefty list of songwriters, producers (like Phil Spector), and more than 160 music businesses. An aspiring artist could conduct business in one location. For instance, an artist could go from floor to floor to do things such as cut a demo, find a publisher, hire musicians and singers, locate record companies, or solicit radio promoters to play their songs. There was also a nearby building at 1650 Broadway where lots of music was produced and indie labels were housed. In fact, due to the culture and nature of both Brill and 1650, they were often lumped together as the "Brill Building Sound," because of their locations being noted for collaborative songwriting approaches to music.[2] The term also came to be associated with the rise of the many girl groups of pop music in the sixties who had songs written by Brill writers, including the husband-and-wife songwriting team of Ellie Greenwich and Jeff Barry, noted for their songs with girl groups like the Crystals ("Da Doo Ron Ron [When He Walked Me Home]"); the Ronettes ("Be My Baby"); the Dixie Cups ("Chapel of Love"); and the Shangri-Las ("Leader of the Pack"). Though 1650 was smaller and didn't have the same name recognition as Brill, 1650 was actually where most rock and roll and R&B labels were housed, including Aldon Music, which featured top songwriting teams who also penned hits for girl groups, such as Carole King and her husband, Gerry Goffin ("Will You Love Me Tomorrow" by the Shirelles and "One Fine Day" by the Chiffons); and Cynthia Weil and her husband, Barry Mann ("Uptown" by the Crystals).

Preparation required that Sylvia scope out the Yellow Pages in advance. Sylvia had never been to New York, but she knew this was a numbers game, so she jumped right in and hit as many record labels as she could find. Though her efforts were aggressive, she managed to land only a few auditions.

And even then, to say that her early auditions were discouraging would be an understatement. She specifically recalled being told by a White record company president, "Young lady, I like your voice. You're not a bad singer, but I want to give you some advice you can use for the rest of your life. Listen to me. You will *never* be a writer. Forget it."[3]

Another group of White New York music executives simply had no interest in her whatsoever. In the middle of her audition, they rudely turned their attention back to what they'd been focused on prior to her arrival—which turned out to be a Motown record. "It was quite interesting because all those big companies had hired people to sit in back rooms and they were taking records that were done by a little company out of Detroit," explained Sylvia. "They were slowing them down to try and figure out the Motown sound."[4]

Though their words about her songwriting stung, Sylvia wasn't totally surprised. At the time, songwriting was largely considered a man's profession in the music industry. In addition to her gender, Sylvia's race was also a problem. With two strikes against her, things did not appear promising. She left the office with her confidence shattered. She wasn't looking for a career as a songwriter back then, but she knew that she still needed an impactful song to turn heads and land a record deal for herself—and that goal seemed further away than ever.

Crestfallen, Sylvia traveled back home to Detroit, sobbing uncontrollably as she walked into her parents' house. As she had so many times before, she turned to her dad for support and wisdom. "She was discouraged terribly," said her sister Angel. "Daddy encouraged her to carry on and not stop writing. He told her if that's what she wanted to do, she should put her heart and soul into it because she could do it."

Another piece of advice Sylvia's father imparted to his daughter was that no person had control of her or of her destiny. "Keep the faith," he reminded her. As long as she believed in herself, she alone had the power and the ability to make her dreams come true.

And so, after brushing herself off and drying her tears, Sylvia decided to keep trying.

## CHAPTER 5

# Hitsville U.S.A. and the Motown Sound

The sixties were a time of great turmoil, with African Americans being denied basic citizenship rights at every turn. Though Sylvia's parents, Melvin and Hazel, had dealt with these very issues decades ago in the South, not much seemed to have changed in the years since—and now, their daughter faced the same obstacles in Detroit as she worked to make a way for herself.

This was also a time when something new was making waves and stirring things up in Motor City. An indie record label called Motown had taken the world by surprise. Everyone was fixated on how its founder, Berry Gordy Jr., revolutionized the lily-White recording industry. With New York being noted as the hub of several major music labels, all eyes were now turning toward Detroit—the heart of the Midwest.

In 1955, Gordy was a former assembly-line worker at Ford Motor Company's Lincoln-Mercury plant, though he dreamed of creating another kind of factory—similar to the automotive industry—where hit songs would be created. He shifted gears and moved in a new direction, from motors to music. With a bright blue wooden sign hanging over the front porch of a little two-story house on 2648 West Grand Boulevard, Gordy christened his company Hitsville U.S.A. and hit the ground running.

A former pugilist turned factory worker turned songwriter, Gordy had first learned about the business of music after joining forces with another songwriter, Roquel Billy Davis, when they met at a music company, and Roquel soon started dating Gordy's sister Gwen, who was already a songwriter. Davis, who also used the pseudonym Tyran Carlo, began cowriting hits with both Berry and Gwen such as "Reet Petite," "To Be Loved," and "Lonely Teardrops," all for Mr. Entertainment himself, the handsome soul singer Jackie Wilson, who was Davis's cousin. Gordy also unexpectedly received a crash course on dealing with the shadier side of the record industry when a New York publisher refused to pay songwriter's royalties owed to him. Though Gordy prepared to sue, his lawyer told him that he'd inevitably spend more money on legal fees than what he'd get from a settlement. Disappointed and frustrated, Gordy questioned how companies stayed in business without paying their writers. "[The lawyer] explained that the owners pay themselves big salaries and expenses, go out of business, collapse the corporation, and start the whole game all over again. There were always new writers eager to write for their new corporation."[1]

Even when Gordy did get paid for his work, it often wasn't nearly the amount he felt he deserved. One such royalty check offered him a measly $3.19 to account for his contributions on a song called "Got a Job," performed by an eighteen-year-old singer and songwriter named

Smokey Robinson, who fronted a group called the Miracles. The song was written as an answer to doo-wop/R&B group the Silhouettes' hit song, "Get a Job." Fed up when he saw the check's amount, Gordy was encouraged by Robinson to start his own record label so he could determine his worth and how much he'd get paid.

In 1959, the thirty-year-old took matters into his own hands to secure his financial interests for future recordings. In studying the business of music, he knew that publishing companies are responsible for ensuring that songwriters and composers are paid royalties when their music is used commercially. In exchange for managing the songs and making sure royalties are paid out, a publishing company takes a portion of the income from songs. So Gordy started his own publishing company, Jobete—named after his daughter and two sons, Joy, Berry, and Terry.

The same year, after securing an $800 loan from his family's savings fund, Gordy founded Tamla Records to sign artists and make music. He selected a name inspired by singer Debbie Reynolds's tune "Tammy," which was the #1 pop song in the country at the time. That same year Gordy and Robinson cowrote a doo-wop tune, "Bad Girl," which landed at #93 on the Billboard Hot 100 chart. A few months later, Janie Bradford, Gordy's first receptionist, cowrote a hip new tune with her boss called "Money (That's What I Want)," performed by singer and songwriter Barrett Strong with Gordy playing piano. "Money" was one of the first tracks recorded at Tamla Records—and became its first hit record. However, Gordy wanted more traction, so Anna Records—co-owned by Gordy's sisters Anna and Gwen, along with Roquel Billy Davis (aka Tyran Carlo)—then licensed the song, which was distributed nationwide by Chess Records.

In 1960, Gordy decided to rename Tamla, because he admitted that the name was "commercial enough but had been more of a gimmick [initially]."[2] Inspired by Detroit's nickname as the "Motor City," he decided to call the company Motown—and history changed forever.

Motown succeeded by understanding how to procure and produce Black talent for the masses, but it wasn't the only record company catering to Black artists. Around the same time, Chicago-based companies like Vee-Jay Records and Chess Records were popping up in the Midwest, while popular Southern labels included Peacock Records, based in Houston, and Stax Records, based in Memphis. In fact, Stax, known for its Southern soul and funk music, was nicknamed Soulsville U.S.A. While these labels were influential because of their artists, ranging from Etta James and Chuck Berry on Chess to Jerry Butler and Gene Chandler on Vee-Jay to Big Mama Thornton and Little Richard on Peacock to Otis Redding and Isaac Hayes on Stax, none left record execs in a conundrum about their signature sound quite like Motown did. Under Gordy's leadership, the distinctive Motown blend of pop and soul stood apart from anything else on the radio, and Motown quickly gained a reputation for its artists' refined performances, which included tight vocal arrangements, polished appearances, magnetic stage presences, and dynamic choreography.

Gordy was intentional about ensuring that his label live up to its name by creating pop stars and producing Top 40 singles in the studios, an assembly line that resembled the model Ford followed with its cars. To do this, he actively taught the art of writing songs with the structure of a beginning, a middle, and an end. "He told me a song has got to be a short book, a small movie, or a short story," recalled Smokey Robinson.[3] In order to keep new music coming out on a constant basis, he instructed musicians to compose the music first and then had songwriters pen lyrics to accompany the track, because it saved time and money. Most others at the time were doing the opposite; lyrics were written first and music came later.

On September 27, 1960, Motown released a new song that quickly stormed up the charts: "Shop Around," performed by Smokey Robinson and the Miracles. The catchy, up-tempo pop tune, cowritten by Robinson and Gordy, became the label's first song to sell a million copies. Talent across the country started flocking to Gordy's blossoming company, which soon boasted a roster of impressive names that included Mable John, Mary Wells, Marvin Gaye, the Temptations, Tammi Terrell, the Contours, and the Four Tops. Gordy also acquired a number of girl groups (which were on the rise in the sixties), including the Supremes, Martha and the Vandellas, and the Velvelettes. Another of his girl groups, the Marvelettes, helped the label make history with 1961's hit "Please Mr. Postman," which became Motown's second song to sell a million copies and its first to solidify crossover status by landing at #1 on Billboard's Hot 100 pop charts.

In addition to concentrating his efforts on artists in front of the microphone, Gordy sought out key executives to assist them behind it. Gordy recruited a man named William R. Stevenson to head up the A&R department. Known by some as William R. but to most as Mickey, his nickname, Stevenson was a fast-talker who was no stranger to hustling and street life. He ran a tight ship, as he was the one responsible for putting the right artists, songwriters, producers, and musicians together to make hit records. Gordy said, "It was really with Mickey that I began something that was unique to my management style, building the structure around the person rather than fitting the person into the structure."[4] Stevenson was a master at ushering in, identifying, and securing talent for the company, and Gordy gave Stevenson free rein to do as he pleased in the department.

On the third Thursday of each month, Motown held open auditions for new talent, meaning there was always a long line of hopefuls trailing for blocks down the sidewalk. Finding the best of the best artists, producers, songwriters, and engineers, and then strategically positioning them and pairing them up, was like playing a game of sonic chess. *Everyone* wanted to be invited into the Motown fold. But not everyone had what it took to get there or even stay. "Motown only took the cream of the crop," explained singer Barrett Strong, who later became one of the label's top songwriters, winning a Grammy Award for his work with the Temptations' tune "Papa Was a Rollin' Stone" (along with his writing partner, Norman Whitfield).

Songwriter Janie Bradford was one of Motown's original five—she'd been there since day one—and she couldn't help but notice Motown's quick ascent in popularity. "Everybody was wanting to sing with Motown; you knew Motown was the thing," said Bradford. "People didn't care what record label they were on. People were leaving their record labels to come and be on Motown, so that's when it hit me that the company became a company."

A common, yet often overlooked, denominator of Motown's success was that while the artists, songs, songwriters, and producers changed from record to record, two variables were forever consistent: the Andantes and the Funk Brothers. The Andantes were Motown's in-house female background singers, composed of Louvain Demps (soprano); Jackie Hicks (first alto); and Marlene Barrow (second soprano). This trio of unassuming ladies sang backing vocals on just about every song the label produced. The Funk Brothers, on the other hand, were Motown's in-house rhythm section of jazz musicians. Stevenson had personally rounded them up exclusively across Detroit from nightclubs, bars, and joints that had live music. Some were classically trained, but most were not; in fact, few of them could even read music. But that didn't stop them from laying it *down*. Regardless of their backgrounds or training, both the Andantes and the Funk Brothers provided the secret sauce—the steady heartbeats—behind the now recognizable Motown sound.

Though not always well-known to the public, some of these artists were considered indispensable by the men in charge. Drummer Benny Benjamin, also nicknamed "Papa Zita," was so phenomenal that Gordy refused to do recording sessions without him; he even played the drums on Gordy's first hit, "Money (That's What I Want)." The problem, however, was that one would be hard-pressed to find Benjamin sober or arriving on time. In spite of that, he was so good at his craft that he could play the drums and bass wouldn't be needed—*that* was the magnitude of Benjamin's muscle. "He was the only addict I knew of who never missed a beat. High, drunk or sober, he was a human metronome," recalled Stevenson.[5]

Stevie Wonder went so far as to call Benny "one of the major forces in the Motown sound. Benny could've very well been the baddest. He was the [Bernard] Purdie of the sixties." Despite his talent, Wonder acknowledged that Benny, like his fellow Funk Brothers, remained "unknown. Because for the most part, these cats'd be in the studios all day, and as musicians they weren't getting that recognition then. People weren't interested in the musicians."[6]

Though the Funk Brothers remained anonymous and uncredited, and were paid only $5 to $10 a session since Motown wasn't union (notably, the standard union rate back then was around $52.50 per session), they played as if their lives depended on it.[7] Trombonist Paul Riser recalled making a mere $2.50 per song at the start, which later increased to seven bucks per track. Ironically, when Motown first began, Gordy initially wanted to be a union signatory in the musicians' union in Detroit; however, due to racism, they weren't allowed. "The union didn't consider Motown a part of the music world. The union had no interest in us whatsoever," said Stevenson. "We were just 'a bunch of Negroes making some of those R&B records,' which wasn't even considered real music in its estimation. As long as we didn't bother anybody or get outta hand, who cared?"[8]

Undeterred, these musicians made a way out of no way to create mind-blowing music. Like the time they converted the downstairs bathroom's hollow enclosure into the company's first echo chamber, since it naturally produced prolonged reverberation. They were relentless, using a variety of instruments to create unique sounds, like tambourines, bells, blocks, vibes, congas, violins, handclaps, or anything else that could make a unique echo on countless different songs.

"Those musicians are just as important as Berry, if not more so. There would be music but it wouldn't be the Motown sound. *That's* the difference," said Paul Riser, who earned the label its first-ever Grammy Award in the Best R&B Instrumental Performance category for his work as an arranger and conductor on the Temptations' 1972 song "Papa Was a Rollin' Stone." Riser was fresh out of Cass Technical High School when he arrived at the label and joined the Funk Brothers as a trombonist. Classically trained on both strings and horns, Riser mastered being able to merge soul with classical horn and rhythm arrangements to contribute to the Motown sound.

When it came to making music, though, just about everyone at the label was tapped to help out in the studio. It wasn't unusual for other artists to perform background on one another's sessions. It wasn't even unusual for regular employees to join in the creation of sound if they could keep a beat by clapping their hands or stomping their feet. "The love we felt for each other when we were playing is the most undisputed truth about our music. I sometimes referred to our sound as a combination of rats, roaches, soul, guts and love," said Gordy.[9]

Motown's headquarters were located in a section of Detroit that also housed a considerable black market for drugs, like many of the other Black neighborhoods in the city during this time. Depending on the time of day, there were also gangs to contend with like the Shakers (and their female counterparts, including the Shakerettes), which was one of the largest groups, with about seven hundred members—all of whom were aggressively protective of their turf area, the North End neighborhood in Detroit. Some local musicians even joined gangs themselves; singer Jackie Wilson, for example, was one of the Shakers' most famous members.[10] Whenever he performed in areas controlled by rival gangs, the Shakers often showed up to add extra security. Whether or not they were tied to a specific gang, many of the artists at Motown could hold and handle their own, as they'd grown up in housing projects or low-income areas and were no strangers to confrontation.

If they needed a sense of belonging, after all, they didn't have to look much further than Motown itself. As the founder and one of the elder members of the company, Gordy took on a fatherlike role at Motown; in fact, many of the artists and staff were teens and young adults. Also, at least initially, the company was based in a small house, one that didn't look like much from the outside but served as the headquarters and recording studio. Gordy's wife at the time, Raynoma, and their kids lived on the second floor, but the rest of the house was reserved exclusively for Motown.

Though small, the house was welcoming, with a large picture window at the front and a nice reception area. Other rooms in the building were for writers, including the writers' department and the A&R department. Part of the dining room was converted into the control room and another house section was the tape library. The previous homeowner had been a photographer and had put a photo studio in the back, which Gordy still used. Reel-to-reel tape recorders and pianos were available in each room so that anyone entering—particularly the creatives—could immediately find inspiration should they seek it out. Seven days a week, twenty-four hours a day, there was always something going on at Motown's home base.

One of the house's most pivotal transformations was the garage, which Gordy turned into a recording studio called Studio A. Studio A was often referred to as the "snake pit" because of the wall-to-wall cables on the floor. The small rectangular space with hardwood floors included an 1877 Steinway grand piano; the nine-foot instrument was made of Victorian rosewood. Then, adjoined to Studio A was the control room (in the living room), which notably included an eight-track recorder. At Motown, the music itself was always completed and recorded on a track first. Songwriters were then given the track and instructed to fit the lyrics to the tune. The vocals were recorded and added only as the last stage of the process. And this was how Motown was able to successfully produce a steady stream of hits—just like an assembly line.

By 1962, just two years after Motown's founding, that conveyor belt was lining up a succession of smash tunes that kept the world talking. Motown's first superstar was the sexy singer Mary Wells. She released three songs, all written by Smokey Robinson, which included "The One Who Really Loves You," "You Beat Me to the Punch," and "Two Lovers." Robinson also put his own buttery-smooth falsetto to use as the lead voice for his group; Smokey Robinson and the Miracles released two songs of their own, one called "I'll Try Something New," which was cowritten by him and Gordy; and another called "You've Really Got a Hold on Me," which was written by just Robinson.

With all these hit songs taking the country by storm, Gordy was keen to ensure that he was fully capitalizing on the label's success. Not only did he want audiences to hear all of this new music on the radio, but he wanted them to be able to experience their favorites performed live. So, at the urging of Motown flutist and saxophonist Thomas "Beans" Bowles (also a bandleader and early Funk Brother, who later became an assistant to Gordy's sister Esther Gordy Edwards), Berry Gordy started the Motortown Revue in the fall of 1962. Initially calling it the Motor Town Special, Bowles had grown tired of waiting for White promoters to take an interest in Motown's artists and book them for gigs around the country; instead, he assembled a roster of the label's finest talent, cobbled together a rough itinerary, and assumed the role of "tour manager" himself as the Revue hit the road. For two dollars, audiences enjoyed acts like Mary Wells, Singin' Sammy Ward, Martha and the Vandellas, the Contours, the Supremes, the Marvelettes, the Miracles, Marvin Gaye, and Little Stevie Wonder. In turn, these acts were able to sell a lot more records and gain invaluable national exposure.

Over the course of three months, the Revue played more than ninety-one evening shows, starting out at the Howard Theatre in Washington, DC, where they performed in front of a sold-out audience. The Motortown Revue primarily traveled along a specific route called the "chitlin circuit," a term that described a select group of smaller, but still crowded, Black performance venues along the Eastern, Southern, and Midwestern parts of the United States. Importantly, all of these locations were handled by Black promoters and had been deemed as safe spaces for Black entertainers to perform during segregation. Just about all the Black entertainers up to this point played this circuit; now, in the 1960s, the Ray Charles Revue, James Brown, Curtis Mayfield and the Impressions, the O'Jays, the Joe Tex with His Skinny

Legs and All Revue, Harold Melvin and the Blue Notes, and Sam and Dave were among the hottest shows traveling along the circuit. However, Motown's music—which was mainly pop-based and infused with R&B—managed to appeal to both Black *and* White audiences, meaning their broader audience often resembled more of a mixing pot than anything like the chitlin circuit where it was solely Black.

Though Motown was eager to broaden their mass appeal to audiences of all colors, they still had to contend with racism in many parts of the country while on tour. Until 1965, Jim Crow laws in the South prevented Black and White audiences from intermingling. In order to monitor this, a guard had to literally stand in front of the stage and police the crowds during these shows. In some Southern states, a rope would even be strung across the middle of the audience, dividing the races in half.

Though Motown artists fought hard to convince people that they could succeed in front of diverse audiences outside of the chitlin circuit, they still faced considerable challenges on their tours. Onstage, the Motortown Revue performed brilliantly, shining like diamonds in resplendent outfits and dancing with precision choreography. Offstage, however, rocks were often thrown at them, shotguns were pointed at them, and they were declined service to eat in restaurants and even to use the same public toilets as White patrons. In Birmingham, Alabama, members of the Revue once were mistaken for Freedom Riders and their tour bus was attacked by bullets. During another performance in Macon, Georgia, a Confederate flag hung menacingly over the stage, warning the Black entertainers of the state's dark history. "We had this cat, Gene Shelby, and he told this one guy, 'Our big star Marvin Gaye ain't gonna like that flag,'" Stevie Wonder later recalled. "This guy says, 'Hey, boy, see the way that flag's blowin' in the breeze? If you don't get your tail out of here, your tail's gonna be up in a tree blowin' just like that flag.'"[11]

In spite of the perils of performing in certain states, Motown was able to grow and succeed precisely by uniting audiences of all colors. Gordy wasn't overly concerned with divisive lines, whether they be related to race *or* genre; in fact, what made Motown stand out above its competition was that Gordy was always focused on creating new ways for his artists and their music to cross over into the pop charts. Historically, up to this point, most songs performed by Black artists relied on repetitive lyrics without much deeper meaning, including hits like "Please, Please, Please" by James Brown, "Personality" by Lloyd Price, and "Shimmy, Shimmy, Ko-Ko-Bop" by Little Anthony and the Imperials. Gordy wanted more from his writers, and he told them specifically that they needed to hook audiences by the twenty-second mark. Lyrics couldn't just be monotonous, either; they needed to form a story, with a beginning, a middle, and an ending, a story that reflected something tangible and real that the listener could relate to. "Motown *educated* people through song," said Gordy.[12] This happened by being deliberate with lyrics, recalled Smokey Robinson about what he learned directly from Gordy: "Berry sat me down, and he explained to me that a song is like a short book—or a short film, or a short story, or a short poem—where everything is tied together. He said a song needs to have a beginning, a middle and an end, and it needs to mean something. And since that moment, I've always written with that in mind. I always try to make my songs mean something."[13]

Fortunately, the fruits of Gordy's efforts extended far beyond Motown, paving the way for how other Black music was merchandised and packaged, too. For instance, Black artists were typically not featured on the album covers themselves until their songs became hits.

This way, the audience could fall in love with the music outside of any racial prejudice they might harbor.

Then, when his artists *were* visible, Gordy made certain they were class acts by looking every bit the part, investing in their style and stage presence. Coaches were brought in to help the performers finesse their skills, starting with Maurice King, a former musical director for the popular Flame Show Bar, one of the hottest Black nightclubs in Detroit. In 1963, Gordy hired King as the musical conductor and director in charge of voice and music for live performances. In this role, he conducted acts like Marvin Gaye, the Miracles, and the Supremes. In addition to making certain that his artists were taken care of, Gordy managed to help his songs attain longevity by having different musicians cover songs that were previously recorded by other Motown acts. He used this strategy until a different rendition became popular or experienced the same level of success as the initial version. This happened with songs down the line, like "I Heard It Through the Grapevine," first performed by the Miracles, Gladys Knight and the Pips, and then Marvin Gaye; and later on, "With a Child's Heart," written by Sylvia Moy and first performed by Stevie Wonder and then Michael Jackson.

Merchandising and packaging weren't the only hurdles to successful sales for Black artists. *Billboard* magazine was considered the crème de la crème of the music industry, so to make the charts for that publication was a vast boost for any career. But right around the time Motown was coming into its own in 1963, *Billboard* suddenly decided to stop publishing its R&B charts—after twenty years. The exact logic underlying this decision remains unclear; supposedly, the R&B chart was becoming "the mainstream for American pop music," which meant there was no longer a need for two distinct charts.[14] Whatever the reason, from November 1963 to January 1965, sixty-two issues of

*Billboard* did not include the R&B chart.[15] Consequently, the presence of African American artists, who were already scarcely featured on the pop charts, became virtually nonexistent on any of the charts during this period. When *Billboard* reinstated the charts in 1965, R&B songs were permitted to cross over to the pop charts; however, this usually took place only after a song first topped the R&B chart. This meant that Black artists had to be *twice* as good. The clarity behind the chart's subsequent resurgence is just as confounding as its disappearance, though supposedly it was reinstated because, according to a contradictory assessment made long after the fact, "many R&B records continued to record hits that did not show up on the pop chart."[16]

Despite this period of uncertainty, Gordy's indie label remained undefeated, because Gordy had positioned his artists in such a way that they were well situated to turn this obstacle into something that worked in their favor. While similar artists from other record labels faded from listings once the chart was removed, Gordy's music had crossover appeal with different races and people of various ages and musical tastes. As 1964's "British Invasion," led by groups like the Beatles and the Rolling Stones, began dominating *Billboard*'s pop charts, the Motown sound gained even more exposure. As it turned out, Gordy's Detroit label was a major influence on these foreign artists, and in turn, foreign audiences. In the late spring of 1964, Mary Wells's song "My Guy" helped her to become one of Motown's first artists to have a hit song in the UK. A few months later, the Supremes also landed on the UK charts with the tune "Baby Love," signaling the first time that either a Motown group or a girl group topped its charts. Back home in the United States, five of Motown's artists made *Billboard*'s Year-End "Hot 100 Singles" chart in 1964, including "My Guy" by Mary Wells (#7); "Dancing in the Street" by Martha and the Vandellas (#17); "Baby Love" by the Supremes (#33); "Baby I Need Your Loving" by the Four Tops (#57); and "The Way You Do the Things You Do" by the Temptations (#71).

What made these accomplishments so remarkable was that, since Motown was a budding label, Gordy didn't have a blueprint to follow whenever problems arose, whether in Motown itself or the overall industry. Everything was handled in-house, so he had to figure out different ways to overcome these obstacles all on his own. Though Motown's independent label status meant it lacked significant financial resources, Gordy was still able to implement unique strategies that he'd learned from previous jobs. For instance, back when he sold Guardian Service cookware, while trying to reach his sales quota he'd learned that competition was an effective way to generate results. He noticed how internal competitions helped the business achieve higher profits, because the competitiveness challenged employees to work harder. Whoever sold the most earned the most. People were forced to think outside the box in order to succeed, and in turn, morale was boosted when those who won were rewarded and recognized for their efforts.

So, to keep his songwriters on their toes, Gordy consistently implemented songwriting battles, where his creatives vied for the next big hit. Gordy kicked off the first one three years earlier, in 1961, by challenging his writers to go against *him*. To no surprise, Smokey Robinson, who was Gordy's first writer, rose to the occasion. Though Gordy was already producing Mary Wells, Robinson set out to write a hit just for her. And he did with the 1962 tune "The One Who Really Loves You." Soon others followed with hit songs, hoping to dethrone the previous person with an even bigger chart-topper. The wheels were set in motion, because Gordy wanted his songwriters to be *twice* as good as everyone else, and he'd reminded them that "competition breeds champions."[17]

Another inspiration came from his days working on an actual assembly line. Every Friday in his office, Gordy held invite-only "quality control meetings" that usually included songwriters and producers, in which they discussed songs that the label planned to release next and why. These gatherings were to ensure that every single detail about the tunes was top-tier, but before they even made it there, these songs had to first make it past the approval of Billie Jean Brown. If Brown didn't approve it, a song never crossed the table for discussion. Gordy had placed the aspiring young attorney in charge of the quality control department because "she was strong, opinionated, honest, witty and had a good ear."[18]

Because of the internal pressure stoked by Gordy, rivalries were already steep by 1963—a year before Sylvia Moy arrived at Motown. By then, in-house hitmaker Smokey Robinson had plenty of competition when it came to those songwriting battles. Norman Whitfield, an up-and-coming songwriter and producer, was working to make a name for himself. He had already helped place Marvin Gaye on the pop charts in 1963 with his first Top 10 hit, "Pride and Joy," a ballad dedicated to Gaye's then-wife, Anna Gordy, who was also Berry's sister. The label also scored big that year with the Martha and the Vandellas hits "Heat Wave" and "Come and Get These Memories," along with the Miracles' "Mickey's Monkey."

With just fewer than one hundred employees by 1963, Motown had grown into a force to be reckoned with—and yet, it still felt intimate. It had a family feel both figuratively *and* literally, since there was a Gordy in every department. Motown was basically an extension of the Gordy family with all of its "fierce closeness and fierce competition and constant collaboration," said Berry.[19]

Despite the industry standard of men at the top of the chain, it was no surprise that Gordy's sisters held top positions at his company. His sisters, who held their own long before him in entertainment circles as socialites, songwriters, and entrepreneurs, were instrumental as he entered the music industry. It was only natural for him to have them by his side. Esther Gordy Edwards, Gordy's eldest sister, served as senior vice president; and Loucye Gordy Wakefield, Gordy's third sister, was named Motown's first vice president until her death at the age of forty. And it wasn't just his sisters and direct female relatives, either. In fact, from the company's beginnings, several women were placed in key executive roles across Motown. As previously mentioned, Billie Jean Brown, who got her start writing liner notes and being a general assistant, ran the quality control department. Frances Heard was the tape library director, Fay Hale headed the processing department, and Maxine Powell directed the in-house finishing school for all its artists. "[Gordy's] willingness to open doors for women was because he had so many sisters," explained receptionist-turned-songwriter Janie Bradford. "This might have attributed to him being open to allowing those kinds of opportunities, especially during the time when people felt like a woman's place was in the kitchen. The Gordy women were not that type. They were always strong women."

Raynoma Gordy Singleton, Berry's second wife, who helped him build up the company during its infancy, was actually the first female producer and arranger at Motown. Gordy didn't mind allowing her to be in this position, because her training had come from Cass Technical High School, which was renowned at this time for a curriculum that rivaled the collegiate level. In addition to working with the Rayber Voices singing group, Raynoma did everything from helping musicians learn to read music to speaking up so that people could make more money to making sandwiches for the hungry teens. She was considered Motown's backbone in its early days.

Raynoma's position as a top creative was a noted anomaly, not just in Motown but across the industry. Aside from Raynoma and Janie Bradford, there weren't *any* single female in-house songwriters or producers before 1964 at the label. During the sixties, female songwriters who won acclaim generally did so only by partnering with their husbands. And becoming a producer as a woman? That was simply out of the question at Hitsville or just about any other record label.

But Motown always managed to stand out from the rest and lead the way. And just around the corner, the label was on the brink of creating more music history with yet another female.

## CHAPTER 6

# Change of Plans

By 1963, Sylvia—like Motown—was well on her way to achieving the musical success she'd been dreaming of. As it so happened, the same week her confidence took a low blow after rejections in New York, Sylvia booked a major gig downtown. After another White female singer fell ill, Sylvia was called to fill in during a weekend at the Caucus Club, one of the city's most renowned supper clubs, which was located in the heart of Detroit's financial district.

The Caucus Club first opened in 1952 as an overflow for its sister restaurant, the London Chop House, which was across the street and at one point regarded as one of the best restaurants not just in Detroit, but in the whole country. Located on the ground floor of the Penobscot Building and known for its distinguished dark paneling and brass sconces, the Caucus Club earned a reputation as the place where Detroit's prominent celebrities and leaders, including decision-makers, politicians, and barons of industry, came to see and to be seen. Conducting business and making deals were the norm during the many power lunches that took place. One never knew who was dining there. The back room of the posh downtown spot was a place where a person could make a grand impression and get discovered.

At one time, the Caucus Club was a private establishment for gentlemen only.[1] Before it was opened to ladies in the late sixties, not many women were even allowed to perform there, and when they did, it was only for a special occasion. This is where a then unknown nineteen-year-old Barbra Streisand launched her professional career in 1961 as a lounge singer. She became one of the early female performers there, so this was a big deal.

Two years later, Sylvia became one of the first Black women to grace that same stage. She initially performed as part of a trio that featured front man Johnny Griffith, the renowned pianist and member of Motown's in-house studio band, the Funk Brothers.

By 1964, things seemed to be looking up for not just Sylvia and the musicians at Motown, but African Americans in general, when President Lyndon B. Johnson signed the Civil Rights Act, which legally ended the segregation that had been institutionalized by Jim Crow laws. It was a time for celebration and exploration. While most Black people had long visited the popular Flame Show Bar for live entertainment, with more downtown Detroit establishments now welcoming Black people, more Black folks increasingly felt comfortable hitting the high-end Caucus Club. On occasion, those who could afford to do so were front and center—including Motown's A&R head, Mickey Stevenson, and a soul singer named Marvin Gaye.

On the same night that the club was about to feature Sylvia's highly anticipated special performance, these two tall, dark, and handsome friends strutted into the joint and sent her life spiraling in a new direction. Marvin and Mickey enjoyed each other's company just as much as they enjoyed the nightlife, and it wasn't unusual for them to visit hot spots together to scope out potential talent. There weren't many Black women allowed to perform at this place, so the two made it a point to check out the new singer who was making a buzz in the city and in the *Detroit Free Press* for having soloed with the Detroit Symphony.

Standing six foot one with a slim build, Gaye was an attractive attention-grabber who was rising in the ranks at Motown as one of the label's most promising crooners. Before he was a singer, Gaye worked as a session drummer for Anna Records—cofounded by Gordy's sisters Anna and Gwen—and initially moved over to Motown only to travel as a drummer with Smokey Robinson and the Miracles. Often wearing sunglasses and smoking a corncob pipe, Gaye was also a gifted pianist—but what he really wanted to be was a jazz singer. In 1961, he released his debut album, *The Soulful Moods of Marvin Gaye*; however, it was his 1962 hit song, "Stubborn Kind of Fella," that put him on the map after reaching #10 on the R&B chart and Top Fifty on the Billboard Hot 100. The song was cowritten with Stevenson and Gordy's brother George, who also worked in the A&R department. That same year, he also played the drums and received his first writing credit on a song for the Marvelettes called "Beechwood 4-5789," cowritten with Stevenson and George.

Though Stevenson was a high-ranking executive at the label, that didn't stand in the way of hanging out with his close pal for a night on the town. Unlike Gaye, who was a bit shy and introverted, Stevenson was bold and confident, immediately owning whatever room he stepped into. Like Gaye, he was also attractive and hard to miss. His silver-streaked hair was styled in smooth, perfect finger waves and he wore a finely tailored silk suit. Stevenson also held one of Motown's most commanding positions as the director of A&R. That night in the Caucus, the producer had all the power, and everyone around him *knew* it.

Sylvia's appearance and performance of a jazz standard captured Stevenson's attention right away. As a classically trained vocalist, her voice wasn't particularly soulful or gritty, but it commanded power. She was a songstress with her own style. Also, because few women of color performed here, it wasn't hard to figure out that Sylvia was a person who had something special. Her beauty captured most people's attention, but it was her voice that kept it, particularly on this night in the smoke-filled establishment. And once he caught wind of her talent, Stevenson knew he had to bring her to Motown. "I was the kind of person that if I saw something that interested me, I would immediately set up to talk to you whether you were ready or not," said Stevenson. "Whatever hit me, that's what I dealt with."

Immediately after the set, Stevenson handed Sylvia his business card and suggested that she come in to audition for him. At Motown, auditions took place every third Thursday. *Nobody* could just waltz in whenever they wanted to, recalled songwriter Janie Bradford, who worked as a secretary and later as director of writers' relations at Motown. Even if you knew somebody who worked there, you had to follow protocol. "Everybody was auditioned by somebody and listened to and agreed upon by whoever was in charge of that particular field to bring the person on board," said Bradford.

Sylvia was thrilled and went in to audition with the first two songs she'd ever written—"I'm Still Loving You" and "A Little More Love." Though both songs had been rejected by record executives in the Big Apple, she knew they'd stand a fair shot at Motown. "New York couldn't understand. They didn't have that ear," she later explained.

"But here at Motown, you had people with raw talent and people with the ears to understand, to feel and hear the raw talent that I had."[2]

Upon first arriving at 2648 West Grand Boulevard, Sylvia laid eyes on the tiny house with a carved wooden sign out front that was hand-painted blue and read "Hitsville U.S.A." Nervous, Sylvia took one last puff of her cigarette before pitching it to the ground and stepping on it. She steadied herself and prepared to walk in, eager to show the label "the same two songs at Motown I was playing in New York."[3]

Because Motown was still small in 1964, it wasn't unusual for someone to audition in front of two or three other songwriters and producers. Sometimes, they were listening to the artist's performance to assess their vocal skills, but just as often, they evaluated the candidate's other skills as well, especially if they wrote their own material. Since she didn't have anyone to play for her, ever self-sufficient, Sylvia drew upon her childhood days of banging on pots and pans with her siblings and beat on the table to keep her own rhythm as she sang. And so it was that the shy young woman performed her first song, "I'm Still Loving You," written about her first love, Al, and how she continued to love him even though she knew they could never reconcile.

With all eyes on her in the tiny room of the audition, Sylvia belted out:

*I'm still loving you.*

*No matter what you say or do.*

She then started beating on the table, singing the next verse.

And as she continued, something magical happened. "I think Eddie and Brian Holland, Lamont Dozier, Mickey, Hank Cosby and Ivy Jo Hunter were there. Quite a few people, and I sang and they joined in with the rhythm, beating on the table. That was the beginning of it all."[4]

In that audition space, Sylvia knew in her gut that this place—Motown—was where she really belonged. "For once, someone understood where I was coming from. They all stood up and started knocking on the table with me," Sylvia later recalled. "Most of the record companies just didn't understand my material. I met with very little success until Mickey Stevenson and Marvin Gaye told me to come over to Motown and speak with Berry Gordy."[5]

What she didn't know at the time was that not only was the assembled crew listening to her vocal abilities, but they were also impressed with the songs themselves. When she informed them that she had written both, and without any formal training as a songwriter, it became clear that Sylvia was more than just a good singer. "She started singing and I thought, 'That's pretty good.' She had the gift," said Stevenson, who maintained that he was impressed with the lyrics of both love songs more so than her voice itself. "I was instrumental in signing ninety percent of the people there. She wasn't singing like the female singers like we had. She wasn't hitting it where we needed to go, [but] she had the gift as a songwriter. That's what I went with. End of conversation."

After her audition, Gordy talked to her about signing a contract with Motown and coming aboard as a songwriter. Gordy relied on Mickey's foresight to help him build the role around the person individually rather than fitting a person into a preexisting role. Everyone present heard Sylvia's potential. And so it was that Sylvia became the first woman in Motown's A&R department to go toe-to-toe, pound-for-pound, with the male-dominated in-house songwriting staff, working alongside the likes of Smokey Robinson, Holland-Dozier-Holland, Norman Whitfield, Barrett Strong, and Ivy Jo Hunter. She was now officially recognized, or "certified," as Motown arranger Paul Riser called it.

However, her career at Motown didn't start off quite as she'd envisioned. In truth, she was totally caught off guard when Gordy agreed with Stevenson and suggested that she pursue songwriting over singing. She'd never thought to put singing on the back burner before, as up to that point, it had been her primary source of income. "Motown came forth with a recording contract for me, a management contract, and a songwriter's contract—which shocked me. Then I was told, 'Sylvia, we'll get to you as a singer. But in the meantime, we've got all these artists and they have no material. You're going to have to write.' I said, 'OK,' because I was kind of shy anyway. And so that's what I started doing."[6]

Though she'd agreed to be a songwriter, it took Sylvia a while to warm up to the idea of that role being her primary focus at Motown. She'd always been shy prior to getting on a stage, but once she hit the limelight, she came *alive*. The only reason she'd started writing songs in the first place was to improve her own chances as a singer by creating material for herself so that she could record songs to earn money for college. And now, she was being told to focus *only* on that.

Fortunately, though Sylvia had auditioned on her own, she quickly formed friendships with her new colleagues—and even reunited with long-lost friends. As it so happened, Sylvia's childhood buddy Louvain Demps had been recruited to Motown as a member of the Andantes. The two had lost contact after Sylvia left Pershing High School and were delighted to be brought back together.

While Sylvia was initially fairly reserved, she also had a pleasant personality and laid-back demeanor, which made her both likable and approachable. In addition to Demps, Sylvia counted Janie Bradford as someone she'd later consider a close friend at the label. As Sylvia's polar opposite, Bradford was the life of the party up at Motown: loud, boisterous, and known for not taking *any* shit. Sylvia was tickled by Bradford's unapologetic nature. "We just took to each other. It was natural. Maybe it was because we were both songwriters," explained Bradford.

Sylvia forged other close friendships at Motown with women in different departments, like Patricia Cosby, who was both the wife of songwriter and producer Henry "Hank" Cosby and the first cousin of Janie Bradford's husband. Patricia was also the assistant to Frances Heard, Motown's director of the tape library. Patricia and Fran, as everyone called her, met Sylvia together on the same day. Patricia spotted Sylvia on her first day of work, sitting in the Motown lobby, and she never forgot how Sylvia informed her of what her role would be. "She had her little yellow writing pad and a tape recorder," remembered Patricia. "I walked over to her and introduced myself. She responded, 'I'm Sylvia. I'm going to be singing and I'm working with Mickey Stevenson.'"

Though Sylvia never became an official recording artist at Motown, Patricia later heard Sylvia sing for herself and remarked that she "had a lovely singing voice." Since the tape library was directly across the hall from the studio, Patricia and Fran had one of the best offices in the place. As Patricia later recalled, the two of them could "hear everything that was going on" behind the Dutch door that had a window with a hole in it that could be opened and closed. Patricia remembered overhearing some of the guys talking about a writer named "Sylvia" and she wondered if this was the same woman she'd just met in the lobby. A few weeks later, Patricia received a call sheet that identified who was going to be in the upcoming quality control meeting. Patricia's suspicions and questions were answered when she saw Sylvia's name pop up on that very list.

Fran and Patricia immediately noticed how quiet Sylvia was, so they decided to break the ice and take her to lunch. Patricia called it the "Motown way"—whenever somebody new came on board in general, they wanted to embrace that person and make them feel like they were part of the family. Fran and Patricia invited their newest colleague to join them at Cunningham's, a popular drugstore in Detroit that sold everything from medicine to lawn chairs to a good meal. Not wanting to come off as antisocial, Sylvia accepted their invitation. She was also receptive to meeting new people, even if it took time for her to open up.

"She did not have much to say. She was just a quiet person, but not in a bad way," said Patricia. "She did say that she had the desire to sing and that she thought she was coming to Motown to sing, but they wanted her to be a writer." Fran encouraged Sylvia to take advantage of the opportunity, because this might "be a gift." Sylvia agreed, but she made it known that she felt like "they tricked me into signing all of these contracts," as Patricia remembered her saying. Fran reminded Sylvia that if anyone desired to do something creative, Motown was the place to be. Sylvia nodded her acquiescence, seeming to resolve that she had no choice but to come to grips with this change in career plans.

Though she didn't fight back against her new designation at the label, there was always a part of her that wondered why she couldn't be both a singer *and* a songwriter. Of course, Motown employees were generally not encouraged to fill the roles of both performers *and* creatives simultaneously, making Smokey somewhat of a rarity in the Motown world. Moreover, most of the songwriters on the payroll had started out as singers at one time or another, before then shifting over to writing full-time.

That didn't make it any less confusing in Sylvia's case, though. Patricia Cosby was perplexed as to why Sylvia could not have been given the same consideration as Smokey. "Why couldn't she have written songs and performed if she wanted to?" asked Patricia during a 2022 interview. "So many people [at Motown] played so many games. Some figured she would not make it as a writer [since no woman had ever been hired as an in-house writer]. It was almost like they were setting it up for her to fail."

There were other challenges to contend with, too—central among them that Sylvia had to figure out how to work in a tiny house with limited space. At the time, Motown's smaller headquarters meant that the label didn't have rehearsal halls or even offices for most of their writers. Certain writers and producers, such as Hank Cosby, Brian and Eddie Holland, Lamont Dozier, and Smokey Robinson, had their own spaces, but a brand-new writer like her would be out of luck. "Sylvia was usually in the lobby," said Patricia, who remembered that Sylvia mostly greeted her with a shy smile and not much else. Then one day, Sylvia said something to Fran, who couldn't wait to get back to the tape library to tell Patricia.

"I know I got some songs that can be hits!" Patricia recalled Fran telling her about Sylvia's comment and excitement on that revelatory day. Patricia said that Sylvia, who could be "feisty," told Fran that if they wanted her to be a songwriter, then that's what she would do.

She was finally ready to see where this road would lead her.

---

Sylvia witnessed how the label became a symbol of not just Black excellence, but excellence—*period.*

Most of the artists at Motown were still teens and had grown up in housing projects or lower-income neighborhoods. They were young and rough around the edges—no strangers to the mean streets of Detroit. Still, Gordy didn't want them to seem unpolished. Black people were constantly being judged and frowned upon as inferior. He knew they had to always be ten times better than others, so Gordy brought in people to refine them in all the areas that were lacking.

To help his artists, Gordy created a department called Artist Development. Musicians were expected to attend sessions there twice a week and pay for their own training, because they were essentially investing in themselves. Lessons in style and grooming were led by etiquette coach Maxine Powell, who was hired in 1964. Powell was the main force behind the glamorous girl-group image presented by the Supremes and their peers: exquisite matching gowns, dainty heels, flawless makeup, and coiffed wigs. Unlike other teen-girl groups of the day, the Supremes were not only beautiful, but they were also graceful and elegant—the epitome of style. The guy groups held their own in matching suits and shoes. In addition to maintaining their appearance, Powell instructed everyone in how to conduct themselves on and away from the stage. She believed they would one day perform in front of royalty, so *they* had to be regal, too.

Also in 1964, Gordy hired Charles Atkins, known by the nickname Cholly, as the in-house choreographer. Because he was a seasoned veteran in the industry, he became another father figure for the artists and was also lovingly called by another name, "Pops." As one half of the top vaudeville dance act, Coles and Atkins, in the forties, Atkins was brought in to teach dance routines and stage presence, such as entering and exiting. Artists like the Supremes, the Temptations, the Four Tops, and Gladys Knight and the Pips all benefited and became renowned for their smooth dance moves and perfect synchronization, thanks to Atkins. The artists had raw talent so he studied their abilities and tried to fit choreography to groups or individuals by mapping out what he called vocal choreography so there was a harmonious flow between the singing and the dancing. Usually for six hours a day, six days a week, for eight weeks, they'd practice. But if they weren't as polished as Atkins hoped for, he'd go on the road with them to rehearse before and between shows.

Above all else, Gordy wanted his artists to be the *best.* "It was us against the world," Sylvia explained. "It was hope for us, kids from the projects, that otherwise might not have had hope. We were the rejects of the music industry. We were those that would've been turned down by many of those major companies that were happening out there. They actually, the Gordys, took what would've been the rejects of the music industry and proved the point."[7]

Inspiration was all around at Motown, and Sylvia had a front-row seat to witness historical moments right as they happened. After Smokey penned Mary Wells's 1964 #1 Billboard chart-topping tune "My Guy," she was hailed as the "Queen of Motown" and the label's first female star. In the same year, Smokey's songwriting skills remained a force to be reckoned with, as hits like the Temptations' "My Girl" and "The Way You Do the Things You Do" played on repeat across radio stations nationwide.

But the cherry on top came via the songwriting trio of Holland-Dozier-Holland, who took home the prestigious BMI "Songwriters of the Year" award. As hard as it may be to believe now, there was a period when the Supremes were nicknamed the "no-hit Supremes," with one flop after the next. Between 1961 and 1963 they released eight singles without any charting in the Top 40 positions of the Billboard Hot 100. However, their patience and persistence paid off when Lamont Dozier and brothers Brian and Eddie Holland helped turn the ladies into superstars with three #1 Billboard pop-chart-topping singles in a row, including "Baby Love," "Where Did Our Love Go?," and "Come See About Me"—all from their second album, *Where Did Our Love Go?* They went from being on the bottom to right on top as one of music's most acclaimed groups period, let alone girl groups.

Sylvia first met Diana Ross, lead vocalist of the Supremes, when they were both kids and the internationally acclaimed performer still went by her birth name, Diane. Sylvia recalled, "She always said she was going to be a star and would go through whatever changes she had to with a smile! They would often tell her she couldn't sing as well as say, Brenda Holloway, but Diana didn't care. She was determined to be a superstar, no matter what."[8]

Since Motown's limited budget meant that everyone had to step up and help out in the studio, Sylvia quickly became part of the behind-the-scenes team that helped the Supremes make their music. At the time, Motown was really into sound effects and made instruments out of all kinds of things, which reminded Sylvia of her childhood. As she pitched in with sound effects at the studio, she had to learn how to do multiple actions at once while being recorded. For example, on the Supremes' hit "Baby Love," Sylvia and her colleagues had to stomp and clap their hands at the same time. "We stomped on boards all the way through songs…on almost all the Supremes' things, we'd lay boards out on the floor and wear shoes with steel in the heels. There would be a whole group of us on those boards stomping all the way through and they would mike that up."[9]

And Sylvia helped out with more than just sound effects. According to her friend and in-house background singer Louvain Demps, on occasion if one of the Andantes wasn't available to do backup work, Sylvia could step in as a soprano. She also assisted on work with lead vocals. "For the singers, sometimes she would do a vocal track," said Cornelius Grant, the Temptations' musical director and arranger. "She would sing some of the lyrics and then some of the singers would copy the lyrics." Whenever she was asked to fill in for backup vocals, she was paid $7. However, in at least one instance, just to be a good friend, she offered her services for nothing in return. Her buddy Demps couldn't hit her high soprano note on a song and she had to have Sylvia step in on her behalf. "Not too many people there had our voice. I can't remember the song, but I was having trouble. I just could *not* hit that note. Sylvia did the song for me. She never mentioned it to anyone," said Demps.

Sylvia had a lot of respect for the Andantes; she quickly recognized how essential they were to refining the Motown sound. "[The Andantes] did the polishing on all of the products," explained Sylvia. "They were that special piece of Motown, just as the musicians were. They were what made it Motown. You would never have to fix anything you recorded on them. They never took the studio into overtime to do a track. Time was money in the studio and you wanted to get finished quickly if you were the producer."[10]

She respected the street-smart Funk Brothers just as much. Sure, some were gun toters. A few of them talked shit, got high, got drunk, did drugs, and fought sometimes. But they had heart and were also the best damn musicians in Detroit. "If a fly flew by the music paper and did something on the paper, they were musicians that would play that spec as a note. Then there were those who couldn't read [music] hardly at all," said Sylvia. "But they could play with so much soul and so much feeling that they could bring goose pimples out on a rock. So, the church, that influence was there."[11]

When it came to her primary task of songwriting, Sylvia got a master class in watching the esteemed trio of Holland-Dozier-Holland turn up the heat and make magic. The same year that Sylvia got hired, the group wrote Marvin Gaye's "How Sweet It Is (To Be Loved by You)" and the Four Tops' "Baby I Need Your Loving." The Four Tops had long provided background vocals for other artists, and this pop single was the first time they'd had a chance to shine and launch themselves into the Top 20.

And the songwriting trio wasn't the only group pumping out the hits. Songwriter Ivy Jo Hunter was on top of the world after scoring a major smash with Martha and the Vandellas' new song "Dancing in the Street." Hunter was the brains behind the record; he maintained that Marvin Gaye only provided him the title, and Stevenson received a songwriting credit because of his A&R position and a deal Hunter had with him. "When you came into Motown, you were admitted by Mickey Stevenson and it was his [modus operandi] to take a piece of whatever you wrote in order for you to get in. His deal with me, we had a fifty-fifty sharing of whatever either one of us did."

This period also ushered in Motown's new label Soul, which had just signed its first artist, Shorty Long. His new bluesy tune, "Devil in the Blue Dress," was cowritten with Stevenson. Shorty, whose feet could barely touch the piano pedals, was a raw talent. Like Smokey Robinson, he was one of the few people at Motown allowed to write and produce their own music, because it was so unique that not everyone could figure out his style and sense of humor lyrically. Stevenson, however, did, and more importantly, he respected that Shorty wrote about what he believed in. "That's the kind of guy he was," said Stevenson. Shorty had a particular love for women with height and stature, for example, and it was often reflected in the songs he wrote. Stevenson recalled how one time, Shorty, ever animated and naturally funny, boasted to some of the Funk Brothers along with himself about the type of women he desired. Shorty talked about how "he saw a chick in the club with long legs and a big ass. I used to say, 'Shorty Long, man, you like them big girls?' He would say, 'William R., when you lay down, you're the same size,'" said Stevenson, chuckling. "His music would fit right in today, but it seemed a little out of place then. He was so different."

While Shorty Long never made an appearance on any TV shows during his ephemeral career, other Motown acts continued building their broad fan base. A benchmark for success in show business was an appearance on *The Ed Sullivan Show*, which was television's biggest prime-time variety show, on Sunday nights. Luckily for Motown, acts such as the Supremes, the Temptations, and Smokey Robinson and the

Miracles all made several appearances on the program and received widespread praise for their performances. Print media helped catapult these acts even further, especially since John H. Johnson, the pioneering African American publisher of two major Chicago-based Black magazines, supported all of the Motown acts. It wasn't long before the Supremes landed their first national covers on the monthly publication *Ebony* and its weekly sister publication, *Jet*. Both magazines were trailblazing media leaders, and soon, White mainstream print followed with articles in magazines like *Look* and *Time*.

Sylvia was thrilled with the label's momentum. She realized that songwriting was a viable career within the music industry, and she didn't need a formal education at the collegiate level to make a living that way. "I didn't have to worry about a job anymore," she said. "The powers that be here realized my talent and my value to what was here. And I was told, 'Okay, we'll advance you X amount of dollars per week so that you will not have to go job hunting so you can just concentrate on your music.'"[12]

Thanks to a mix of talent, tenacity, and circumstance, Sylvia had found herself in a different kind of classroom and she was ready to get a different kind of education—the Motown kind.

# CHAPTER 7

# And Then Came You

Hiring women into creative roles at Motown was one thing, and Gordy clearly had no problem doing that. Unlike many other labels at the time, Motown had hired females from day one for administrative roles. As a result, many of the women who were allowed to write songs were also expected to fulfill other positions within the company, meaning they couldn't focus solely on their writing. As a result, their writing contributions were at best overlooked and at worst disregarded by their male peers. According to longtime Motown employee Patricia Cosby, even when the women's riffs and rhythms held serious promise, their male colleagues did not consider them to be serious competition, and they didn't shy away from letting the women know. In addition to doubting their talent, the men were also skeptical about the longevity of their female coworkers at the label; Sylvia reportedly overheard whispers from certain men about "not helping her" because she probably wouldn't last long around there anyway.

Sylvia wasn't the only female writer who struggled in this environment; Vicki Basemore was another example. Patricia argued that Basemore and Janie Bradford were both "very good writers and the few releases that they got were really significant." Bradford had proven her songwriting abilities early on in 1959, when she joined forces with Gordy himself to cowrite the song "Money (That's What I Want)," which became Tamla Records' first hit. Basemore, on the other hand, wasn't even officially on the staff roster at Motown as an in-house songwriter but was allowed to write music. She was a young woman with connections to Mickey Stevenson, but she lacked a strong support system. As Patricia saw it, "She was another victim. There were other female writers who had very worthy material and it went nowhere." Her biggest hit would be a song cowritten with Sylvia, "With a Child's Heart."

Even women with family connections struggled to gain the recognition they craved. Raynoma Gordy Singleton, Berry Gordy's second wife, was one of the first women to write and arrange music at the label. In addition to playing the organ on the Marvelettes' song "Someday, Someway," she assisted with chord charts for "Money (That's What I Want)" along with singing background vocals on the Barrett Strong tune. Unfortunately, much like Basemore, Gordy Singleton's accomplishments weren't always acknowledged. Her time being short-lived at the label didn't help either. Still, her existence opened doors.

One of the main obstacles was that the head of the A&R department, Mickey Stevenson, was determined to run the business on his own terms—and those terms often excluded the women at Motown. Gordy told Stevenson that as head of A&R, he didn't have to report to anyone, and if Stevenson got trouble from someone and it wasn't Gordy, he should ignore it. This meant that Stevenson could do as he pleased, because Gordy trusted him to make the right decisions. "Getting into Motown was on [Motown's] terms. You couldn't even take the contract out of the building," said songwriter Ivy Jo Hunter. "So whatever you were going to do at Motown, you were going to do it the Motown way. As far as the A&R department is concerned, that was Mickey's baby."

Stevenson was a shrewd fast-talker who took his job seriously and never minced words with anyone, male or female. Stevenson showed no remorse or regrets about being selective in how he conducted business in the A&R department. As far as the department's dealings with women, the way he was treated by them determined how he'd act toward them. If he felt that he was unfairly being scrutinized without being given a fair chance, he didn't take this lightly and used his power to his advantage. "I ran the music division, so if you couldn't get along with me, it wasn't going to happen," Stevenson explained. "If you had an attitude about me because of what somebody told you and you brought that to me, it was going to change things. You got further away [from the goal]. I didn't want to deal with you. That gave me another reputation. They had all kinds of names for me. I was a dictator. I wasn't none of that."

This denial is at odds with accusations made by both men and women at Motown, including the Funk Brothers. Whenever they had sessions that needed to be finished, Stevenson would position himself in the control booth so that everyone in Studio A could see him standing high and looking low. It wasn't unusual for the Funk Brothers to work all-nighters because Stevenson refused to allow anyone to leave until everything was completed to his satisfaction. Drummer Benny Benjamin went so far as to nickname Stevenson "Il Duce," an Italian term that meant "the leader" but was more obviously a reference to Italian dictator Benito "Il Duce" Mussolini.

Benjamin wasn't the only one with an unflattering nickname for Stevenson; because of Stevenson's sexist attitude and practices toward women, the ladies had come up with a few nicknames of their own. "Some of the women of Motown had much nicer names for me, names that made 'Il Duce' sound like 'baby love.' They called me a chauvinist pig or 'that asshole,' and a few other choice words that even I'm too proud to mention," Stevenson said. He didn't have any misconceptions about why they disliked him, either, noting that "they called me all those undignified names because I wouldn't allow them to produce any artists."[1]

In Stevenson's eyes, the biggest problem with most of the female songwriters and women colleagues in general at Motown was that they did not understand what the positions required, and he felt that their skill sets were lacking in comparison to those of their male counterparts. "If I gave you something to do and you didn't bring it up to the level I thought it should be, nobody considered that part. They only considered what they did. Female writers didn't consider things had to reach a certain level," said Stevenson, justifying his actions. "We were not there to enjoy ourselves. This was a job. We had a whole world out there trying to stop us. So everything we came out with had better be not good but fantastic. Nobody understood that but the Berry Gordys, the Smokey Robinsons, and the Holland-Dozier-Hollands."

Though he admittedly did not engage with the majority of the women at Motown, Stevenson held Sylvia to her own standard and deeply respected her work ethic. "She wanted results. She wanted to know what she could do to make herself better. She came with conversations about making things better," explained Stevenson. "What could be done about this part of the song? She had another approach. One of learning, acquiring knowledge, and gaining information. That's what I was there for."

Observant but quiet, Sylvia stayed mostly to herself and formed her own opinions, which was another thing that set her apart from many of her female colleagues (in Stevenson's eyes). "She had an independent attitude, which was very good for me, because most of the females around there had a whole other way of looking at everything, especially me," Stevenson said and laughed. "Sylvia had a certain respect for me that was admirable for me when I talked to her. If someone had a problem with me, that was that person's problem. Don't bring it to her. She would stop you. That, I loved about her. You couldn't talk to her about me because she was working *with* me."

When conflict did arise, Stevenson trusted her instincts. "She had the ability, I would say a third sense, another way of dealing with things, which was very attractive to me," said Stevenson. "I could reach her with what was happening at the company with something I needed to have done. She would be an example, because I was known to not deal with any female writers. She looked past that and dealt with me one-on-one. I respected that...Sylvia was more of a warmer person. I sensed that about her. We would sit at the piano for hours. Sometimes we wouldn't be working on a song but talking. I wanted to get inside of her head because I could see she could be better. I did not waste my time with people doing that. I was inspired to do that with her. We wrote songs together. You know I had to be inspired to write songs with her."

Regardless of Stevenson's or his male colleagues' opinions about their female counterparts, it was obvious that women were on the rise in the early sixties—especially when it came to the girl groups blasting to the top of the pop charts. In 1961, a youthful quartet called the Shirelles hit it big with the crossover tune "Will You Love Me Tomorrow." Bolstered by a sweet melody, the song's lyrics came from the perspective of a young woman who was contemplating whether or not to have premarital sex with her beloved. It quickly caught on with audiences across the nation and became the first #1 pop single by a girl group, let alone an African American girl group. Encouraged by this success, labels everywhere hopped on the girl-group trend and launched hundreds of (mostly teen) girl groups over the next decade, including the Crystals, the Ronettes, the Chiffons, the Chantels, the Dixie Cups, and the Shangri-Las.

As it turned out, the music for "Will You Love Me Tomorrow" was actually written by a woman—the legendary singer-songwriter Carole King—who'd teamed up with her then-husband, lyricist Gerry Goffin, to finish the tune. By the early 1960s, a select few White women—including King, Cynthia Weil, and Ellie Greenwich—were making names for themselves by cowriting with their husbands and delegating responsibilities between themselves and the men, since women still weren't able to get writing credit on their own. In addition to allowing women to get their foot in the door in such a male-dominated industry, the male-female dynamic of these coupled partnerships meant that there was also greater diversity and range in the songs themselves. For example, King and Goffin's music was often soft and syrupy, such as the Chiffons' hit "One Fine Day," but they were also capable of writing bold and powerful tracks like the Crystals' "He Hit Me (And It Felt Like a Kiss)," which was one of the first pop songs to openly discuss the taboo subject of domestic abuse. Meanwhile, Greenwich and her husband, Jeff Barry, explored various facets of love across their songs, which included the likes of "Be My Baby" by the Ronettes, "Da Doo Ron Ron (When He Walked Me Home)" and "Then He Kissed Me" by the Crystals, "Chapel of Love" by the Dixie Cups, and "River Deep–Mountain High" by Ike and Tina Turner.

At the end of the day, female creatives in the music industry back then just didn't have as many options. A few of them, such as the little-known yet prolific African American songwriter Rose Marie McCoy, refused to sign with major labels and chose to stay independent—but even that came with its own concessions. As one of the only African American women to have her own office in the historic Brill Building during this era, McCoy was positioned right among rock and roll's key movers and shakers, and wrote more than eight hundred songs over the course of her career. Though titan labels like Atlantic and Stax sought her out, McCoy had seen the concerning inner workings of the music industry up close and maintained her distance. As was customary with female songwriters, though independent, she had to partner with a male, Charlie Singleton, in order to receive any writing credit at all because that was how things worked. However, McCoy was clever and forward-thinking, and to ensure she received her royalties, she used a male pseudonym, James Lee, when she copyrighted her work. In fact, Lee is the name co-credited on Ike and Tina Turner's 1961 hit, "It's Gonna Work Out Fine."

Sadly, the people who ultimately ended up drawing the shortest stick of the bunch were the performers themselves. Naive young women who often didn't have the proper resources and business savvy to protect their financial interests were often the ones left in the dust. "We would record songs, and listed on the [recording] as the writer would be his [the owner/producer's] eight-month-old grandchild! It was just ridiculous," said singer Nona Hendryx, a former member of the 1960s girl group the Bluebelles, which later became Patti LaBelle and the Bluebelles, and eventually Labelle. "He owned the recording studio, he owned our contracts, we had his lawyers...I mean, talk about conflict of interest! But I didn't know anything about conflict of interest. I was fifteen years old. What do I know about...making a recording contract deal? We got ripped off badly over the years, especially from the Bluebelles era...We ended up with nothing but our name."[2]

Though girl groups were on the rise, feminism was still often a distant concept in music industry encounters—and nowhere was that more obvious than in the clubs where Sylvia sang. While label execs did frequent nightclubs in the hopes of scouting for new talent, and their wealthy friends and business associates often accompanied them for a fun night out on the town, there were also fervent rumors of men in powerful positions taking advantage of young women who were naive to the ways of the industry and willing to do anything to break into it.

Sylvia was not exempt from experiencing these kinds of encounters. Luckily, she could speak French from her studies in high school, and she knew the romance language of Italian as a classically trained vocalist. Ronnie, one of Sylvia's younger sisters, recalled some of the situations Sylvia found herself in—and how she made her boundaries clear right from the beginning. "She sang in Canada. Once while performing in a French club, she sang for a group at a high-business kind of place. What they didn't know was that she understood French. When she got there, there were a lot of men. These big businessmen, rich businessmen, started talking. They said when she got through singing, see if they could be with her in another way. She knew what they were saying and when they finished, she went over to them and said, 'I will sing for you but there will be nothing else going on. I'm here as a singer not as a person to be going to bed with anybody.' They were astonished because they didn't know she understood French. She told them how she felt and left. She dealt with men wanting her to sing and do other things a lot."

Fortunately, there was one man who immediately recognized Sylvia's potential: arranger and songwriter Hank Cosby. Both Hank and Sylvia knew that if she wanted to succeed at Motown, she needed a male mentor who could speak up on her behalf and advocate for her. As it so happened, Hank was an in-house favorite, mainly because he'd been working with Gordy for so long. The two knew each other from back when Hank was a session saxophonist for Jackie Wilson, and Hank had also once played in the Funk Brothers' horn section.

That's not to say Hank received a lot of support from his colleagues when he decided to take Sylvia under his wing. "Sylvia overheard a conversation once," Patricia Cosby, Hank's wife and colleague, later said. "They didn't know she was within earshot. Someone argued with Hank because that person didn't want Hank to form a partnership with Sylvia because she was a woman." Another time, Patricia added, "one of the guys pulled him aside and said, 'Don't be trying to feed her all of that information. She doesn't need to know it. She won't be here that long no way.' Hank responded, 'She'll be here as long as I'm here.'"

True to his word, Hank stepped up and eventually became one of Sylvia's closest friends. "Sylvia truly cared about Hank Cosby and his wife...and considered Hank a close musically talented friend and confidant," said her sister Celeste. "She often shared with Hank her anger and complaints about others who did not cowrite her songs, but demanded interest in them." More than just lending her a sympathetic ear, Hank—one of the few producers and arrangers at Motown who could actually read music—was also generous in sharing his knowledge and experience with the eager pupil. Thanks in part to Hank's tutelage, Sylvia was proud to say that she "could lay the tracks, come up with the melodies and chords for the tracks—because I could play piano—and some guitar and drums. I can arrange for strings, horns, drums."[3]

It wasn't long before her peers, like fellow songwriter Ivy Jo Hunter, started taking notice. Trained in orchestral music on trumpet and keyboards, the Cass Technical High School graduate had served for a short while in the US Army. Like many of the men at Motown, he'd tried hitting on Sylvia early in her time there, before he learned that she was a writer. "I always thought she was attractive," he said. "I think she had other commitments. But she was nice to me. She didn't just say, 'Get the hell on away from me.' She was like that with everybody. She didn't really turn people away. She was a very warm person. She would just let me down easy. She was always treating me like I was kidding without damaging the friendship or anything. She was a lady."

Over time, Hunter started to respect her for her natural talent and work ethic as much as her beauty. After getting hired as a songwriter, Sylvia took initiative and recalled how she started the process on her own. "I went home and wrote and wrote…I brought my songs in," she recalled. "I said, 'I'm ready for work. I've got my songs,' and they said, 'No. Here,' and gave me a track."[4]

Thanks in part to his military background, Hunter was no-nonsense and a straight shooter, and he made it clear to Sylvia that he wasn't going to go easy on her because of her gender.

"[Hunter] threw a track at me on tape and told me to take it home and write a song on it," she later recalled. "Well, I took it home and played it and there was nothing on it but music. I took it back to Ivy and told him that it was the dumbest thing ever. I'm not going to do it backwards and that we should write the song first, then arrange and cut the music to it. I'm not going to do this. So Ivy said, 'Don't do it then.'"[5]

When it came to songwriting, Hunter didn't really care *how* she wrote her songs ("It's your business!"), as long as she got it done. After some thinking, Sylvia "had to go back more humbly than the first time and ask for the tape back. I figured out eventually how to write a song on that thing."

Without formal songwriting training, Sylvia's best asset was her dedication to the craft, and she was willing to do whatever it took to get her songs to pass muster. Eventually, she realized that in order to succeed at Motown, she needed to be versatile. "I did learn how to do it all, any way that you'd approach it," she said. "I could write the song first or work up the chord progression to lay the tracks."[6]

Though many men at the label were initially attracted to her as Hunter had been, Sylvia never entertained any of their advances—but neither did she try to embarrass them in her rejection. As a result, she started earning their respect as a creative in her own right. Songwriter Eddie Holland, the chief lyricist of Holland-Dozier-Holland, said that Sylvia was humble and thoughtful, friendly but silent, with a level of professionalism that was bar none. "She had a quiet way of moving around and working with people. She was easy to work with," said Holland. "To be honest, she almost had like an angelic way about her. That's how it struck me. She was very, very quiet and attractive. I always thought she was a unique individual because she was always [keeping] to herself and didn't create any kind of disturbance. She moved through the system or whoever she had to deal with very quietly, very smoothly, and that always intrigued me. She would smile often and go about her work. She pretty much stayed to herself unless she was doing her work and had an idea. She was who she was...a wonderful person."

Maintaining a balance between being friendly with her male peers but not too friendly was tricky, but Sylvia made it somewhat easier on herself by choosing to write the majority of her songs at her parents' house, right on the piano she grew up playing. This proved beneficial for her in a number of ways. Her sister Celeste later noted that men at Motown were always "trying to get her in bed. They were all over her. She was clever at how she would navigate that. A lot of things were going on between everybody else, but she managed to avoid it because she didn't hang around."

More than that, however, the distance between Sylvia's family home and the Motown headquarters allowed Sylvia to develop her own distinctive style. "When you have everybody writing there [at the Motown house] in different rooms, you are hearing everybody else's sound and their lyrics," Celeste continued. "Songs will kind of still come out much the same. She did not do that…She would go down to Motown and pick up her tracks, and then she would go to my mom's house and write her songs. That's the way she maintained her distinction from the rest of the sound."

And with a strong songwriting foundation in hand, Sylvia's ability to tap into that distinctive style would soon be put to the test.

Back in 1961, three years before Sylvia joined the ranks of Motown, a promising young singer named Kim Weston found herself signing a contract with the label. Weston had one of the most powerful voices at Motown and also happened to be Stevenson's wife at the time. There were high hopes all around that her career might echo the skyrocketing success that singer Mary Wells was experiencing in 1962 with a slew of Smokey Robinson–penned tunes like "The One Who Really Loves You," "Two Lovers," and the Grammy-nominated "You Beat Me to the Punch." However, when Weston finally released her debut single, "Love Me All the Way" (which was written by her then-husband) in February 1963, the song reached only #88 on the pop charts and #24 on the R&B chart. Though disappointed, Stevenson was confident that she just hadn't found the right track to rocket her to the top. After hearing Sylvia's original song "A Little More Love" during her audition in 1964, however, he decided to pair the two up, hoping that Sylvia could adapt the tune to better fit Weston's vocals.

Sylvia was delighted. "A Little More Love" was one of the first songs she had ever written, and she must've loved the irony that one of the very tunes a big-shot music executive in New York had once scoffed at was to be the tune that earned her the first liner credit of her career. Sadly, her celebration was short-lived when she realized that Stevenson's name was listed alongside hers as a cowriter—even though she'd written the song long before she ever came to Motown. Her disappointment expanded after the song, once slated as a featured A-side single for Weston that would be released in October 1964, was pulled for unknown reasons.

Shortly afterward, Sylvia learned that Weston's version of another one of her original songs, "I'm Still Loving You," was scheduled for release in January 1965. But again, all hopes were dashed when the song failed to chart. "Usually, when an artist had a hit, they would have a record," explained Weston years later. "Before the hit died down, they would release another record. That never happened with me. I don't know what the problem was. Maybe because I was real quiet back then. People just didn't know how to take me."[7] To make matters worse, Sylvia was forced to share writing credit with not only Stevenson, but also another songwriter: Ivy Jo Hunter.

Resilient as ever, she kept pressing forward. In September 1965, eight months after the release of "I'm Still Loving You," Sylvia was happy to see Weston experience some success when she scored her first big hit with the Holland-Dozier-Holland song "Take Me in Your Arms (Rock Me a Little While)." Later that same month, Weston released a duet with soul crooner Marvin Gaye called "What Good Am I Without You," which was cowritten by her husband, Stevenson, and Alphonso Higdon.

Motown had experienced great success in the past with duets made up of established talent and rising stars, and Gaye had quickly proven himself to be a solid partner. In 1962, Gaye's track "Stubborn Kind of Fellow," cowritten with Stevenson and Berry Gordy's brother George, had won over audiences across the country. Two years later, Gaye joined forces with the Queen of Motown, Mary Wells, for their 1964 duet album, *Together*, which was another smash hit. Stevenson hoped that same magic could be replicated with a duet between Gaye and Weston.

Tapped to write a duet for the pair, Sylvia got right to work and wound up with "It Takes Two," a sweet pop song about how wonderful an intimate relationship can be when two people mutually agree to unite and prioritize their partnership. Sylvia had been fortunate enough to witness such a union between her parents during her childhood, and she knew it was indeed possible for a relationship to go the distance if the two people in it were committed to making it work.

Though the song was initially recorded in 1965, it took more than a year for Motown to actually release it because of the label's overcrowded roster. During this time, Sylvia's anxiety only worsened. She had yet to write a bona fide breakout hit, and though she enjoyed writing for singers like Weston, she hadn't yet established an exclusive partnership with anyone in particular. The stress of it all only worked to aggravate her stomach ulcer, which made the situation even trickier.

Sylvia knew that if she was really going to succeed at Motown, she needed two things: an untapped vocal talent and an opportunity to craft something truly special.

Luckily for her, those two things were already on their way—in the form of a promising young musician named Little Stevie Wonder.

## CHAPTER 8

# Little Stevie

At first glance, young Stevland Hardaway Judkins might've appeared to be a typical eleven-year-old kid. He climbed trees. He played games. He even rode a bike—as long as one of his brothers sat behind him and steered it. Despite the fact that Stevie was blind, he didn't consider himself any different from the other boys and never saw his disability as a handicap. He had just as much reckless abandon as any other kid.

Born on May 13, 1950, in Saginaw, Michigan, Stevie's mother, Lula Mae Hardaway, named her son "Stevland Hardaway Judkins" because, to her, the odd spelling symbolized strength and power. The tiny baby needed to be tough; he'd arrived six weeks premature, weighing just under four pounds. He was initially placed in an incubator to give his lungs a chance to develop and to make certain he could breathe on his own. However, receiving too much oxygen inside led him to contract retinopathy of prematurity, a disease in which his retinas detached from his eyes, resulting in blindness at the hospital not long following birth.

The third oldest of Lula's six children, Stevie was raised in a rough section of west Detroit's inner city. His family lived in a tiny one-story house. When walking up the three small wooden steps to the front door, a person had to be especially careful; with boards missing on the porch floor, moving across it required the skill of a tightrope walker. The woven plastic screen door covering wasn't hard to miss, either. There was a large hole in the center. "I wasn't sure whether it was due to the ghetto conditions or Stevie," his private tutor, Ted Hull, later admitted. "I knew from experience that blind kids could be hard on screens."[1]

Once inside, the house was neat and clean, though the few pieces of furniture were worn down and had certainly seen better days. Even so, the tidiness reflected the vigilance of Stevie's single mother, who devoted herself to keeping an orderly house and ensuring that her kids were well cared for and safe—above all else.

Lula was extremely protective of all her children but especially Stevie; she was wary that others might try to take advantage of him due to his blindness. Still, she acknowledged that Stevie couldn't *always* be under her watchful eye, so she allowed him to visit the homes of people she trusted, like her friend Ruth Glover. Stevie loved going over to the Glover home on Twenty-Fifth Street, where he did flips and somersaults along with young John Glover, who was three years his senior. John's older sister, Margaret, was fond of the kid, too

Though tiny, the Glover house was always filled to the brim with music. Stevie was mesmerized by John's guitar playing, but he was especially captivated whenever Margaret played the Wurlitzer upright piano that rested in the corner of the family's living room. Stevie fell in love with the instrument right away, and it wasn't long before he was banging around on it and playing tunes for himself. Initially, he tickled the keys with one finger, until Margaret showed him how to play the instrument properly, using two hands. She told him it would sound better—richer—and once he'd mastered this technique, Stevie was hooked.

Though John and Stevie played all kinds of games together, it was obvious early on that their true passion was music, and the duo eventually formed a group called Steve and John where Stevie played the bongos, which he learned to play and had mastered long before the piano, and John played the guitar. Stevie ended up channeling all of his excitement and excess energy into this outlet; he particularly liked playing songs by Jackie Wilson and would always imitate Jackie's electric stage performances with his own flips and acrobatics.

It was clear that pint-sized Stevie had real star potential. At least Stevie's mom, Lula, always thought so. Around 1961, the Motown sound was blasting from every radio station. Stevie got a real kick out of comparing himself with Smokey Robinson to anyone who would listen, claiming that he was a much better singer than Smokey, who was admired for his satiny falsetto. It was a small world in Detroit back in those days, and as it so happened, the Glover family was related to the White family, including Ronnie White, a member of Smokey Robinson's background singers, the Miracles. Gerald White, Ronnie's younger brother by ten years, was close to his cousin John and was over at the Glover house often, so the three boys became fast friends.

One day in 1961, John invited Stevie over to the basement of Gerald's house on Vicksburg Street, where eleven-year-old Stevie sang a few songs in front of Ronnie himself. Ronnie was impressed by Stevie's high-pitched, soft range. As the boy sang, his head swayed from side to side, a repetitive behavior called blindism most commonly found in congenitally blind kids. But beyond his vocal talent, which might not have been such a big deal on its own, Ronnie recognized that Stevie's skills as a musician were downright otherworldly. At the age of four, even before setting a finger on the Glover family piano, Stevie had taught himself how to play the harmonica. He spent days walking around in circles, playing until he perfected his use of the instrument, which he later compared to a small saxophone. By the age of nine, he'd also mastered piano, drums, and percussion—no small feat for any musician, let alone one as young as Stevie. Ronnie already knew what John was capable of doing, so this was a full-circle moment for the duo. Ultimately, Stevie's musical ability was such that Ronnie decided to bring him and John into Motown to audition in front of Gordy himself. Though both arrived for the audition, one of them made a bigger impression than the other.

"I was there when Stevie Wonder was brought in the door [on his first day]," recalled singer Martha Reeves. She'd heard a lot of stories about the boy wonder prior to his arrival, like the one that told about when an eight-year-old Stevie had conducted an adult Pentecostal church choir from behind a Hammond organ. "It's impossible to even kinda imagine somebody that young, having that much talent, that much genius, that he could conduct a Pentecostal choir, because they [are known to] shout."

Upon arriving at Motown headquarters, the rambunctious Stevie wasted no time boasting to everyone that he could sing better than Smokey. He was "mischievous but at the same time so talented," said Andantes singer Louvain Demps. "He had more confidence than he had the actual singing voice. He spoke that into existence. His voice ended up matching his confidence."

Before he met Gordy, Reeves, who was Stevenson's secretary at the time, had Stevie wait in her front office. She could not keep up with the youngster, who tore through the space like a tornado. When Gordy was finally ready for the audition, Stevie sang a few songs and played the bongos while John strummed the guitar. Coincidentally, members of the Supremes were in the studio at the same time, and when they had a break in their recording session, they came in to watch the duo perform alongside the Motown exec. Like everyone else, they were a bit excited and curious to see what the kid could do.

A scrawny, skinny youngster, Stevie was bold and brave, and though he couldn't see, he didn't miss much of what he heard going on around him. He was well aware that his mother was distrustful of the music industry, and she often talked about hearing horror stories about artists being taken advantage of financially. Quick-witted and feisty, the precocious boy didn't hesitate to inform Gordy that "I understand you cheat people out of their money."[2] Then, without slowing down or thinking twice about what he'd just said, Stevie was on to his next mission. Like a kid in a candy store, he could hardly contain himself in such a stimulating musical environment.

After signing with the label in 1961 along with John Glover, it became apparent that folks at Motown saw real potential in the child prodigy Stevie, and he became their focus. Around that time, singer Clarence Paul was working alongside Mickey Stevenson in the A&R department. In his pre-Motown days, he'd performed with Stevenson as a duo called Clarence Paul and Mickey Stevenson (similar to the contemporary R&B duo Sam and Dave), and Stevenson trusted his longtime collaborator's judgment. So when Clarence requested to take Stevie under his wing and promised Stevenson that he'd keep a watchful eye on the kid, Stevenson agreed to give Clarence a shot.

After the two got better acquainted, Clarence led the youngster into Studio A, where the Funk Brothers were just finishing up a session. Clarence first guided Stevie to William "Benny" Benjamin's drum set, where the man watched as the little kid felt his way around the instrument. Benjamin then got up and allowed Stevie to sit down. Right away, he picked up the sticks and joined the Funk Brothers' bass player, guitarist, and organist, who'd been messing around post-session. It didn't take long for him to find the pocket and home in on the groove. When Stevie stopped playing and got off the drums, Benjamin and Stevenson immediately looked at each other, surprised and impressed with what they'd just witnessed.

Clarence then walked Stevie over to where organist Earl Van Dyke was playing. Van Dyke got off the Hammond B-3 organ so Stevie could sit down. After running his hands across the keys and familiarizing himself with the instrument, Stevie busted out another tune that knocked Van Dyke's socks off.

Finally, Stevie got up and made a beeline over to one of the hanging microphones, pulling out a harmonica. By this time, the Funk Brothers were on fire with what had now turned into an impromptu jam session. The tiny dynamo began playing the harmonica and doing runs across his lips, gripping the instrument tightly with both hands. Suddenly, he placed it back into his pocket and started belting out a song with all his heart and soul. After the seasoned vets witnessed the boy wonder in action, Gordy remembered, "His voice didn't knock me out, but his harmonica playing *did*."[3]

Gordy wasn't the only impressed exec in the room. Stevie's innate gifts reminded Mickey Stevenson of Frank Isaac Robinson, a Detroit jazz pianist in the 1940s who'd taught himself how to play the instrument by the age of three. Sugar Chile, as he was known, had even appeared in a 1946 musical called *No Leave, No Love* at the age of eight. "[Sugar Chile] was one of the most gifted kids that I'd ever seen," recalled Stevenson. "When I saw Stevie, I said he's got that kind of gift like Sugar Chile."

Thankfully, Stevie's audition couldn't have come at a better time. Another young talent by the name of William Edward John—better known as "Little Willie John"—had quickly risen in the ranks to become the hottest act in Detroit. Little Willie John's powerful, soulful vocals gained him national attention with songs like "All Around the World," "Need Your Love So Bad," and "Fever," which became a #1 hit in 1956 when he was just eighteen years old. Gordy was impressed with Stevie, whom he considered to be a wonder, and was eager to set him up just like Little Willie John, which is how he got the stage name "Little Stevie Wonder." Lula liked it, but she warned her son that if he put "Little" in front of his name, he'd "better be as good as Little Willie John."

Fortunately, Stevie was up to the task.

Since Stevie was still a minor when he signed the contract, Lula handled the financial side of things. She received $200 a month, and in order to protect her son's financial assets, Lula legally changed Stevie's surname from Judkins to Morris, "an old family name, as a preemptive strike against any attempt by Judkins to cut in on their sudden good fortune."[4] The deal also included an allowance of a few dollars that was set aside each week for Little Stevie to spend however he wished. Requesting that he be paid in quarters, Stevie eagerly put this money right back into the label's vending machine, where he eagerly scarfed down all the sweets and candy he could stomach.

"The candy machine is in the Motown Museum. That was almost Stevie's own private machine," explained arranger Paul Riser fondly. "He *loved* Baby Ruth candy bars. Right now, he owes me about five dollars in change. He would always say he didn't have any money and say [to] give him a quarter. The people at Motown used to give him so much change. He knew his candy bar was over so many slots to pull and get it. They kept the machine stocked just for him. He always knew where it was."

But it wasn't all fun and games. Little Stevie needed real mentorship for his career to flourish, and in addition to Clarence Paul, he also teamed up with Hank Cosby, an early saxophonist with the Funk Brothers, who was now a songwriter, arranger, and producer. "For whatever reason, Little Stevie latched on to both Hank and Clarence Paul," said Patricia Cosby, Hank's wife. "They were like his go-to people of the musicians that put their hands on him, so to speak. Stevie was like a sponge."

Whenever you saw Clarence, Little Stevie was nearby—just as he'd promised Stevenson. Though he was a great songwriter and producer in his own right, Stevenson admitted that Clarence's contributions were primarily used as "filler," or the material on an album that rounded it out but was usually skipped over. Determined to rise in the ranks, Clarence wholeheartedly took on the role of Stevie's music director. As it happened, his right-hand man was singer Marvin Gaye, a skilled drummer and pianist who collaborated with Clarence on most of the songs he wrote for Stevie. "CP," Marvin's nickname for Clarence Paul, quickly became like a father figure to Little Stevie, and the group set to work.

The first song Stevie recorded at Motown was titled "I Call It Pretty Music but the Old People Call It the Blues." Cowritten and coproduced by Clarence and Berry Gordy, the tune was released in June 1962 and featured Gaye on the drums. The song received a tepid response from the public, as people weren't quite sure what to make of Little Stevie Wonder singing and then playing harmonica. Still, Gordy had faith in Stevie, and so Motown released a second single, this time an up-tempo, jazzy R&B groove called "Little Water Boy." Written and produced by Clarence, with Gaye giving the drums a total workout, the song featured Stevie's youthful, high-pitched voice set against Clarence's powerful baritone delivery. The comedic lyrics chronicle a little water boy's negotiations with a man eager to quench his thirst but not as eager to part with fifty cents. Though catchy, clever, and cute, the song didn't perform particularly well on the charts either.

Undeterred, Stevie's first album, *The Jazz Soul of Little Stevie*, was released in September 1962 on Tamla. Interestingly enough, unlike his first two songs, the project did not include any vocals by the twelve-year-old. Instead, Gordy wanted Little Stevie to lean more into his instrumental abilities across the harmonica, bongos, piano, organ, and drums. One song, "Paulsby"—a clever tribute to his mentors, combining their last names—even featured him playing both the harmonica and the organ. The album also featured a song called "Fingertips," which showcased Little Stevie on the bongos and Marvin Gaye on drums. Though Clarence and Hank were co-credited as the only songwriters on the jazzy, mellow tune, flutist and saxophonist Thomas "Beans" Bowles is prominently featured as the song's driving force, with his high-pitched flute leading the rest of the band along.

Gordy wanted to keep the train moving with Little Stevie, so even though the first album had yet to really resonate with audiences, Motown released a second album from Stevie the next month, called *Tribute to Uncle Ray*. Though the album had actually been recorded before the first one and paid homage to blind superstar singer and pianist Ray Charles, it didn't really inspire more publicity or sales, and Stevie's career threatened to lull.

Finally, the release of his third single offered a glimmer of hope. "Contract on Love" was cowritten by one of Motown's first female songwriters, Janie Bradford, along with Brian Holland and Lamont Dozier. The pairing was a lucky coincidence in some ways; the song hadn't been written with any particular artist in mind, and Little Stevie was in need of something that might stand a fighting chance on the charts. The punchy tune featured handclaps and doo-wop-styled backing vocals provided by members of the Temptations. Even though Little Stevie delivered a passionate vocal performance on the track, the song didn't exactly vault the singer to stardom. It did, however, sell a few more records than his first two single releases had, and it also received more favorable reviews. And that, at least, was a start.

Gordy felt this tiny bit of momentum might be the thing to move the needle forward. Keen to ramp up his young prodigy's exposure, Gordy signed Stevie to the concert roster for the label's then-brand-new chitlin circuit–traveling Motortown Revue, with Clarence right by Stevie's side as his music director. Stevie was as excited as he was anxious about connecting with audiences across the country, but he wasn't the only novice in the bunch when it came to performing in front of a large crowd. Before the Motortown Revue launched that year, most Motown artists had performed only locally in a club or in a school auditorium. They were *all* learning on the job.

Although unpolished as a performer, Little Stevie impressed the higher-ups with his exuberant stage presence, especially since he was the first to open the shows (due to labor laws involving minors). "[He] never failed to get a crowd going. So much so, he was a difficult act to follow," admitted Mary Wilson of the Supremes.[5] It was exhilarating for him to the point that the teen often didn't want to leave the stage at the end of a set. According to Wilson, Clarence noticed this as well, so they devised a routine around Stevie exiting the stage. Clarence would come up to escort Stevie offstage, but he would "break free," return to his beckoning audience, and perform another song. "Man, I'd never heard noise so loud. It scared me," Clarence reflected later on. "I picked him up and took him off the stage. But them kids were hollering and he wanted to go back onstage. He jumped right back out there."[6]

For the most part, the audience bought into the supposed spontaneity, but alas, nothing lasts forever—especially when it's contrived. Eventually, "[Stevie] got too heavy," and the pair were forced to retire the ploy.[7] Though Stevie was growing by the day, he was determined to find new ways to work the crowd into a frenzy—for as long as he could.

## CHAPTER 9

# No One-Hit Wonder

In June 1962, the Motortown Revue decided to hold the final performance of their run at Chicago's Regal Theater. Located on the city's South Side, in the Bronzeville area, the Regal was one of the most prominent entertainment venues, and it was particularly popular among Black audiences. For the chitlin circuit, it was truly considered regal with its plush carpeting, velvet drapes, and velvet seats, comfortably accommodating some three thousand people. The theater's interior had been inspired by New York's Savoy Ballroom up in Harlem and featured movies and live stage performances by entertainers such as Ella Fitzgerald, Ray Charles, Duke Ellington, Nat King Cole, B. B. King, and Miles Davis. In Chicago, the Regal was the place to be—and well-dressed Chicagoans were anxious to see the lineup of Motown's hottest acts.

Berry Gordy decided to send a camera crew to the Windy City for Little Stevie's performance in hopes that he could record some of the fervor and excitement the boy stirred up in an audience. Some of the other acts in the Revue, however, weren't too pleased with the decision. After all, Stevie hadn't even had a hit break out on the charts yet. Even so, Gordy instinctively knew this would be a golden opportunity for Little Stevie to delight everyone with his electrifying instrumental performances on harmonica, bongos, and piano—and he was determined to get it on tape.

On the day of the performance, everything started off without a hitch. Though Stevie usually kicked off the show, this time around he wasn't first. Sharply dressed in a cropped black tuxedo jacket and pants, Marvin Gaye had just delivered a spellbinding performance that kept the audience whooping and hollering. As he bowed, threw the audience a kiss, and headed offstage, host Bill Murray walked over to the bandstand to grab a chair and bongos that he placed on top of it, situating both in the center of the stage. Once everything was set up, Murray went on to introduce "a very outstanding young man," someone he called "more or less a genius of our time," who was only twelve years old. Murray urged the audience to "make him feel happy" and, with that, he brought Little Stevie Wonder up to perform. Strolling arm in arm with Clarence by his side, Little Stevie, all dressed up in a suit and tie, greeted the audience with his megawatt, slightly dimpled smile. Clarence then picked up the bongos from the seat so that he could place the drums between Stevie's legs, and then positioned himself in front of the band behind him as the conductor. With rapid-fire speed, Little Stevie's thin hands pounded on the bongos as if warming them up before suddenly slowing down the pace to jibe with the rest of the band.

In a soft yet confident voice, Little Stevie then told the ladies and gentlemen before him that he wanted to record a song called

"Fingertips" for his live album. To help him along, he asked the audience to "clap your hands. Come on, everybody. I want you to clap your hands, stomp your feet, jump up and down. Do anything that you want to do! Yeah! Yeah! Yeah!" After a minute, Murray returned to the stage to remove the chair and adjust the microphone in front of Little Stevie. As he stood up, Murray discreetly pulled a harmonica out from his left suit pocket and carefully placed the instrument in Stevie's right hand.

Seconds later, Little Stevie was playing the harmonica and mimicking the *exact* flute solo that Thomas "Beans" Bowles wrote and played on the studio version of the song. After a fiery two-minute solo, Stevie then summoned the audience with a call-and-response. Raising his right arm in the air to signal for them to join along, he yelled, "Everybody say yeah!" The band stood in unison and began swaying back and forth with glee. The audience erupted with screams and applause as Stevie encouraged them to "clap your hands just a little bit louder!" before launching back into his harmonica solo. Pleased with the audience's enthusiastic response, he played for another minute before seamlessly segueing into a playful bit of the nursery rhyme "Mary Had a Little Lamb." After Murray ran out to signal that it was time to exit, Stevie flashed his winning smile and offered a couple of bows as Clarence took his arm to escort him from the stage. As they neared the curtain, Stevie suddenly stopped and took another bow as Clarence patiently waited. Then, to everyone's delight, not less than a second later, both returned to the stage, with Clarence walking Stevie to the microphone as the crowd cheered wildly. Murray was still at the microphone and positioned it for Little Stevie to perform a harmonica solo.

As effortless as this encore might've appeared to the audience, it was anything but calm backstage. Singer Mary Wells was set to perform after Stevie, and her band had already taken to the stage when

Little Stevie left the first time. Since each act had its own conductor, Wells's bass player, Joe Swift—also her conductor—had already started getting ready to play Mary's set. Joe was ill-prepared for the unexpected adjustment on bass, and, as Stevie later recalled, he cursed and shouted, "'What key? What key?'"[1]

But Little Stevie didn't let that mishap distract him and kept up his pace, singing, "Goodbye, goodbye, goodbye, goodbye, goodbye. I'm gonna go, yeah. I'm gonna go, yeah, but let's, let's swing it one more time!" Finally, Clarence grabbed Little Stevie by his arm and they both walked offstage, with Little Stevie's instrument glued to his mouth all the while. After a final smile and bow, Stevie headed backstage at last, with Murray exclaiming, "There he goes, ladies and gentlemen. Stevie Wonder!!!!"

It was truly a night to remember, and Gordy had successfully captured and recorded history—flaws and all. "We're not sure why the record was such a big hit, but leaving that mistake in didn't hurt," acknowledged Gordy. "There are certain kinds of mistakes I love. They sometimes give things extra life and magic because of their raw, real quality."[2]

And when it came to Motown, there was no one more raw or more real than Little Stevie Wonder.

---

After *Recorded Live: The 12 Year Old Genius* was released in 1963, Little Stevie was on the fast track to becoming a household name, just like his labelmates at Motown. At the time of its release, Little Stevie expressed some concern that he was now *thirteen* instead of twelve, but fortunately, it didn't really matter in the larger scheme of things. The live version of "Fingertips—Pt 2" spent three weeks in the #1 position and fifteen weeks on Billboard's Top 100, with seven of those weeks in the Top 10. And he was *smoldering* for another six weeks after that, as it hit #1 on Billboard's Hot R&B chart. Motown was over the moon; this was the label's second #1 pop single and the first live single ever to go #1 on Billboard. It also was the label's first time placing an album at #1 on the Billboard pop chart, with his accomplishment making Little Stevie Wonder the youngest artist at the time to ever do such on Billboard. The historic moment was documented when *Ebony*, the top-selling, pioneering Black monthly magazine noted for chronicling celebrities, gave him his first national media exposure in its July 1963 issue with a five-page article titled "Wonderful World of Little Stevie Wonder."

Little Stevie was scorching and *everyone* knew it.

In addition to dominating the charts, Little Stevie had learned a lot about stage dynamics from his first tour and had gained more confidence in front of a crowd. As he later recalled, "The first time I began to feel I was exciting to people, I threw my glasses out into the audience. I used to have a bow tie on, I threw that out, and that all stemmed from the time I did 'Fingertips.' It was so exciting that I wanted to get them to do it again, so the next time I tried it again and it was still exciting."[3]

As people started listening to his music and showing up in droves to watch him perform live, he developed a rabid cross-country fanbase that was increasingly eager to see him perform on television. It was only a matter of time before Dick Clark, a popular TV personality and producer, reached out to ask Little Stevie to perform on his top-rated nationally televised dance show, *American Bandstand*. The weekly mainstream show was filmed in front of a live audience but mainly featured White teens, all dancing to tunes from the Top 40. The show's highlight moment would occur when an artist performed their current hit, followed by a brief interview with the show's host, Clark.

From the outside, it might've seemed like Stevie was only getting hotter and hotter, but as quickly as his success came, things suddenly took a dramatic turn for the worse. Some at Motown still weren't quite convinced that Little Stevie had long-term potential. Aside from the live album and "Fingertips—Pt 2," Stevie's music just wasn't selling or turning any kind of profit for Hitsville, and his follow-up songs flopped over and over again. A period of sharp decline was on the horizon, though Gordy remained steadfast in investing a lot in him. To no avail; it seemed as if the "no-hit Wonder" nickname, bestowed upon him earlier on in his career, would be coming back to haunt him.

Though he could carry a decent tune, Stevie's real power came from his instrumental genius, and there was concern that audiences were flocking to him as more of a novelty act. And it wasn't just outsiders, either; in fact, some folks at Motown started becoming more vocal that they considered Stevie's success from the live recording more a stroke of luck than anything else.

Stevie was feeling the pressure in other areas of his life as well. The sixth grader had missed a lot of school while he was out on the road, and his grades were slipping at the public school he attended, Fitzgerald Elementary. It didn't help that Stevie's biological father flagged Stevie's truancy to the Board of Education. The Board of Education then contacted his mother, Lula, and told her son in no uncertain terms that Stevie needed to finish his schooling before he could continue performing.

Stevie was, understandably, devastated by the news. "I'll never forget that day," he later said. "I was miserable. I remember going to the bathroom and crying, praying that God would allow me to remain in the industry. But I just knew it was impossible."[4] Troubling matters compounded when a White teacher warned Stevie that without education, he would not make it very far in life. "One of my teachers told me that I had three strikes against me that must be considered. I was poor, Black, *and* blind. I was told to buckle down and forget about music, because there would be nothing for an uneducated blind man to do but make rugs and potholders. You can just imagine how painful this was for a kid to hear—*any* kid!"[5] Moreover, in spite of his early success, it seemed like none of the adults at school understood or valued his musical prospects. "The teachers didn't understand my goal, which is to be an artist. My life is music but the kind of music I like they didn't think much of."[6]

Providentially, a solution arrived in the form of Ted Hull, a twenty-five-year-old tutor and graduate of the Michigan School for the Blind and Michigan State University. Hull, who was White and considered legally blind, could relate to Stevie's visual impairments; though he still had 20 percent vision in his left eye, he was totally blind in his right. What's more, thanks to his special degree for teaching the blind, Hull could guarantee that Stevie was able to complete his schooling, even though they were out on the road "seventy-five to eighty percent of the year."[7] During the day, Hull carved out the proper amount of time for Stevie's studies so that he could meet the requirements of the Board of Education and the Michigan School for the Blind; the two studied together three hours, usually beginning at ten in the morning. Stevie's "field trips" on the road were just as unique as his scholastic circumstances, and often consisted of the duo bringing things like "a cue board for arithmetic, a typewriter, tape recorder, braillewriter, slate and stylus for braille writing, paper, a talking book machine, talking books from the Wayne County Library…and a small organ which can be hooked into a car's cigarette lighter for practicing and composing."[8] More than just helping him with his academic studies, Hull also taught Stevie how to read musical symbols in braille, because Stevie hoped to one day do his own arranging. The advanced pace of Hull's curriculum not only ensured that Stevie kept up with his studies, but it actually put him ahead of his peers—and he was able to complete three years of school in just two.

Though Stevie loved performing, he wasn't initially fond of life on the road. After all, he was still just a kid and often missed his family (especially his siblings) back home. However, as time pressed on, he grew to deeply appreciate the opportunity to travel around the country with such seasoned performers. As he recalled, "Marvin Gaye was a very well-read man, so he and Smokey would be on the bus having discussions about the Bible, Greek mythology, Egyptian history, playing different kinds of music."[9] Even when he wasn't studying alongside his tutor, Little Stevie was still listening, learning, and absorbing everything he could from the adult friends in his life.

For the few months he wasn't on the road, Stevie was required to attend classes on campus at the Michigan School for the Blind, and he tried to make the most of his limited time there by joining clubs and activities along with the other kids. According to his mother, who always encouraged him to explore his likes and dislikes, he joined the wrestling team, ran track, and participated in activities like swimming, boating, and skating.

Still, when it came to Stevie's true passion, nothing ever came close to music.

Following the success of Stevie's live album, Gordy advised the teen to record standards, including Disney songs such as "When You Wish Upon a Star," "Smile," "Put on a Happy Face," and "Get Happy." Stevie wasn't the only one at Motown who received this advice; Gordy believed that his artists could establish more crossover appeal by covering standards like many of their peers in the industry. In Stevie's case, however, this turned out to be a particularly poor decision. Stevie brought down the house back when he was traveling the chitlin circuit, and those audiences—consisting of mostly Black adults—had no interest in listening to the cheesy remakes on his next album, *With a Song in My Heart.* Stevie was also growing up and no longer marketed himself as "Little" Stevie Wonder, but audiences familiar with the young virtuoso hardly paid attention. During one performance, he even became indignant when referred to by his old nickname, and a blind singer and songwriter named Lee Garrett remembered him cursing behind the scenes, lamenting, "'Little! Little! Little Stevie Wonder! I'm *not* fucking going on that stage. I'm *not* Little Stevie Wonder!'" Ultimately, it was up to Lee to calm Stevie down by reminding him that it would take people time to recognize that he was growing up before their eyes.[10]

This, however, was only a minor concern for Motown, as there were more-pressing issues to contend with. Prominent among them was that a lot more people at Motown had lost confidence in Stevie's ability to put out another hit record, due to his dismal sales track and seemingly limited prospects.

Fortunately, Berry Gordy was not one of those people. He still felt that Stevie had something special—and he wasn't the only one. Stevie's mother, Lula, had taken a very active role in her child's career from the moment he stepped foot inside of Motown. She had developed a reputation as being very no-nonsense, and when she spoke, people in high-ranking administrative positions listened and respected what she had to say. "Lula was all hands on deck when it came to her Stevie," remembered arranger Paul Riser. "When she was on her way up there at Motown to wake up the powers that be about her son, they would say, 'Lula is on the way.' They fixed things up and got ready for her. When she walked in, she walked in like she had a machine gun in her hand. She said, 'You're gonna listen to me. What is going on?' Lula ran things when it came to Stevie. She didn't let anybody mess with him."

But it wasn't just naysayers that posed a problem. As Stevie's career stalled, something that no one could prevent from messing with him began to take over: puberty. After being considered short and small for his age early on in his career, around the age of fourteen he was finally sprouting taller and taller, now headed toward six feet tall. And that was far from the only physical change he had to contend with.

Around the age of thirteen, it is common for a boy's voice to change or even crack as their larynx (voice box) grows larger. This process typically lasts only a few months for most, but for adolescent entertainers like Stevie, whose high-pitched voice was getting progressively deeper every day, the timing was critical. Thankfully, Motown execs had anticipated that puberty would eventually catch up to him and planned ahead. As Stevie explained, "Luckily, I had a lot of records in the can which they put out…while my voice was changing keys."[11] Sylvia would later jokingly refer to the aforementioned can as "the garbage can," because if an artist's prerecorded track did not pass a quality control board, it wouldn't end up going anywhere *but* the can.[12] Even so, audiences remained eager to see Stevie perform during these years. Fans couldn't get enough of the energy and excitement he brought to the stage, and the label couldn't hold them off forever. And so Stevie continued touring and even made his first trip to Europe with Motown artists in 1963.

Still, it was far from smooth sailing for Stevie and his team. In addition to growing increasingly agitated by any pitying or babying, he also started facing vocal complications from strain and pain while speaking or singing, which resulted in severe physical discomfort. Wade Marcus, Stevie's music director and arranger, noticed that he was having a hard time hitting high notes and worked diligently to rewrite music to accommodate the teen's changing vocal range. Nonetheless, the physical strain still made it impossible for him to reach certain notes.

It wasn't long before the show's promoter took notice. On the third day of their show in Paris, the promoter made an executive decision that shocked everyone: He moved Stevie's time slot. Now, instead of closing the show, Stevie was opening it—just like he did at the *beginning* of his career. Over the years, he'd developed a reputation as the star attraction of these shows, which was why he'd always been saved for last. According to his private tutor, Ted Hull, this sudden switch-up rocked Stevie, putting more and more pressure on the teen.

Even adding in elaborate choreography wasn't enough to buoy Stevie's spirits. "We used to do finales that were out of *sight*," said Stevie. "Martha Reeves used to show me all the new dances to do. She would say, 'Yeah. This is ba-ad. This will make you look sexy on stage'...Martha always showed me the baddest steps."[13] In spite of this, Stevie was profoundly disappointed and, according to claims by Hull, "upset by Wade's decision. He took it as confirmation that 'everyone' at Motown was against him."[14]

In reality, this couldn't have been further from the truth.

# CHAPTER 10

# Trying Times

Folks at Motown, Gordy leading among them, were actually working harder than ever to save Stevie's career. And this is exactly why Gordy set out to break Stevie into the film industry—via a relatively new genre that was geared specifically toward teens.

From 1963 to about 1968, "beach party movies" such as *Beach Party* and *Surf Party*, which featured happy-go-lucky White teens who liked partying and surfing, were all the rage. This novel genre was concocted by legendary B-movie-studio American International Pictures, with films featuring the likes of Frankie Avalon and Annette Funicello.

In 1964, Gordy arranged for Stevie to make his film debut in a quirky beach party film called *Muscle Beach Party*. The storylines of beach party movies were often thin, centering around the mishaps and mayhem of White high school teens or young college students, usually on or around beaches in Malibu, often without a Black person in sight.

There was always plenty of comedy, lighthearted romances, fast cars, drinking, and, of course, partying.

Typically, the flicks always made it a point to end with a dynamic, upbeat musical performance, and that's where Gordy saw an opportunity for Stevie to make history—as the first Motown artist to appear in a feature-length movie. Stevie is introduced toward the end of *Muscle Beach Party* by an elevator operator donning blue pajamas, red slippers, and a cartoonish creature mask. "Now, children of the surf," the operator announces, "you think there are seven wonders of the world? Well, here's the eighth, Little Stevie Wonder," before switching the large lever inside the gold-railed elevator. In front of a packed house of White teens, Stevie hits the stage, clapping his hands and twisting his hips while excitedly singing a feel-good, corny song called "Happy Street," surrounded by a band of White guys. When he finally pulls the harmonica from his pocket and begins to play, some of the partygoers lose control of themselves, jumping on top of tables and dancing wildly.

After being backed by the hardcore members of the Funk Brothers for so long at home in Detroit, this sunny, squeaky-clean ensemble provided quite a stark contrast. Still, Stevie enjoyed being out in California, and four months later, he made a second silver screen appearance in *Bikini Beach*, which came out in July 1964. Like the previous film, he appears toward the end of the film, but this time, he is introduced as "Little Stevie Wonder" by actor and comedian Don Rickles, whose face is covered with paint to match his colorful shirt. The audience, still filled with White teens (plus an old man and two old women), is giving the dance floor a real workout as the revelers try out their best moves on the tabletops. Stevie claps his hands and bounces up and down to a party groove called "Happy Feelin' (Dance and Shout)," which is backed by yet another White band (though, this time, they notably hired one other Black musician). In the midst of all the dancing and singing, there's even a surprise cameo by a monkey character. Utter foolishness at its best.

Though Stevie liked the film world, he initially hoped for more than what he received in the end—at least according to his tutor, Ted Hull. "He did two pictures in Hollywood and it was fun, but he was disappointed. He wanted to be an actor. Singing and playing were fine, but he wanted a line."[1] Even so, Motown spotted early signs of success and tried to capitalize on it by releasing a full "beach" album of similar tunes, titled (fittingly) *Stevie at the Beach*. One song, "Hey Harmonica Man," made it up to #5 on Billboard's Hot R&B chart and peaked at #29 on the Hot 100 chart. Unfortunately, however, this targeted album was of no interest to Stevie's core audience—and even as a teen, Stevie disliked this new direction, considering it deeply uncool. Years later, Stevie admitted that he was embarrassed about his appearances in those short-lived flicks, because, as he supposedly complained to Hull, he was "forced to do some incredibly dumb numbers."[2]

On top of all that, Stevie soon had additional worries: mounting vocal issues. Though Gordy wasn't crazy about Stevie's voice as much as he was about his harmonica playing, he recognized that it was an instrument just as important to Stevie's career as his harmonica. After he visited some specialists to get his throat checked out, doctors explained that Stevie had two nodules on his vocal cords that would require surgery.[3] Following the procedure, the loquacious teen was forced to remain silent for two weeks as his body healed.

During this torturous recovery period, everyone wondered how the procedure might affect Stevie's singing—and tensions were high. It didn't help matters that as a result of the procedure and doctor's orders, he also had to sit out most of the year, which reportedly led to "bouts of depression and isolation," along with "more anxiety."[4] With nothing to focus on, Stevie grew increasingly restless. As he gained more autonomy as a teen, he also longed for more creative control over his career, but he struggled to stay focused. On a good day, he was able to offer "a lyric here or a strand of melody there," Hull recalled, but for the most part, "it really didn't go much further than that."[5]

Time seemed to be quickly slipping away. Since people did not know what to do with him and what direction his career should take, Stevie no longer seemed to be much of a priority for the label. As Gordy himself even admitted, "As hard as it is to establish an act, once you do, once you open that door, you just have to march right in. With Stevie we hadn't and now it seemed we couldn't."[6] It was exasperating for Gordy because with all the things done in attempts to establish him up to this point, marching in *and* staying there for the long haul with measured success appeared elusive. Instead, Motown was choosing to focus their time and efforts on the Supremes and the Temptations, whose popularity was taking off.

Relegated to the sidelines, Hull claimed that Stevie grew increasingly resentful about "Motown's nonchalant attitude toward his career."[7] And when fifteen-year-old Stevie finally walked back into the studio in 1965, it was obvious that things would never be the same as before. "You have a kid and then that person gets a grown person's voice," explained singer Louvain Demps of the Andantes. "You don't know where to place him, so it wasn't his fault that's what was happening."

The truth of it was this: None of the singles that Stevie had released after "Fingertips—Pt 2"—including "Workout Stevie Workout," "Castles in the Sand," "Hey Harmonica Man," and "High Heel Sneakers"—had ushered him back onto the charts, and thus it was time to talk about Stevie's future at Motown.

Patricia Cosby, the wife of producer Hank Cosby, knew that Stevie's days were numbered, recalling, "I was working in the tape library.

I knew there was a lot of money spent recording material for Stevie. Generally, people don't realize all of this was a new experience for practically everybody at Motown. Who had the experience of working with this little blind baby? He was mysterious, and you had to really keep your hands on him because he was all over the place...A lot of the people wanted to do things with Stevie, but [the company was growing and] they had started doing things with other people. Smokey was focusing all of his attention on his own group and having his attention on the Temptations. Holland-Dozier-Holland was having their attention on the Supremes."

And Patricia wasn't the only one who sensed the clock ticking. As songwriter Janie Bradford later confirmed, "I did hear...that [Mr. Gordy] was thinking about letting him go at some point when he ran cold. We were not getting hits." Arranger Paul Riser agreed that he "absolutely" remembered that Stevie was on the possible chopping block. Even Stevie's mother recalled how "Gordy maintained faith in Stevie's career, but there were factions within Motown that argued that Stevie's contract not be renewed...Cut the losses now, the thinking went, and don't look back."[8]

Despite his obvious struggles, when asked about it years later, others at Motown refused to admit that Stevie's career was ever in jeopardy. A&R director Mickey Stevenson denied Stevie was ever at risk, and Smokey Robinson proclaimed the same after being directly asked in 2022, saying, "Let me tell you something, Motown never thought about dropping Stevie. Never ever in *life* did we think about dropping Stevie. I don't know where that came from or who told you that, but that is an out-and-out lie. We never thought about dropping Stevie. Whoever told you that is a barefaced lie. [Berry] said when he brought Stevie to Motown, he didn't think Stevie was a great singer, but he never thought about dropping Stevie." Songwriter Eddie Holland backed this assertion as well, claiming, "This information…I never heard of it before. It's not true."

Although there were mixed opinions about Stevie's future at Motown at that point, most agreed that literal growing pains were slowing Stevie down considerably. "It was not a slump. He was in development," explained Stevenson. "That didn't bother me at all. It was just a matter of time before he started breaking out. In those three years, he was developing how to create himself. He didn't do it in five minutes. It takes time."

Some people hoped that Stevie wouldn't notice the growing pressure around him. Bradford explained that "when he came [to Motown], he was too sheltered," and reasoned that it was possible he didn't know what was going on at the time. But to his credit, Stevie always had a feeling something was up.

"I knew I wasn't as productive as I had been," Stevie later admitted. "One guy at Motown, who eventually got fired, recommended that several Motown acts be dropped…'His voice is changing, he's getting taller, we gotta buy him new clothes…where's Michael Jackson when you need him?'"[9] Though he didn't want to be let go, Stevie understood the pressure that the label was under and was well aware that he wasn't "really making any money for the company. My voice was hanging… they didn't know what to do."[10]

Around the same time, Motown was going through growing changes of its own, shifting its direction to focus on the hot new hitmakers who'd proven themselves with moneymaking abilities, thanks to the genius of Holland-Dozier-Holland, the "golden" trio of Motown's in-house team of songwriters. Unfortunately, this meant that older songwriters, like Stevie's longtime mentor, Clarence Paul, were left in the lurch. Though he had an exclusive relationship with Stevie, he hadn't written any new hits for the teen—and the label thought it

Dad Melvin Moy in Detroit circa 1944
Courtesy Estate of Sylvia Moy LLC

Mother Hazel Moy in Detroit circa 1944
Courtesy Estate of Sylvia Moy LLC

Grandmother Rosalie Ridgell in Detroit circa 1947.
Courtesy Estate of Sylvia Moy LLC

Little Sylvia, six (center), with sisters Ronnie, four, and Lazoe, eight, posing for a studio portrait in Detroit circa 1944
Courtesy Estate of Sylvia Moy LLC

Relaxing at the piano while holding sheet music in Detroit circa the mid-sixties

Klaros Inc./The James D Wilson Historical Images Collection

Sharing a musical moment with Stevie Wonder along with some of the Funk Brothers (l-r), James Jamerson, Early Van Dyke, and Robert White, in Motown's Studio A in Detroit during 1967

Motown Records/*Detroit FreePress*/ZUMA Press

**CLOCKWISE FROM TOP LEFT:**

Conversing with Motown founder Berry Gordy at a music awards gala circa the late sixties

Courtesy Estate of Sylvia Moy LLC

Demonstrating her production skills at the mixing board in a Detroit recording studio circa the late sixties

Klaros Inc./The James D Wilson Historical Images Collection

Showing off some of the many BMI Awards she received at her Webb Street home in Detroit circa the early seventies

Klaros Inc./The James D Wilson Historical Images Collection

Spending a moment singing in a Detroit recording studio circa the late sixties

Klaros Inc./The James D Wilson Historical Images Collection

**CLOCKWISE FROM TOP LEFT:**

Relaxing and looking stylish at her Webb Street home in Detroit circa the early seventies

Klaros Inc./The James D Wilson Historical Images Collection

Meeting with nephew Jackie (sitting) and Oscar Smith, one of her first assistants and recording engineers, while talking in the dining room at her parents' home circa 1971

Courtesy of *The Jacksonville Free Press*

Hugging the inspirations behind most of her music, her loving parents, Hazel and Melvin, at the Prince Hall Grand Lodge in Detroit circa the early seventies

Klaros Inc./The James D Wilson Historical Images Collection

Greeting Smokey Robinson at a music industry gala circa the early seventies

Courtesy Estate of Sylvia Moy LLC

**CLOCKWISE FROM TOP LEFT:**

Relishing a delightful evening in celebration of Sylvia with her sister Ronnie and their dad at the Prince Hall Grand Lodge in Detroit circa the early seventies

Courtesy Estate of Sylvia Moy LLC

Looking up to a painting of a child laughing while playing music in her private music room at her home circa 1973

Klaros Inc./The James D Wilson Historical Images Collection

Working on vocal arrangements with her group, Opus IV, during a session in the private music room at her home circa 1973. Sylvia produced and co-wrote their funk-soul tune "If It Don't Fit," arranged by Paul Riser and released by Cotillion Records in 1976

Klaros Inc./The James D Wilson Historical Images Collection

Joyously playing piano in her private music room on the second floor of her Webb Street home circa 1973

Klaros Inc./The James D Wilson Historical Images Collection

Spending quiet time alone sitting on the front porch and enjoying nature in Detroit circa the late seventies

Klaros Inc./The James D Wilson Historical Images Collection

Showing off her model good looks and dimpled smile at a gathering in Detroit circa the late seventies

Klaros Inc./The James D Wilson Historical Images Collection

Sylvia (standing, second from right) celebrating family time with her parents (sitting second from left and sitting third from right), along with all of her siblings: (standing l–r) Melvin, Christopher, Francetta, and Lazoe, (sitting l–r) Angel, Anita, Celeste, and Ronnie, at the Detroit house they grew up in circa the mid-eighties Courtesy Estate of Sylvia Moy LLC

Singing in the recording studio at her Masterpiece Sound Studios in Detroit in 1995
Pat West/*Detroit Free Press*/ZUMA Press

Arriving at the 37th Annual Songwriters Hall of Fame ceremony with her brother Melvin and one of her best friends, Rita Carter Perry, at New York's Marriott Marquis in 2006

Nancy Kaszerman/ZUMA Press

Celebrating at the VIP cocktail reception and backstage at the Marriott Marquis in New York during the 37th Annual Songwriters Hall of Fame ceremony in 2006. As an honoree, she poses with fellow honorees and other musical luminaries (l-r) Trace Adkins, inductee Will Jennings, John LoFumento, Paul Shaffer, inductee Mac Davis, Lise Davis, Del Bryant, inductee Thom Bell, and Hal David

Getty Images/L. Busacca

Receiving congratulations from Stevie Wonder after he helped to induct her along with the late Hank Cosby, whose honor was accepted by his wife, Patricia Cosby, at the 37th Annual Songwriters Hall of Fame ceremony in 2006

Getty Images/L. Busacca

Surrounding herself with some of her biggest supporters, (l-r) sister Celeste and best friends Dr. Barbara Wilson and Rita Carter Perry, at the 37th Annual Songwriters Hall of Fame ceremony in 2006

Courtesy of *The Jacksonville Free Press*

Embracing warm wishes from Stevie Wonder following her induction into the Songwriters Hall of Fame in 2006

Courtesy of *The Jacksonville Free Press*

**BELOW:**

Sharing a moment and receiving congratulatory wishes from her Motown colleagues and songwriting greats, including (l-r) Nikolas Ashford, Janie Bradford, and Valerie Simpson, at the 37th Annual Songwriters Hall of Fame ceremony in 2006

Courtesy of *The Jacksonville Free Press*

Spending time with two of her siblings, Melvin and Celeste, who provided support during her journey to New York for the prestigious ceremony in 2006

Courtesy of *The Jacksonville Free Press*

Taking in the spectacular evening with renowned lyricist Hal David (left), inducted into the Songwriters Hall of Fame in 1972, and her fellow inductee Will Jennings at the 37th Annual Songwriters Hall of Fame ceremony in 2006

Courtesy of *The Jacksonville Free Press*

Joining Harold Bowles, who later did some work with Sylvia at her Masterpiece Sound Studios and was the son of legendary Motown musician Thomas "Beans" Bowles, at an affair in Detroit circa 2011

Courtesy Estate of Sylvia Moy LLC

was time for a change. According to Stevie's mom, Gordy "decided that Stevie should start building relationships with some of the other writers and producers."[11]

The sudden separation from Clarence ended up being a fairly traumatic experience for Stevie. From the very first day that he'd arrived at Motown, Clarence had been Stevie's main producer, and the two became so close that Clarence was like a father to him.

And now, in a time when the ground under his feet seemed shaky and uncertain, Stevie was suddenly all on his own.

"I remembered the day he came crying to me. He said, 'They took Clarence from me! They took Clarence from me!'" recalled singer Louvain Demps about the emotionally charged incident. "When they took Clarence away from him, he cried and cried. I felt so bad for him. Clarence could work with him. He could pull things out of him that others might not have known how."

Discouraged but not defeated, Stevie knew that he'd have to fight for himself if he wanted to stay in the industry—and at Motown. "I felt bad because I wasn't successful in writing or singing, but that didn't discourage me. It never made me feel like giving up...it made me try even harder. You must have bad times to know what the good times are."[12]

In the face of mounting obstacles, Stevie remained hopeful that something good was on the horizon. "I had the confidence that something good was gonna happen," he later explained, "but I didn't know when."[13]

And fortunately, though unbeknownst to him at the time, he'd caught the attention of another person at Motown who was eager to jump-start her career: a young songwriter who was just as determined to prove herself as Stevie was.

A young songwriter named Sylvia Moy.

Both Sylvia and Stevie had a lot to prove—not just to the label, but to themselves.

"During these times I was watching Stevie, he was sitting around banging on the piano, just as I was hoping for a chance with the producers, and sometimes he looked a little discouraged," Sylvia later said. "But he hung in there. I watched him and some of those ditties he was playing on the piano, I thought they were good."[14]

Sylvia deeply empathized with Stevie's plight, as she was growing increasingly concerned about her own future at Motown. Though Kim Weston had released her rendition of Sylvia's audition song, "I'm Still Loving You," in January 1965, the song didn't fare well on the charts—and many of Sylvia's other pieces failed to even get beyond the cutting-room floor. Besides, writing songs was never Sylvia's end goal. "What she really wanted to do…was to produce, an ambition that was constantly frustrated in a typically male chauvinistic way by Mickey and the other producers," explained singer, producer, and Gordy's second ex-wife, Raynoma Gordy Singleton.[15]

Ever since she first stepped foot into the recording industry, she'd heard all about the limitations faced by her female peers. "I was told at one time, 'Women don't do this. Women don't produce.' My dad told me, 'Do it anyway. You want to do it? You do it! And if you don't think it's gonna be hard, because it's called life and life is hard. And if you can't deal with that part of it, you might as well dig a hole and get in it.' If it's your dream and you love doing it and God has given you those talents…you do it."[16]

To her credit, Sylvia believed that where there was a will, there was a way—and she was determined to start producing music *her* way. "I wanted the freedom to do as the guys were doing and that was produce, oversee my [own] music."[17] But despite her ambitions, women simply weren't allowed to produce music on their own, and as her friend Raynoma later recalled, Sylvia was explicitly "told she could co-produce with one of the guys and receive royalties. She *still* couldn't get label credit."[18] Despite the fact that she was being invited to—and attending—the producer meetings every week, every week Sylvia was repeatedly brushed off whenever she tried to advocate for herself. "I'm doing the same thing that the guys are doing. Can I get what they're getting?" she later recalled asking the management. "[But] they told me that I couldn't have that because I didn't have a producer contract. I said, 'Give me one and I will sign it.' So it continued like that," Sylvia said. "I kept going to the producers' meetings and I kept praying that one day I would get my propers."[19]

Keeping women shrouded in secrecy and denying them credit as producers wasn't just a Motown rule, either; it was an industry standard even at mainstream record labels during this era. That didn't make it any easier for Sylvia to swallow, though.

"If you walk through the history of this country, you realize that women have had to struggle to be in leadership roles. This is built into the way that our society operates and not just in America but other societies as well," said Charles E. Sykes, a doctor of music education and the retired executive director of the African American Arts Institute at Indiana University, who conducted extensive research on the history of Motown and spoke with Sylvia. "Our society, the standard is defined primarily by White males. They're the ones who have historically been in leadership positions and have set the standards, so why would Black men be different in terms of the way that they view women? That's the way it was and, in some ways, still is."

If anyone else could empathize with Sylvia's frustrations, it was singer Valerie Simpson, who began writing and producing at Motown in 1966 alongside her husband, Nickolas Ashford, as one half of the legendary New York–based duo of Ashford and Simpson. They'd scored big in 1966 with their hit "Ain't No Mountain High Enough," an inspirational duet performed by Marvin Gaye and Tammi Terrell. Despite this success, however, Simpson's achievements were consistently linked with her husband; even when she became the first woman at Motown to actually receive liner credit as a producer on 1968's "Ain't Nothing Like the Real Thing" (performed by Gaye and Terrell), she was still credited alongside Ashford.

Even so, Simpson acknowledged the credit opened doors for her that other women struggled to walk through. "I think the hardest thing was getting a producer's contract. Because for a woman at that time, there were very few of us working as producers...So when I finally got that, it made things a lot easier because then you could instruct how you wanted your song to come out."[20]

Sylvia longed for this kind of autonomy—and she remained on the lookout for any opportunity that might present itself. At Motown's weekly producer meetings, Mickey Stevenson would routinely go down the roster of artists and hand out assignments to the in-house producers, though as Sylvia later clarified, "For a while there, it was about seventeen men producing and one woman—me."[21] Though she technically had the same title as her male peers, it was assumed that Sylvia would never be given an assignment of her own, and that she would instead write under one of her male counterparts.

"I didn't like this," she later admitted of the process, "but it was just one of those things."[22]

However, this all changed during one particular meeting of the producers in 1965.

As usual, Sylvia and her male colleagues were sitting in metal fold-up chairs in Studio A as they awaited Stevenson's orders. Dressed to the nines as ever, Stevenson diligently handed out assignments to the fellas—but when the meeting was coming to a close, Stevenson realized that he'd forgotten to hand out one assignment. The particular artist hadn't even really been at the forefront of his mind, due to his lagging career, and Stevenson wondered aloud if anyone would be willing to donate their time instead.

"'I'm going to ask for volunteers and that's [for] Stevie Wonder,'" Sylvia recalled Stevenson saying. "He made that announcement and all the guys just turned it down. So he says, 'Well, I think we're going to let him go. We're going to release him. He's made some money and it's over for him."[23]

The meeting was adjourned quickly thereafter. But then, amid the bustle of folks walking, talking, and shuffling their feet, and the loud clanking of metal chairs being folded and put away, Sylvia did something she had never done before.

She mustered up the nerve to approach Stevenson and informed him that she didn't agree with his assessment of Stevie, and "didn't think it was over" for him. She asked that he be her first assignment under her own name and recalled, "I was begging. 'Give him to me. *Please* let me have him.'"[24]

To see quiet and soft-spoken Sylvia this fired up about anything—let alone a performer whose career was on the rocks—was unusual. And so Stevenson agreed that he would go to the quality control board and make a suggestion on her behalf. Later in the day, Stevenson came back and told her, "Sylvia Moy, you got your first production assignment, Stevie Wonder, but I'm going to tell you this: You come up with a hit on him, we'll keep him. If not, we'll let him go."[25]

This was the moment Sylvia had been waiting for.

"The shot to take Stevie when no one else would was her big opportunity, and she had stipulated that she'd do it if she could produce and get the credit," remembered Raynoma Gordy Singleton proudly. "[And] finally, Mickey gave her the green light."[26]

"When it came time for people to work with him, everybody had their doubts and droughts. Sylvia didn't have that," Stevenson later reflected. "So to me, that's a natural marriage. She saw some of the natural gifts." If she felt like she could do something with Stevie's voice and career that others could not, well, Stevenson was curious to see what might transpire. Ultimately, Stevenson and Gordy were about making money—and if Sylvia thought she could turn Stevie into a chart-topper, they'd let her have at it.

Sylvia was thrilled and itching to show everyone at Motown just what she was made of—but not everyone at the label was as delighted by Sylvia and Stevie's new pairing. Up to this point, Sylvia had worked alongside Hank Cosby, who then got credit on Sylvia's projects by default. Hank's wife, Patricia, recalled that when Stevenson allowed Sylvia to collaborate with Stevie, some producers and songwriters balked. "Hank was the only guy that was willing to work with Sylvia to work with Stevie," said Patricia. "The other guys were like, 'Why don't you just let him go? Why is she trying to hold on to him?'"

No one doubted that Stevie was a skilled musician. "He always had the genius gene. He was efficient on three or four different instruments at the time. But being a genius and getting hit songs are two different things," said Cornelius Grant, a songwriter, guitarist, and bandleader for the Temptations. The male producers at Motown consequently were hesitant to give any of their own songs to Stevie.

Even so, they weren't too excited about Sylvia making an attempt. "They didn't want to see a woman come in there outright and get a song on Stevie Wonder," explained singer Martha Reeves. "Couldn't nobody else do that for him." Reeves reasoned that Sylvia had the patience in this moment to reach inside of Stevie and pull out his untapped abilities. The men, on the other hand, were so focused and busy with their own successes that they didn't have time to stop and assist someone who'd been mainly struggling up to that point in time.

Though Sylvia was excited and eager, she was also incredibly emotional about the task set before her. When she finally told her dad about the opportunity, she couldn't stop crying. Her dad told her to pray and to remember that *nobody* at Motown was bigger than God. "My father was very firm on not holding back or allowing anyone to hold you back on what you could do or could not do," said Sylvia's youngest sister, Anita. "He did not believe in that. If there was something that you could do or wanted to do, he felt you had to do it."

This would be the moment of truth for not just Sylvia, but Stevie, too.

And this new partnership had the potential to make or break them both.

# CHAPTER 11

# "Uptight"

Everything was riding on this moment for Stevie and Sylvia. He needed a hit song; she needed to help him get one—and fast.

Determined to make this new partnership work, Sylvia made a personal trip to Lula Hardaway's home to speak with Stevie's mother about him. Sylvia confirmed to Lula what she had already suspected about certain people at Motown who wanted to cut Stevie loose, but she also informed Lula that she, Sylvia, had just been assigned to Stevie, and she was determined to help him succeed.

Lula had never been crazy about many of the folks who worked at Motown—but when it came to Sylvia, things were different. Lula never felt threatened by Sylvia; rather, she *trusted* her son with Sylvia, because she respected Sylvia's integrity and dedicated commitment in having her son's best interests at heart. And so, Lula gave her blessing for Sylvia to work with Stevie.

Sylvia immediately brought Stevie into the studio, explaining that she was going to be the one to work with him going forward. Stevie felt Sylvia's spirit immediately and felt safe. "I loved Sylvia from the moment that I met her," Stevie said. "[I appreciated] her heart. Her passion. Her desire to not only do music great but to do great things with my music."[1] What's more, the fact that Sylvia—a woman—had stepped up to work with him when no one else would really stood out to Stevie. He saw their union as a divine intervention, and, like his mother, he trusted both Sylvia and the process they were about to embark upon together. Though Sylvia previously spoke directly with Lula about Stevie when she visited her, Sylvia never had a one-on-one conversation directly with Stevie about the matter. She didn't want to upset him or impact his confidence any further. However, the teen was wise—and he had impeccable hearing, too. He knew what was on the line.

The first thing Sylvia requested was simple: She wanted to hear Stevie's "little ditties," a term she liked to use to describe unfinished melodies. "I had a bag of [my own] songs at the time, but I told Stevie, 'I want you to play everything, all of the little ditties you have, play them for me,'" Sylvia later recalled. "He went through everything. He said, 'That's all I have,' and I thought I was going to have to start working from my bag. I asked him, 'Are you *sure* you don't have anything else?'"[2]

Sylvia knew that whatever they made together, that song had to be a hit—and so far, none of Stevie's ditties were cutting it. She was resigned to calling it a day and going back to the piano. But just as she was walking out of the room, he started playing a melody, one that captured her attention and made her turn right back around.

"Play it again," she told Stevie.

He started playing and then singing, "Baby, everything is alright, uptight." That's as much as he had at the time, but there was *something* about it that clicked for Sylvia.

"Stevie, that's *it*!"

Somewhat taken aback by her enthusiasm, she said Stevie initially brushed her off. "What? That ain't nothing."

But Sylvia knew in her *gut* it was something—and so, she told him, "*That's* the one we're going to work with."[3]

Reenergized, Sylvia took the ditty home to start fleshing it out a bit more and adding more lyrics to go along with Stevie's vocal melody. An avid music listener, she'd already noticed that British music was starting to rise in popularity stateside, and she appreciated how much more elaborate and diverse their lyrics were. "At this time over in Europe, they were putting more words in a phrase. I used that style for this [song]," explained Sylvia.[4] In addition to having increased word counts and being more poetic, the British songs also contained deeper meanings and more thought-provoking messages—something that Sylvia strove to emulate in her own music.

Within a few weeks, the pair began collaborating on the song in earnest. Since Sylvia didn't typically write at the Motown office, she would go over to Stevie's family home and pick him up, then bring him right back to the piano at her parents' house—the environment that made her feel most at ease. Over the course of many such long days together, the two developed a personal and professional rhythm that really worked for them. Though she was more introverted and he was more extroverted, he followed her lead when it came to the songs—and she, in turn, welcomed his input.

Also at the Moy home was Sylvia's nephew Jackie, who was just a kid during this time and had grown particularly attached to Sylvia while his mother was away working in New York. As it so happened, he'd been present while they were working on "Uptight" and loved watching the two work magic together. "They worked on melody because she wanted to know where he could sing, because his voice was changing," Jackie said. "They would test different things. She was trying to find a new register for him to not sing using the old voice but find another way, because Stevie was singing from his throat as a kid."

It was important to keep Stevie's primary instrument healthy. After all, years of screaming and general mismanagement of his voice had taken an almost career-stopping toll on the young singer in the past. Ever mindful of this as a trained vocalist herself, Sylvia wanted to make certain that Stevie had the proper tools to both land a hit in the near future *and* sustain a long-term career. "Sylvia learned opera. She started teaching him [Stevie] how to breathe properly and sing properly," remembered Jackie. "She taught him how to sing from [his diaphragm] and helped him work on his new register and how to hit those notes."

Though she had twelve years on Stevie and a lot more experience, Sylvia never belittled or talked down to Stevie; rather, she encouraged him to bring his own strengths to the table. This meant that while Stevie often crafted the melodies of the music and the inspiration or story behind the notes, Sylvia was the one who would craft the engaging lyrics.[5] Though she was writing the words down, she was intent on including the words Stevie himself used in everyday life, like "far out," "groovy," "outta sight," and "uptight"—which is where the title of the song came from. Nowadays, the term "uptight" usually refers to someone who is nervous, tense, or stressed out. Back in the sixties, however, the word also had a place in modern slang, where it was used to describe someone who was excellent or happy, while "outta sight" was another way of saying something was cool.[6] Far from looking down on Stevie's teenage vocabulary, Sylvia loved what she referred to as his "Stevie-isms" and made them a signature part of the music.[7]

Another thing that really set "Uptight" apart from other music in Stevie's past was the fact that Sylvia had managed to incorporate more words and backstory, similar to the European music she'd been hearing lately. The poppy lyrics of "Uptight" may sound light and upbeat, but they also talk about class from the perspective of a boy so poor he owned only the shirt on his back. In the song, the boy is talking to his wealthy sweetheart, a "pearl of a girl" who has been brought up in a mansion with butlers and maids. Though the boy admits he doesn't bring a lot to the table financially, the girl assures him that "everything's alright" because she sees his real value: the fact that his "heart is true."

To bring everything all together, producer and arranger Hank Cosby stepped in at the end and helped the pair tighten up the chords. Since Sylvia had already been working on the lyrics, she was a bit ahead of the game by the time she received the polished music track back from Cosby. "I used four or five horns. We gave it to her, and in a couple of weeks, it came back," Cosby later recalled. "Bit by bit, the song just grew. That's the way she would write."[8]

Though Sylvia and Stevie had great chemistry, they also had their share of obstacles when it came to working together. One thing that Sylvia hadn't fully considered when she asked for the assignment in the first place was the fact that Stevie's first Motown mentor, Clarence Paul, had worked with him by whispering the lyrics to Stevie, which he then sang back on the recording. This bespoke technique worked for them for a while, but eventually, Clarence wanted to be able to work from the control booth while Stevie was in the studio. Fortunately, Mike McLean, a top Motown engineer, had designed an efficient wiring system to allow both Clarence and Stevie to wear earphones.[9] By doing this, Clarence could remain in the control booth and recite the lyrics a line or two ahead of Stevie, just as Stevie listened in the studio to the music track and recorded his voice alongside it.

As if Sylvia's hands weren't full enough already, she had to learn how to work this same method, because that's what Stevie was most comfortable with. When it came time to record "Uptight," Sylvia stood in the control booth, overlooking Studio A, and recited the lyrics a line or two ahead of the track into Stevie's headset:

*Baby, everything is alright.*

*Uptight, out of sight.*

Luckily, they quickly fell into sync; the pair never missed a beat as he repeated everything she recited to him like an echo. Everyone marveled at how Sylvia was able to pick up right where Clarence Paul left off. "Clarence could work with him. Then Sylvia got him. It was like this connection...If you got hot peppers in there, something's coming out *hot*!" remembered singer Louvain Demps, who sang background vocals on "Uptight" with the Andantes. In addition to the supporting female vocalists, two of Stevie's favorite Funk Brothers—drummer Benny Benjamin and bass player James Jamerson—contributed their talents to the track as well. This was a deeply special moment for him; though others at the label had doubted him at times, Benjamin and Jamerson never wavered in their support for Stevie, so their presence on the song instilled him with confidence.[10]

When the song was completed, many were impressed by Stevie's deeper tone; after years of practice, his vocal range had grown significantly steadier, and he now had the power to perform songs with more depth and emotion. Even Berry Gordy liked what he heard. "[Stevie's] voice changed for the better," Gordy said. "That young, undeveloped, high-pitched sound that I hadn't loved when I first met him turned into a controlled, powerful, versatile instrument. Stevie's confidence soared."[11]

After formally ditching the "Little" moniker ahead of his stage name, Stevie Wonder was ready to usher in a new era, starting with the single "Uptight," which was released on November 22, 1965. The track was a scorching success, burning up the Top 40 by late January and hitting #3 on the Billboard Hot 100 pop chart. Two months later, the song was #1 on the R&B chart and even came in at #14 on the British singles charts. After selling a million copies, it eventually went platinum. And as "Uptight" continued its reign over the radio and an album was released, Stevie signed a new contract that would keep him at Motown until the age of twenty-one. As Demps later summed it up, with that single track *alone*, "Sylvia saved Stevie."

But Sylvia was confident that the song would work in her favor, too. In addition to giving her more credibility when it came to songwriting itself, a part of her even hoped that her male colleagues would come to respect her enough to look beyond her gender, and maybe, just maybe, see her as their equal. "I said to myself, 'OK. This is the chance. If they believe in it this much, this will put me in a position to at least negotiate something for myself after it goes out and it is a hit,'" she explained.[12]

Unfortunately, despite all of Sylvia's hard work, most of her colleagues at Motown ultimately ended up celebrating Stevenson's and Cosby's contributions to the hit over her own. And as these men were lauded for their part in reviving Stevie's career, Sylvia's role was minimized almost out of existence.

Although Stevenson had allegedly promised her that she could produce the song and put her name on it if it worked, he changed his tune when he realized what a big hit it was going to be. According to Raynoma Gordy Singleton, "Sylvia cut a demo and proudly presented it to Mickey, who took one listen and said, 'That's great. I love it. Sylvia, thanks a lot but...it's going to take a real pro to produce this record the way it should be done.'"[13]

Sylvia felt as if she couldn't breathe. She'd kept her end of the bargain and expected the rest of the agreement to be fulfilled. "This was my first production, but it didn't quite work that way," lamented Sylvia later on. "After doing it, I must admit, the guys changed their minds.

Mickey changed his mind and decided it did sound like a hit. And I got it as far as going to the arranging department. Hank Cosby was head. And the two of them ended up splitting a production on that song."[14]

Indeed, while Sylvia was credited as a writer on the hit song (alongside Cosby and Wonder), her contributions to the production were ignored. Immediately after she learned about the exclusion, she fought to maintain her composure in her colleagues' presence. But once she was finally alone, she let everything go.

"I stood outside the door and cried. I was upset," she admitted. "They never knew it."[15]

When she went home and told her parents about it, they advised her to "stick it out at Motown."[16] But it was clear the situation never sat right with her—especially when, decades later, she talked about the situation with Charles E. Sykes, retired executive director of the African American Arts Institute at Indiana University. Though he'd conducted extensive research on Motown, his interview with Sylvia really pulled at his heartstrings.

"It's a heart-wrenching story," Sykes acknowledged, "because think about it. First of all, you had this woman who was working with someone who was still essentially a child and helping him to grow, being part of his transition to becoming a young man and being able to help him extend his career. She understood that as talented as he was, he was going to be dismissed by Motown because they were not able to produce a hit with him. It was *very* heart-wrenching, and when she mentioned that she cried outside the door, I was tearing up with her."

Though friends like Raynoma Gordy Singleton remembered Sylvia's devastation that "she would never break that circle," not everyone at Motown was willing to take full accountability for the slight.[17] When asked about Gordy Singleton's statement and if there was any merit to it, Mickey Stevenson later said, "It was not true but in a way it was." According to Stevenson, muscle was needed when it came to being a producer. And women didn't always have the strength, stamina, or intellect required to be in this leadership position over men, particularly in the studio.

"If you're not strong enough to control the musicians in the studio to get what you want, then you're not a producer. That took another learning process. Since that was my point of view and my job, I went at it with a passion," Stevenson said. "[The women at the company] used to call me some terrible names because I would not allow women to produce...I was not into dealing with female producers unless they came to produce, then I could show them something so they could learn something. For me, you had to come with the attitude of really learning how to produce the product."

Though Sylvia Moy was swept under the rug professionally, there were still many at Motown who knew what she'd done. "I don't know whether Sylvia gets credit in the media, but the real factor is she is responsible for bringing the goods," admitted her colleague Cornelius Grant, the Temptations' guitarist and songwriter. "Her lyrics really resounded and created an opportunity for Stevie...She brought him to the forefront."

And once he got there, Sylvia was determined to see things through. After all, she loved working with Stevie and wanted to continue the partnership. "That was her door to Motown, Stevie, and then the hits that he had gotten for her," said songwriter and Motown executive Janie Bradford. "So, they couldn't let this good thing die. They had to keep this going. To me that was very understandable."

Though "Uptight" would be the culminating moment for her after its release in November, this wasn't the only thing she accomplished that year. Three major songs that Sylvia cowrote and worked on were completed but not released until the following year.

On the home front, things weren't much easier for Sylvia. She had recently arranged for her younger brother Melvin to audition at Motown. At the time, the Temptations were looking to add another member to their group. Like Melvin, most of the members were six feet in height or taller, and he could certainly hold his own vocally.

But fate had other plans, and Uncle Sam got Melvin first. The teen received a draft letter in 1965, and instead of auditioning for one of Motown's hottest male groups, Melvin joined the Army and served in the Vietnam War.

Sylvia and the Moy family were crushed. After his initial deployment, she kept in touch with Melvin and offered as much comfort as she could. Eager to lift the spirits of Melvin and his fellow soldiers, Sylvia approached Berry Gordy and suggested sending Motown music care packages overseas. Luckily for everyone involved, Gordy readily agreed. Esther Gordy Edwards, Gordy's eldest sister who served as Motown's senior vice president, assisted in making this possible.

Because of Sylvia's connection to the label, Melvin received a monthly shipment of the latest releases from artists, including the Temptations, the Supremes, and Martha and the Vandellas. An ocean away, he shared the songs with his comrades, setting up concerts for the troops where they could unwind and listen to the records, and also encouraging his fellow soldiers to perform the songs themselves if they were musically inclined. "In the military, he [used] Motown music and promoted peace amongst the soldiers, to calm them down," said arranger Paul Riser. "You know music does that."

To help herself cope with anxiety and grief back home, Sylvia did what she knew best: She put her feelings into song. This time, she teamed up with fellow Motown songwriter Richard Morris to craft the tune "Forget Me Not," which is about a soldier being shipped off to war. The lyrics in the gut-wrenching ballad encourage the soldier to hold on to love and to cherish happy memories whenever he feels lonely or sad. It's unknown why there was a delay of three years before the song was finally released to the public.

While this period in her life was marked by grief and uncertainty, music kept Sylvia rejuvenated—and it wasn't long before she was approached to work on another project. In 1965, Eddie Holland, of the acclaimed Holland-Dozier-Holland songwriting trio, reached out to her and asked if she could help him out with a song he'd been working on for the Isley Brothers.

Trying to catch his breath as an in-demand songwriter for the label, Holland's time was limited—and he knew "This Old Heart of Mine (Is Weak for You)" needed some extra TLC. He had long been impressed with Sylvia's songwriting abilities and style. But even more importantly, her work ethic was impeccable; she was as practical as she was prolific, and she never complained when someone asked her to step up.

Holland later revealed that he could have picked any one of the other male songwriters to help him finish "This Old Heart of Mine," but Sylvia was his first choice. This in and of itself was a huge compliment, as Holland readily admitted that he didn't like many people. "I decided to find someone who could write certain songs with me and I wouldn't have to work as hard," he said. "I thought about Sylvia because of her personality and because of the way she dealt with people. She had a relaxed way. She would kind of smile. She wouldn't do a whole lot of talking. She would do more thinking than talking."

Since Holland knew that Sylvia didn't work out of the office, he invited her to his home on LaSalle to work on "This Old Heart of Mine." During the three or four hours they spent working on the song, they stayed focused on the task at hand, but when it was all said and done, Holland claimed that "neither could come up with anything for the song," which surprised them both.

Fortunately, the following day, he returned to the office with a new surge of creativity. "It all came to me in a flash," he recalled. "I started writing it out. I finished the whole song. When she heard me writing it, she opened my office door, looked at me, and smiled. And she just shook her head in agreement with what I was doing. She thought it was good. She dealt with it with such humility. She didn't get angry about it. She took it in stride, smiled, walked away, and closed the door. So, I just put her name on the song. I just felt like it. Anybody else I wouldn't have done that. But because of Sylvia's personality...she just hit me in a quiet, positive way."

Recognition wasn't always freely given for one's efforts even when earned at Motown; Sylvia saw how things worked around there with producers leveraging their power to subjectively decide how to dole out credit as they saw fit.

## CHAPTER 12

# Credit, That's What I Want

January 1966 kicked off at lightning speed for Sylvia as two songs she'd cowritten finally made their way outside the Motown walls. The first was "My Baby Loves Me," a beautiful sentimental ballad performed by Martha and the Vandellas, which was released on January 4. It was a simple song about one of Sylvia's favorite subjects: love. *Everyone* agreed that love songs were Sylvia's specialty. While the romantic ballad had initially been written for Motown singer Kim Weston (whose husband at the time, A&R director Mickey Stevenson, was credited on the work as a cowriter), the tune was later handed over to Martha Reeves to record. Sylvia's words resonated with her on such a deep level that it was *eerie*, Reeves later said.

"['My Baby Loves Me'] wasn't written for me, but there was a time when I thought [Sylvia] was following me around because the song spoke to what I was going through," marveled Reeves. "I was really in love. I put my heart and soul in it when singing. The song was beautifully orchestrated; however, it had the Andantes and the Four Tops on it. Those are the eight people singing backup. Not a Vandella was on it."

None were the wiser about those really singing background vocals, because just as songs weren't always truthfully credited to those who actually wrote them, the same applied to the artists performing them. Luckily, the song still resonated with music lovers. It hit #3 on Billboard's Hot R&B singles chart while also landing #22 on the Billboard Hot 100 singles chart. Even though Reeves was the one who recorded the track, she respected Sylvia's lovely voice, which she listened to whenever learning a melody for one of Sylvia's songs. "She was a jazz singer and wrote songs with a little bit of a jazz flavor," said Reeves. "I'm sure she was gonna record some of the songs she wrote for me for herself but changed her mind from being a performer."

Songwriter Ivy Jo Hunter added that Sylvia had a few things working specifically in her favor as a songwriter, especially when it came to love songs. He felt that a big factor of Sylvia's success was her upbringing in a loving, two-parent home, since songwriting works best when it comes from an authentic source. "I would have never written the songs Sylvia did because I did not have a woman's touch. All of my stuff was entirely different," Hunter admitted. "Most of it was sad, because I didn't really have a lot of love stories. I had a lot of disappointments and that's basically what I wrote about. It was like a part of me that never fully developed. You can't write things that you don't know about."

The new year was just getting warmed up when Sylvia's second collaboration, the Isley Brothers' recording of "This Old Heart of Mine," hit the market on January 12, 1966. "I didn't think that much of it [initially], but Ronnie Isley thought it was a great song," Eddie Holland later admitted. Despite his initial feelings, Holland still knew it had hitmaking potential and his feeling quickly proved correct as the track flew up to #12 on the Billboard Hot 100 and #6 on the R&B charts.

And then, just when Sylvia was sure her star was on the rise, the ground beneath her feet began shaking once more.

It all started when the Temptations went into the studio that month and recorded the song "Ain't Too Proud to Beg." Sylvia had allegedly contributed to the infectious groove, which was written the year before. However, when the song finally came out in May 1966, her name was nowhere to be found in the credit lines.

It turned out that the young and budding Motown songwriter Norman Whitfield was looking to make a name for himself. At this point in his early career, most of his work had been cowritten alongside Motown legend Eddie Holland. With Holland's help, Whitfield produced and scored his first Top 40 pop tune with the Marvelettes' 1964 song "Too Many Fish in the Sea." But the air at Motown was still thick with competitive tension, and for Whitfield, his sights were set on dethroning Smokey Robinson as the Temptations' sole producer. To do so, he needed to write something that would eclipse Smokey's hot new track, "Get Ready." And Whitfield was sure that he'd found the perfect song—sort of.

Eddie Holland recalled the day Whitfield presented him with some of the "most awful lyrics" he'd ever seen. "'I've got this paper here. This is what I have. What can you do with this?'" Holland recalled of the conversation. "I told him I couldn't do anything with that because there's nothing here. It wasn't called 'Ain't Too Proud to Beg.' It was called something else. I looked at this paper and I think on the third verse, it had a line and all these verses he had. I don't know where he got them from, to be honest...but they weren't that well done, put together."

Was it possible that Whitfield could have spliced together phrases and ideas he possibly gathered from Sylvia? Holland didn't think so.

"I knew that Sylvia wrote way better than that. She made *sense* out of everything she did. Her name never came up with me and Norman. Norman said it was something he had written. And it looked like something he had written, because Norman was not a real good writer at that time."

Though Holland told Norman in no uncertain terms that there was nothing he could do with the lyrics as Norman had written them, there *was* one line in the third verse that stood out: "'Ain't too proud to beg.' I said that's the only thing on here that *makes sense* to me out of all of these lines," Holland recalled. "He asked, 'Can you use that?' I said I could use that and write a song around that. So that's what I did. Norman didn't even have a melody. *I* had to create the song."

Though Holland received credit for the revamping of the song, in actuality, Sylvia was the one who had first planted the seeds of inspiration for the lyrics. Her son's father, Al, was an insanely controlling man who was always desperately begging and pleading to get back with Sylvia, even after she courageously walked away. This man would say *anything* to win her back, going so far as to confess that "I ain't too proud to beg."

According to Sylvia's nephew Jackie, this dynamic inspired the story she contributed in the lyrics of the hit song. "They were having a problem making the song's lyrics and arrangement gel. They asked for Sylvia's advice. She rearranged it, which was the released version," Jackie alleged. "She told me [that the other cowriters] couldn't pull it together in the song's arrangement. They contacted her and said, 'We've got this problem with this song. Would you take a look at it and see what you can do?' She took it and gave it back to them. That was the released version. It was a big hit. She mentioned that Motown had an event in Las Vegas. In the parking lot, she saw [one of the cowriters] when she was getting out of her car and going into the casino. She said he looked at her and he came over and said, 'We didn't do it.' He said to her, 'I apologize.' She said he pulled a wad of money out of his pocket and he handed it to her. He said, 'I'm sorry.' They got the award for the song, but she was nowhere listed on it."

At Motown, opinions were divided on whether or not Sylvia had anything to do with the song. Eddie Holland, for one, never agreed with Jackie's claim, saying that "something must have gotten mixed up" with the account. Holland said he knew Sylvia well and her saying something like what her nephew claimed "was not her personality. It's hard for me to believe that story. Unless you said you heard it from Sylvia yourself, I would never believe that...How the hell would family members know that?!" Others were well aware of the fact that the figureheads at Motown, like Gordy, reached out to her for help when other songwriters got stuck, and so it wouldn't have been out of the realm of possibility. "Berry recognized...that when there was material that he thought was almost there but needed something extra, especially with lyrics or another writer's touch, Sylvia was the first call for that," said arranger Paul Riser. "He would get her to bring quality into the product, the song, or get her opinion." Still, there is no evidence that Gordy ever reached out to Sylvia as it relates to "Ain't Too Proud to Beg."

Whether or not Sylvia was involved in helping the song make its way out the door, even Gordy admitted in his memoir that several revisions of the track were required before the song passed the quality control meeting.[1] Since Smokey Robinson's tune "Get Ready" had hit the top of the R&B charts but reached only #29 on the pop charts (missing the Top 20), it was decided that "Ain't Too Proud to Beg" would be the Temptations' next single—and it was a smash hit. Losing this competition was directly responsible for how Norman Whitfield got the Temptations from Smokey Robinson and became the group's main producer.

According to Sylvia's family, however, the song's success was bittersweet. "We believe she cowrote this song...because it is almost verbatim the story of her breakup with her one and only love," said Sylvia's younger sister Celeste.

In the end, without definitive credits linking her to the song, the truth remains a mystery—both for the general public and for music scholars like James E. Perone, professor emeritus of music at the University of Mount Union, Alliance, Ohio.

As it happened, Perone made an interesting observation that pulled "Ain't Too Proud to Beg" right up alongside Stevie Wonder's hits, without ever realizing that Sylvia may have been the one thing the two had in common.[2]

For starters, Perone pointed out that there was a clear connection between "Ain't Too Proud to Beg" and Stevie's 1965 catchy dance tune "Ain't That Asking for Trouble," which was cowritten by Sylvia, Stevie, and Clarence Paul. According to Perone, it is "worth noting that later soul or soul-influenced songs sound as though they could have been inspired by (or at least relate back to)" this tune or "at least its style."[3] From his perspective, "There's quite a bit of stylistic similarity between those two songs, which is interesting to me because if you look purely at Stevie Wonder's recordings, there's *so* much diversity of style." He elaborated that the basic feel is "a bit more intangible, but there's just some sort of a feel about them that makes them sound like they're not from entirely different worlds."

Might this be possible? One can only wonder.

---

Regardless of how much credit she was or wasn't getting publicly, it quickly became clear to Sylvia's colleagues and fellow artists at Motown that she could really knock out some chart-toppers. As she readily admitted, "I got into it and the hits started coming."[4]

Motown tape librarian Patricia Cosby marveled at how far Sylvia had come in such a short amount of time. After all, she'd witnessed Sylvia's journey from the first day she stepped foot inside Hitsville U.S.A., back when she thought she'd be a singer and could never have imagined her future career as a songwriter. In hindsight, things worked in Sylvia's favor once she began surrendering and making the most of the opportunity before her. "Long story short, in the early days, I think that Sylvia was disappointed with the path that they laid out for her," said Patricia. "But apparently somebody knew what they were doing, because she was absolutely one of the most successful writers."

Though she could've written for a lot of other artists (and did), Stevie remained one of her favorite collaborators. They'd ended up writing a lot of songs together for his album *Up-Tight (Everything's Alright)*, which was released in May 1966. The A-side of the record featured a Moy-Wonder collab called "Nothing's Too Good for My Baby," an up-tempo song that reached #4 on the R&B charts in the United States On its flip side was a tender ballad called "With a Child's Heart," a song that hit #8 on the R&B charts and once again featured the Detroit Symphony Orchestra. That tune was cowritten by Sylvia, Hank Cosby, and another one of Motown's few female songwriters, Vicki Basemore (who was also Mickey Stevenson's sister-in-law).

Interestingly, though Stevie was the initial voice behind "With a Child's Heart," it's the second version of this song—which came out in 1973—that really popularized the tune, and this version was recorded by Stevie Wonder's cousin: Michael Jackson. Sylvia had kept an eye on Michael and his brothers, known as the Jackson 5, ever since their first day at Motown, four years after she'd arrived. She distinctly remembered seeing Michael, the youngest, standing helplessly on the company's front porch and watching the other children outside playing, crying because he wanted to play like them. She had a lot of empathy for the young boy; according to her sister Anita, Sylvia was particularly touched by "his sensitivity. She felt that was part of why he was so talented. She said she felt that the song meant something to him. He did not get that chance to be a child. She could feel some of the things he was going through at that age. That's why he picked that particular one of her songs."

Meanwhile, as 1966 thundered on, Stevie received his first two Grammy nominations, in the categories of "Best Rhythm and Blues Solo Vocal Performance by a Male or Female" and the "Best Rhythm and Blues Recording"—both for "Uptight." Although he didn't take home the gilded gramophones that night (the awards both ultimately went to Ray Charles's "Crying Time"), it was a sign that good things were on the horizon. The same year, Sylvia won two awards as a songwriter for "Uptight"—one in the pop category, and the other in the R&B category—at the legendary Broadcast Music, Inc. (BMI) Awards, a global organization that continues to recognize songwriters, composers, and music publishers.

The most important recognition she received, however, was from Stevie himself. Even if she didn't always get the internal or external recognition she deserved, Stevie continuously credited Sylvia—and Hank Cosby—for his success, especially in the early days.

"It was a great marriage, one that really made it possible for me to continue to be in Motown," said Stevie.[5]

And it was only the beginning.

---

Though the two didn't always seem to have much in common to outside observers, the deep connection that Sylvia and Stevie developed was undeniable. "She learned from him and with her warm side, he learned from her," said Mickey Stevenson. "She came from her voice, her heart, and her feelings with a song." Their strengths and weaknesses complemented one another, allowing them to bypass many obstacles and hiccups. "As he was struggling with lyrics maybe and melody, she would hear it right away. He'd give her an idea, she'd take it and expand it," said arranger Paul Riser, who worked with them both. "They worked together well. It was because of her insight, and they wrote songs together. They had the spiritual connection. And they loved each other. Oh, Stevie loved Sylvia. He did. He trusted her."

"A man needs a woman's touch. [Sylvia] was qualified to add that," added songwriter Ivy Jo Hunter. "I always wondered why [Stevie] felt he needed anybody. But he always did. He was that kind of person."

Another person that Stevie worked well with was producer Hank Cosby, who was one of the few musicians at Motown who'd been trained to read music. And when Stevie, Sylvia, and Hank combined forces, with Hank arranging Stevie's melodies and putting finishing touches on the track? They were a winning trio.

When it came to her part of the equation, Sylvia didn't rush. She wanted to write masterpieces that would stand the test of time, and she was meticulous about ensuring that the rhythm, flow, storyline, and rhyme all worked together. More than a few of her male colleagues—even Stevie, at times—grew frustrated with how slow her process seemed, as they were constantly under pressure to put out hit after hit, and they wanted something fast, almost overnight. "Sometimes she'd be very slow writing a song. She'd be a month and Stevie would be very impatient," remembered Hank. "Everybody would be all upset with her, and we'd get her in the studio, and the song would be half finished. We'd have to finish writing it in the studio."[6]

There were times when Sylvia's patience was tested as well. Stevie's attention span was all over the place when it came to writing melodies.

He had so many ideas that he would often start one, drop it, and switch to another right away. "Sylvia did a lot of writing on the early things. I would come up with the basic idea, maybe a punch line, and she would write the story. I would give her a tape of it," Stevie explained. "I write so many tunes in bits that I really don't get the time to finish them all up, so I just give 'em to someone to do. Usually, I'll write the music and basic idea for the story. Then there are times when I'm so interested in getting down to writing another tune that I give it to someone else to finish up, or I feel that my story isn't strong enough, so I give the song to Sylvia or whoever to finish up."[7]

At that time, Stevie was drawing a lot of inspiration from his love of reading and was whipping out so many tunes that he couldn't realistically figure out where he was from song to song. "Most of the spare time I get I spend writing songs. Reading stimulates me to write more. If you get wrapped up in a book it stimulates you. Sometimes I write as many as 150 songs a month down in my basement at home, then I'll take them to the studio."[8] And yet, despite his innumerable tunes and wavering attention, he had a solid work ethic and spent long hours immersed in the music. "He was very lucky he developed good working habits at an early age," Hank Cosby once told Sharon Davis, a former press manager at Motown. "He is behind the piano every day for twelve to thirteen hours. How can anyone compete with that?"

Another thing that set Sylvia apart from others who'd tried to work with Stevie in the past was her ability to understand and channel Stevie's energy to fit each individual song. According to singer Martha Reeves, "When he had voice trouble, he had to sing ballads and slow down on the fast songs. He was a writing, singing, instrumental playing machine. His energy level was so high. *She* captured it. *She* calmed him down to a point and she didn't want nothing from him. Sylvia didn't want nothing from him but just his talent."

This also meant that she recognized how much Stevie thrived off the live reactions of others in the studio whenever he was recording. "He had to feel the presence of people. If there were none around, his vocal was just dead," said Sylvia. "At times, I had to go outside and stop people who were passing to bring them in, so Stevie could feel their presence. Once we got that, he could fire that feeling."[9]

Moreover, Sylvia inherently understood that Stevie had an increased sensitivity to sound due to his blindness, and she ensured that appropriate accommodations were made for him in the studio. "After all, we dim the lights in the studio to concentrate," Sylvia explained. "Stevie is very sensitive, like an open channel, to what's going on around him. What you might feel or I might feel, he can feel that. He can express through music what others might feel."[10]

And Sylvia wasn't doing all of the accommodation, either; Stevie was equally invested in stepping into Sylvia's world—and that meant literally meeting her at the place she worked best: the Moy family home. Jackie, Sylvia's nephew, served as his aunt's engineer when she first started working with Stevie. Back then, eleven-year-old Jackie's job was to rewind and play back the tape each time she requested him to do so—all while she and Stevie created magic, sitting side by side on the bench before the piano in the family's living room. Too young to fully understand that he was witnessing music history up close and personal, Jackie recalled it simply "being fun" to sit quietly and watch. "At night, Sylvia would be at my grandparents' with Stevie and me. We used a reel-to-reel tape recorder because Motown would put the songs on a reel tape. They would sit down at the piano and they would play. I would be the one that Sylvia would say, 'Oh, Jackie, play that track back. Rewind it to that point again.' So I got to learn how to work the reel. I would sit there quietly watching. I was the little engineer while she worked with Stevie on singing the songs."

Not all members of the Moy household were quite as excited to have Stevie and Sylvia around. As Sylvia's youngest brother, Christopher, recalled later on, "[Stevie] would ask me to go bring him some cookies. I was young and didn't care who Stevie Wonder was. I was younger than him and didn't want to be the bad guy…I would try to sneak in the house because I didn't want to be the one he'd send on an errand to get him some cookies. Then I'd hear him ask, 'Where's my cookies?' All I could think was, 'How did he know I was there? His back would be to me!'"

Still, for the most part, Stevie charmed everyone who came into his orbit, even going so far as to recognize sound and foot patterns, particularly of those at Motown. "Stevie was amazing. He could walk into a room and greet everybody by name," said Sylvia. "I've wondered to this day how he did it. I mean did we all have a special odor or what?"[11]

As Stevie and Sylvia's work relationship blossomed into a solid friendship, Sylvia invited him to the annual cookout at the Moy family home, which Stevie attended along with his kid sister Renee. Hot off the heels of the success of "Uptight," Stevie appreciated how welcoming and down to earth the Moy family was and especially savored Mr. Moy's world-famous barbecue, made from a recipe he learned as a native New Orleanian.

After Stevie finished eating, he entertained guests on the family piano. Before they knew it, word spread around the neighborhood that Stevie Wonder was at the Moys' house. "We knew most of the people in the immediate neighborhood, but these people were coming from miles away," said Sylvia's sister Angel. Before Mr. Moy knew it, there was a steady flow of unknowns coming in and out of the house like a revolving door.

As time went on, everyone around them—even as high up as Mickey Stevenson and Smokey Robinson—could feel that there was something truly special in the friendship that Stevie and Sylvia shared. As Sylvia herself once noted, "Something electric happens whenever Stevie Wonder and I get together."[12]

That power surge had been vital in helping Sylvia stay afloat up till now, but she soon realized that she'd need an energy boost far greater from within as an individual to keep up with her male colleagues' lightning force.

## CHAPTER 13

# Writing to Win

As Sylvia continued to refine her style, she also became better at showing the musicians at Motown exactly *how* she wanted her songs to be performed. "Sylvia could tell the musicians what she wanted, and the masterpieces were the result of it," said Martha Reeves. "That was how you produced the Motown Sound. She was there and got the respect."

Most striking of all, Sylvia managed to get respect on her *own* terms. In a time when women often felt like they had to live up to certain social expectations, Sylvia stuck to her guns and mostly kept to herself, no matter the cost.

"There was a certain mindset of some at Motown…a streetwise mentality…[but Sylvia] was a lady," explained Reeves. "She kept her dignity and poise. I don't think she's ever identified with any of them on a social basis. It was all songwriting…I had to dance around a lot *myself* and get out of there and survive. [But Sylvia] would not attend the little party parties...You don't see any pictures of her in no crowd, at no party. We didn't hang out socially. I only saw her in the recording studio. Never at a house, never at a bar. Never, ever at a community club, nowhere."

So why was Sylvia allowed to break all the rules that other women at Motown were seemingly expected to follow? Most likely because Motown didn't want to disrupt that winning formula by firing Sylvia and losing the songs with potential that she could bring in. After all, at the end of the day, making money was always more important.

By her own admission, Sylvia described herself as "eccentric" and a "rarity in the music business."[1] Still, being one of a kind came with a heavy price. "I have to admit as a woman I suffered as a writer. What was I doing horning in? Finally I gained respect. A woman has to be *twice* as good to prove herself."[2]

Though Sylvia refused to adhere to the social expectations at the label, she was also a shrewd and strategic player when things got political. "She knew how to play the game like the men did. Oh, did she ever know it," marveled arranger Paul Riser. "She had a smart family around her. Her mother was a singer and all the kids were in music. She had good people around her."

No matter the support that Sylvia had at home, she knew the only way to stay on top of the industry was to stay on top of her internal competition. After all, Motown only hired the best of the best; if she could outshine her colleagues, she had a real shot at hitting the charts. "We had a competitive thing here," she admitted. "If I had to compete against Smokey, Eddie, or Brian [Holland] to get a release out on one of the artists here, our music was going to hold its own out there against whoever was doing a writing or producing with the other companies. And usually it did," she said.[3]

Songwriter and singer Barrett Strong, a frequent collaborator with Norman Whitfield, admired Sylvia's hustle. "She was just so good at what she could do," Strong said. He reasoned that men gave her a hard time "probably because it was a competitive place. A lot of women didn't step up because they thought it was too competitive." But in Strong's eyes, Sylvia wasn't just competition for her female colleagues—"she was real competition for *everyone*...she was somebody to reckon with."

Andantes background singer Louvain Demps had recognized the strength in Sylvia going back to their days at Pershing High School together, and she had no doubt that Sylvia could hold her own with the best of them. "Competition is good if it's done well," said Demps. "Sylvia was pretty charming, wise, and to look at her, you wouldn't think that she had that kind of fight in her. But that fight wasn't like the guys had. She wasn't ego-tripping...

"She just stood her ground and she knew what she could do. I don't know if she prayed a lot, but that quiet force that she had, it came through. She didn't give up. She was in a fight with a bunch of guys, but she was wise and talented. You could not talk her down. She knew her craft," Demps continued. "She was stronger than she looked. Just looking at a pretty woman, you know how guys are and some of the older ones, too. But it wasn't about that with her...what amazed me so much is that she walked with her head held high, and she might have felt something on the inside, but she didn't let it show. Not to us. What I'm trying to get at is with this strong inner force and all this beauty that she had, she also gained the respect of these men and women."

Sylvia also believed that we teach people how to treat us. "She had to compete with the guys but stay dignified as a lady. She never let them disrespect her and she never lost her composure," added Sylvia's friend and colleague Martha Reeves. "She was a very pretty woman. Whatever advances were made to her, she always let you know that she was about the music. It was about business. She would come in there just to do the music. She didn't hang about. You had to make an appointment to meet with Sylvia. She was not there after the place closed. She always gave herself distance as just a songwriter."

Part of the reason Sylvia was so adamant about her hours at Motown was that she needed to maintain strict work-life boundaries. At Motown, Sylvia was calm, poised, professional; only at home could she really vent her frustration and "scream out loud," according to her nephew Jackie.

But the second she walked into the Motown headquarters, she was *on*. Songwriter Eddie Holland enjoyed working with her because she was such a team player. "She had a quiet way of moving around and working with people. She was easy to work with. I liked that about her."

No matter how likable she might have been to some, other folks remained a thorn in her side by making her time there complicated.

---

Two years and several successes later, Sylvia continued to face sexism and resistance at the label. A&R director Mickey Stevenson remained reluctant to explicitly credit Sylvia as a producer because he didn't believe Sylvia's approach to songwriting overlapped with the production process. In his eyes, if a person "came with all kinds of things in their heads, or the song in their head, that's not producing." When asked later about Sylvia specifically, however, he seemed to change his tune—and even took credit *himself* for opening the door for her. "I really wanted her to be a producer because she had that ability as well," he claimed. "She was one of the first females that I brought to the light."

Despite Stevenson's claim to have brought Sylvia "to the light," not everyone thought Mickey—or any of the other higher-ups at Motown—was utilizing Sylvia's strengths the best they could have.

Arranger Paul Riser said that Sylvia had a lot of people in her circle who really didn't mean her well, even though they pretended to aid in her advancement when asked about it later in interviews. "[Mickey] didn't help Sylvia like he should have," Riser alleged. "He used Sylvia and then when he didn't think he could use her to his benefit, he tried to hold her back."

On the contrary, iconic singer and songwriter Smokey Robinson, one of Stevenson's best friends, saw things a bit differently. Robinson acknowledged that Sylvia "was one of our top writers and did produce a couple of things. She mostly worked with Stevie. They were really tight and really close." But when it came to discussing Sylvia's work, or the work done by her female peers, it was clear Robinson didn't see them on equal footing with the men at the label. "We had a couple women who produced some records here and there. But basically the women who were working there on a constant basis were either working at the company or they were songwriters."

Regardless of what the higher-ups thought, Sylvia remained steadfast in her belief that she had more than earned the right to be considered a producer and receive some monetary gain. "If you look at the body of work that I wrote, I did more than write them. I was writing the background parts, the bass parts, and I was basically producing."[4] She said, "I didn't get my producing credit, the label credit. I eventually got the producer royalties for two of the songs, but not the label credit. I did get the writing credit."[5]

Louvain Demps backed up Sylvia's claims, saying, "All of these years later it should be known Sylvia produced many of the great songs that she wrote, but they wouldn't give her label credit for producing. She was the first female producer we had, and she was warm and had it together. They gave her a hard time, but you could not deny her place because she was good."

One of the most frustrating aspects of the whole ordeal for Sylvia was that Stevenson received credit for just about *everything*—even things he allegedly hadn't worked on personally—just because he was the head of A&R. Others, like songwriter Ivy Jo Hunter, allegedly worked out their own agreements with Stevenson long before Sylvia ever arrived at the label. "His deal with me, we had a fifty-fifty sharing of whatever either one of us did," Hunter explained. "So, whatever he wrote with Sylvia, he also had to give me part of it. There were songs that he gave me credit on that I didn't contribute anything to, like Kim Weston's 'A Thrill a Moment,' and 'I'm Still Loving You,' and Martha Reeves's 'My Baby Loves Me.'" Though it often benefited him, there were also times when Hunter's deal with Stevenson boomeranged to nip him in the butt, like when he gave away credit on his monster 1964 hit "Dancing in the Streets." According to Hunter, the cowriting credits went to Stevenson based on their deal and Marvin Gaye, whose only real involvement was suggesting the title, since the song was already completed before either heard it.

As the A&R director, Stevenson allegedly received "royalty income from songs he played little part in composing. It was a tax on access to the system."[6] Producers at the time typically received about a one-third share in the profits on any particular song, which cut into the royalties of everyone else who'd worked on the record, though Stevenson himself confirmed that the higher the song placed on the music charts and the bigger it was, the more money he received. "As A&R director, I got an override. That meant I received a royalty from every record that went out; it didn't matter who produced it. The bigger the hit, the more money I made...As the A&R man, I was in a no-lose position."[7]

This didn't exactly sit well with the people who worked under him, even though they knew it was par for the course in the industry. As singer and songwriter Clarence Paul claimed, "Motown had their own songwriting contracts, which were way below the rest of the industry. Tunes were stolen all the time, and often credit wasn't properly assigned."[8] Arranger and trombonist Paul Riser echoed these sentiments, recalling that "it was a lot going on up in there. There was a lot of power and control in that A&R department...[Mickey] had enough talent to actually say, 'Let's act as cowriters.' He did do this with some and others he didn't. He said, 'I want a piece of that.' Sometimes a person could put a couple of words in a song and get a piece of it. He was that kind of person, too. He was the best and the worst at the same time."

Regardless of how common it may have been across the rest of the music industry, Stevenson's percentage was also notable in that it was astronomical, at least as far as many of his employees were concerned. According to songwriter Hunter, Stevenson's command and prestige within the Motown hierarchy allowed him to dictate, and receive, up to a 50 percent share of all of his song royalties during their initial "negotiations," even though, in the bulk of cases, Stevenson allegedly would contribute very little or nothing at all.[9] Even people as high up as Gordy remembered the grumblings that accompanied some of his earnings. "Mickey kept everything running smoothly. I did, however, get a complaint now and then when he wanted a larger percentage of a song than he was entitled to," said Gordy.[10] Still, as long as Stevenson kept making Motown money, Gordy was reluctant to rock the boat. Raynoma Gordy Singleton described Stevenson as "the wheeler-dealer of the decade."[11] Gordy echoed the sentiments: "Mickey was a street cat, a wheeler dealer, but I knew it was that same hustling quality that made him the superstar A&R man he was."[12]

Stevenson had a different perspective on the whole issue and denied taking credit for other people's work, saying, "If I had something to do with it, I had something to do with it. I didn't go around trying to take percentages from nobody. No." On the contrary, he believed that *no* sound or song belonged to a single person, no matter how much that person tried to keep their work private. "My point is when a great idea or something is in the air, anyone that's in tune can tune in to it. I mean, any great lyric, any great thought, doesn't belong to nobody out there. Now who tunes in and makes it happen, that's who gets the credit for it, but it's been there. Are you with me?"

As agreeable and easy to work with as Sylvia often was, her frustrations only continued to grow—and before long, she started standing up for herself and the ownership of her own songs. "To get his name on product, Mickey took from her. He took from everybody," alleged Paul Riser, who'd worked with Sylvia on several of her arrangements. "When he saw he couldn't do that anymore, then she became an enemy." Mickey denied these claims.

No matter the case, Sylvia wasn't content to stick up for only herself, either. "She was a threat to all of them," Riser continued. "She had courage. She said what she meant. If she saw something wrong, she would speak on it, especially if it affected her and it would have affected the other writers. That's how she operated."

In Sylvia's eyes, the most pressing task at hand was to encourage the more novice songwriters at Motown to retain their rights to their lyrics, instead of handing them over by selling them to more-well-established colleagues and unknowingly relegating themselves to the role of a ghostwriter. And Sylvia wasn't the only one who felt strongly about this. Paul Riser agreed wholeheartedly, and he found himself at odds with many at the label whenever he spoke up. "People got mad at me for telling them to stop. You are selling your work and efforts. But they did it all the time. She would pick things up and cut right through the jugular vein to their face," Riser said, laughing. "Some people couldn't take that kind of honesty. She shook them up at Motown. She read them all the time and told them before they even knew what they were doing."

Sylvia sympathized with the novice writers; after all, she'd been at Motown only a few years by that point, and she'd seen firsthand how easy it was to ignore the financial side of things when her job was so heavily focused on the music itself. "We were sheltered. We were really in a situation where we could be creative and not worry about the business," Sylvia said. "Somebody else took care of all of the business. So we were unsophisticated to some degree. It is a business."[13] What's more, she'd also been pressured into handing over credit, and she *continued* to feel the pressure to do so. "She was under the same pressure that anyone else was under to share the proceeds," said Ivy Jo Hunter, who worked closely with Mickey Stevenson. "It was part of the business."

At the end of the day, it was a double-edged sword: damned if you did (retain your own rights) and damned if you didn't. There was also the risk that if you pushed *too* hard against the status quo, you'd be shut out of the game altogether. Ted Hull, Stevie's longtime private tutor, sometimes wrote a few songs for his student. However, after he wrote Stevie's song "Purple Raindrops," which was on the B-side of "Uptight," he was shocked to learn that he would be giving up one-third of his royalties to Clarence Paul, who'd merely suggested that Hull add another bridge to the tune. He was similarly disconcerted by what he referred to as the "credit scam" where it "was customary to share credit with anyone [who] helped get a piece produced."[14] After openly expressing his disdain, however, Hull never received an opportunity to write another song at Motown.

Around this same period, tensions even started bubbling between Sylvia and her longtime mentor Hank Cosby. After years of privately confiding in Hank about all the frustration and resentment she harbored for those who took credit for her and others' work at the label, he eventually showed his hand. "Her professional relationship with Hank became fractured when he started doing the same thing," recalled Celeste, one of Sylvia's younger sisters. As one might imagine, Sylvia felt betrayed.

"She knew what was going on. That includes Hank, too. Sylvia was sharp," added Paul Riser. "He was right there running the A&R department with Mickey. They were in cahoots. Hank was a user. He would use Sylvia to where she was valuable to him. Then, at other times, he would prevent her from doing certain things, because it wasn't what Mickey thought or what Berry thought and what other administrators thought. There was jealousy among other writers when it came to her."

And it wasn't only the songwriters who were growing tired of feeling cheated out of their hard-earned royalties. According to Raynoma Gordy Singleton, "On the road, Motown artists compared notes with singers signed to other labels. Finding their royalty rates substandard, and being treated like children when they questioned those in charge, the artists too were feeling subversive. Times had changed, yet provisions for the artists had not."[15]

However, unbeknownst to all, big changes *were* happening behind the scenes at Motown. Though some loved Stevenson and others loathed him, none could deny that "he was one of the greatest creative forces during our formative years," as Gordy once said.[16] Understandably so, folks were somewhat caught off guard when Gordy decided to move in a different direction in 1966 and hired Eddie Holland, one-third of the award-winning songwriting and production trio of Holland-Dozier-Holland, to replace him.

"I left the chairman's office mad as hell, disappointed and disillusioned," recalled Stevenson about that day. "I called all the writers, producers, and musicians together to make my farewell speech as A&R director. I had to keep my composure as I spoke. It wasn't easy turning everything over to Eddie, and I could see the strange looks on everyone's faces, from shock to confusion."[17] After making his exit, Stevenson took a position setting up and running MGM's records division in Los Angeles. In addition to Stevenson's departure, the Motown family lost another member, as his wife and one of the label's best voices, singer Kim Weston, left, too.

Early on in his new role, Eddie Holland managed to sign one of the company's biggest and brightest writing couples. Instead of having people send in tapes or hold office auditions as the extroverted Stevenson once did, the introverted Holland decided to travel to the music hub of New York to find talent, and that's exactly where he came across a husband-and-wife team of singers, songwriters, and producers named Nickolas Ashford and Valerie Simpson. Earlier that year, a group called the Coasters released a song by the couple titled "Let's Go Get Stoned," but after Ray Charles released his own rendition in 1966, the track soared to the very top of the R&B charts and became a truly recognizable tune.

Sylvia was thrilled. Though the couple chose to keep their primary residence in New York, they flew into Detroit to work with artists and producers at Motown, which meant that she wouldn't be such an anomaly in the A&R department simply because of her gender. Though Sylvia didn't see Valerie around the offices much when she was in town, she was comforted to know that change was on the horizon.

But during the coming year, she'd hardly have time to think too hard about that changing horizon. She'd be too busy flying right over it.

## CHAPTER 14

# Signature Style

By 1966, Sylvia felt comfortable enough at Motown to start including her family members in the creation of her songs. "Angel Baby (Don't You Ever Leave Me)," which Stevie released in November of that year, was cowritten by Sylvia and Angel, one of her younger sisters. Another song, titled "Be Cool, Be Calm (And Keep Yourself Together)," was inspired by a cheerleading chant that Sylvia heard another younger sister, Celeste, performing outside as Sylvia sat in the family's living room. Sylvia was so inspired by it that she included those words in the title and even paid Celeste $35 in gratitude (Celeste would go on to make history a few years later, in 1969, by becoming one of the first two African American cheerleaders at Michigan State University). Both songs were featured on Stevie's sixth album, *Down to Earth*, and both Angel and Celeste were quickly signed to Motown as songwriters.

"Our contracts were not designated for any particular artist," Angel later explained. "Sylvia wanted us under contract because I often helped Sylvia with lyrics. Celeste helped with melodies and new music ideas for songs. [We] both also helped with background harmony for the songs Sylvia wrote and produced."

As the year wound down to the holidays, good things continued rolling in. In December, Sylvia was delighted when her song "It Takes Two" reached #14 on the Billboard pop music charts and reached #4 on the Billboard soul music charts. Written the year before, the duet was performed by Marvin Gaye and Kim Weston and became the biggest hit of Weston's career.

Also, toward the end of 1966, Stevie presented his songwriting partner with another song, one he'd affectionately named "Sylvia." If there were ever any doubts that Stevie didn't write his own lyrics, this song was the proof of it. Even though his intentions were good-spirited and kind, it put Sylvia in a rather tricky position.

"That was interesting. He wanted to write a song for me. He brought me an idea and the title and he wanted me to finish it," recalled Sylvia. "I felt difficulty writing it, so what I had to do to write the lyrics was to forget the title of the song and think about my boyfriend. That one messed with my head."[1]

After digging deep, Sylvia decided to focus the lyrics instead on the love between two friends who must eventually move on and go their separate ways. Though she wanted to remain faithful to the original concept, inspired by their tight bond, she also knew from experience that relationships were ever changing as the people in them grew apart—and she felt strongly that the lyrics should reflect that truth.

Though Sylvia and Stevie worked well together, there were also times when Stevie longed for input from men, who might approach his work differently from a lyrical standpoint. In one particular case, Stevie and Hank Cosby came up with music that they really liked, and Stevie approached Smokey Robinson during the annual Motown Christmas party to get his input on the words. "He wanted me to write some lyrics...And the only thing I could think of was Pagliacci, the clown who made everybody happy while he was sad because he had nobody to love him," Robinson later said.[2] Robinson ended up writing lyrics for the song that would be called "Tears of a Clown," which was released the following year. Ultimately, Stevie decided to hand over the track to Smokey to record with the Miracles, and it became one of the group's biggest songs.

From the sidelines, Sylvia cheered Stevie on as he continued to grow as a songwriter while sharing his work with others.

As 1967 rolled in, the changes at Motown kept coming. After less than a year in his new role, Eddie Holland resigned as the head of A&R, and, for the first time in the company's history, Gordy appointed a White person, Ralph Seltzer, to lead the coveted department, which would be rebranded the Creative Division. A lawyer by trade, Seltzer had already been working alongside Holland (and had previously served as a legal administrator), so he was ready to take up the reins.

Though not many at the label seemed particularly fond of Seltzer, Sylvia stuck to her guns and never let the opinions of others taint how she saw him. "Ralph was a brilliant company man, a Motown man, a Berry man," she later said. "Everything he did was for Motown and for Berry."[3]

As the year moved along, Stevie and Sylvia remained in lockstep. In May, five days after Stevie's seventeenth birthday, Motown released "I Was Made to Love Her," and it proved to be a smashing success. Stevie scored a #2 hit on the Billboard pop singles chart and the song remained on the R&B charts as #1 for four consecutive weeks. In August, Stevie released his seventh album with the same title, and a month later, *Jet* magazine, the top weekly African American publication in the country, ran its first-ever Soul Brothers Top 20 chart, with "I Was Made to Love Her" ranked #3; also, Stevie was listed as the "Artist of the Week." This was a big deal; what the Billboard music charts represented for the mainstream, the Soul Brothers charts represented for Black communities—and it meant the song had deeply resonated with its core audience.

Stevie had written the music for the song in ten minutes. The track began with him playing harmonica and his close friend, Funk Brothers bassist James Jamerson, laying down a distinctive funky bass groove. But the lyrics were all Sylvia. As a youngster, she'd sometimes hear her dad tell her mom how he was made just to love her, and the phrase had really stuck with her—enough to wind up as the title of one of her songs. There were references to her parents' relationship scattered throughout the lyrics, starting from the mention of "Lil' Rock" (where her mom was from) in the very first line. Ultimately, "it was really about my mom and dad, based on stories I heard from them," she later noted.[4]

It was also with this song that Sylvia devised a way to link her songs together, even when others at Motown were passing them off as their own and denying her songwriting and production credits. "There is a little-known way in which Sylvia marked her songs, by including in the lyrics the titles of other songs that she wrote, so there wouldn't be any question that they were her songs," revealed her younger sister Celeste. In "I Was Made to Love Her," she included the lines "I know that my baby loves me. My baby needs me," which were a reference to a song she'd written in 1965 for Martha and the Vandellas called "My Baby Loves Me."

To promote the now iconic tune, Stevie appeared on *The Merv Griffin Show*, one of TV's premier talk shows, and performed "I Was Made to Love Her" live. Griffin said he represented the "best of Motown" and dubbed Stevie the "Prophet of Soul," likening the way that Stevie delivered and served up feel-good music to a Sunday ministry. As charming in interviews as he was onstage, Stevie surprised Griffin when he admitted on-air that he hadn't written lyrics for either of his hits at the time. "I wrote 'Uptight' and 'I Was Made to Love Her.' I only write melodies though. I would never mingle with lyrics," Stevie said. Shocked, Griffin reiterated, "You have no lyrics?" only to have Stevie interject with a laugh, "Oh, I can't do it. I don't rhyme either."[5]

Though Stevie usually was quick to give Sylvia the credit she deserved for her writing, journalists were observant—and it didn't go unnoticed that Stevie's mother, Lula Mae Hardaway, received her first liner credit on that particular song. One time, a magazine reporter who was interviewing Sylvia about her work as a songwriter asked her what Lula Mae Hardaway's exact role was in writing "I Was Made to Love Her." Until this point, the journalist noticed that label credits usually read only the trio of Cosby, Moy, and Wonder—so what did Lula do? Sylvia merely responded that Lula Mae was Stevie's mother and "didn't have anything to do with writing the song."[6] Even worse, Sylvia's name was deliberately left off as the producer, and only Hank was credited for producing the track.

Sylvia's hands were tied; if she wanted to keep working for Motown, she couldn't risk publicly bashing the company's inner workings, so she kept her feelings tucked inside. If the higher-ups were intent on her remaining a ghost producer, she'd make certain that the songs she wrote and produced were distinguishable by her own singular style.

Eddie Holland admired her for this unique approach, and he couldn't help but notice that when it came to writing lyrics, she often incorporated bits and pieces from her Southern heritage. "She had her own way of music. She was a very good songwriter. Only a few of us were really different," explained Holland. "I don't know what it was about the South, but she always [related] to Southern-type things. She had her own way of expressing herself. We all had our differences. She wrote things that almost always had a country twang to [them] which I thought was quite humorous. They would be commercial songs, but they'd have their own little twist."

What's more, as a trained vocalist and singer herself, Sylvia could easily see that her natural vocal chops worked to her advantage as a songwriter, too. "Most of the vocal melodies and lyrics came from songwriters who were also singers. The strong lyric writers such as Eddie Holland, Johnny Bristol, Ivy Jo Hunter, myself and Smokey Robinson—that is where you see those songs with strong lyrics. [Because] a singer wrote them," Sylvia explained. "A musician comes up with chord progressions and singers usually come up with vocal melodies. We hear that when we write. We hear and think lyrically."[7]

Because of this, Sylvia's distinct style set her apart at Motown—even when she was surrounded by other incredibly talented, award-winning creatives. "You were dealing with [certain kinds of] people at Motown. Holland-Dozier-Holland had their style. Smokey had his style. Norman Whitfield had his style. Mickey Stevenson had his style, and Stevie Wonder developed his style. He went on to become one of the greatest songwriters of all time. Sylvia had her style," said Eddie Holland. "Among people that were extremely talented, they evolved. For her to have her niche, that is very, very special. She had her own technique and was successful. She did it in the midst of a lot of other creative talent. She did it around a lot of creative, aggressive males. She did that and that takes a lot of ability. That takes something special." Holland went a step further and suggested the mere fact that Sylvia could find her lane spoke to an aspect of what he considered to be a "spiritual existence."

Another colleague, singer and songwriter Barrett Strong, believed that her writing was actually similar to that of Brian and Eddie Holland, two-thirds of the famous Holland-Dozier-Holland songwriting trio. "She had that kind of style," he said. "She also reminded me of Linda Creed, who worked with Thom Bell [noted as one of the creators of the Philly Sound in the seventies]. Sylvia's sound was R&B and pop like Linda's style," said Strong, who was Norman Whitfield's songwriting partner for a slew of classic monster hits from the Temptations such as "Cloud Nine," "I Can't Get Next to You," "Ball of Confusion (That's What the World Is Today)," "Papa Was a Rollin' Stone," and "Just My Imagination (Running Away with Me)."

More than anything, it was Sylvia's dedication to making sure each and every step of the process was perfect that really made her stand out, whether she was acting in her role as a writer or a producer. Arranger Paul Riser worked with Sylvia often and said the level of care and competence that she demonstrated was impeccable. "I never produced anything with her, but as a writer, she was there. She was there more than not, making sure songs were happening properly. As a producer she had ideas and thoughts. She was one of the greatest minds in music—man or woman. That was Sylvia."

While all this activity was going on inside the label, there were big changes happening in Sylvia's personal life, too. After two years spent fighting in Vietnam, Sylvia's brother Melvin finally came home in July 1967 to a new Detroit. Two weeks after Melvin's return, lingering racial tensions between Black people and White police officers came to a boiling point and the city erupted into what would become known as the

1967 Riots. In all, more than 158 riots took place across America that summer, but none were fiercer or bloodier than the one in the Motor City, which lasted for five days. When the smoke cleared, 43 people had died and 7,200 more were arrested; what's more, there were over 2,500 looted, damaged, or destroyed buildings left in the wake of the chaos.[8]

Amid this background of chaos and turmoil, Melvin was already having a difficult time adjusting to life back home. "You can't just have someone go through that and then drop them back where they came from and things are supposed to be the way they were," Melvin later said.

Like so many teens who went to war, Melvin was hesitant to discuss his lingering trauma. Even so, Sylvia could sense her brother was struggling, and she made it a point to try to help Melvin reacclimate, suggesting that he use songwriting as a form of therapy. She first encouraged him to write because she knew that jotting down his thoughts could be healing and cathartic. She then invited him to travel to the Motown offices with her. By now, everyone at the label was well aware that Sylvia was a hit-writing machine, and they figured the apple wouldn't fall far from the tree. "[Because she was] so prolific in writing all those songs and things, it just made sense that he would try his hand at it," said songwriter and Motown executive Janie Bradford.

At the time, the most promising opportunity for Melvin to work his way into the Motown family seemed to be by partnering him with a new group called Junior Walker and the All Stars, headed up by double-hitter vocalist and tenor saxophonist Junior Walker. They'd been signed to the label's Soul Records, which focused on more traditionally R&B-sounding artists like Shorty Long and Gladys Knight and the Pips. Though Junior Walker's group had a track they were currently working on, they were still struggling with finding the right lyrics for it and Sylvia thought Melvin might be able to help them out.

To get the creative juices flowing, Sylvia asked him about the things he'd missed most about home when he was gone during the war. When he replied that he'd missed good home-cooked meals, Sylvia helped Melvin put his thoughts down in words, and after layering those lyrics over the preexisting track, they came up with a smoldering, down-home tune, "Home Cookin'." Junior's group loved the song, which ended up becoming the album's title as well, and both were released two years later, in 1969. In addition to helping stir up "Home Cookin'," Sylvia also cowrote another song on the album called "Baby Ain't You Shame."

Sylvia's résumé was blossoming with new songwriting partnerships by this point. The previous year, she'd written an up-tempo song called "Ain't No Sun Since You've Been Gone," and it was finally released by the Temptations in July 1967. David Ruffin delivered lead vocals on the song, which was cowritten with Cornelius Grant and Norman Whitfield the previous year. Two months later, Gladys Knight and the Pips tried their hand at a down-home, soulful version of the tune, and later renditions were recorded by artists such as Diana Ross and the Supremes, Dusty Springfield, Chuck Jackson, the Dynamics, and the Undisputed Truth. Grant, who was traveling with the Temptations, praised Sylvia for the storytelling in her lyrics, because Sylvia's songs made people think. "She wrote about reality. She was great in my estimation…She was a great lyricist," he said. "I didn't get a chance to really work with her simultaneously in the studio. She would come in and then the final step would be to put those words to the track…I came up with the hook. Sometimes I would talk to Norman and come up with a good hook. She came up with most of the lyrics for this song. We put in a couple, but she was responsible for the major parts."

August arrived, and Sylvia's collaborations with Stevie once again made headlines as she earned a prestigious BMI award for both "Uptight" and "I Was Made to Love Her." After the full album *I Was*

*Made to Love Her* came out, Stevie released another single, "I'm Wondering," which was cowritten with Sylvia and Hank Cosby. Though it was not featured on the LP for reasons unknown, the song was a big hit with listeners, reaching #12 on Billboard's Hot 100 and #22 on the pop charts.

Sylvia also collaborated with Martha Reeves and the Vandellas, cowriting a smash hit with Richard Morris called "Love Bug Leave My Heart Alone." The song landed at #14 on the Billboard R&B singles chart and reached #25 on the Billboard pop singles chart, making it Martha Reeves and the Vandellas' second-consecutive Top 40 single that year. Buoyed by the success, she and Morris teamed up again that year to cowrite another song for the group called "(We've Got) Honey Love," which ended up being released two years later, in 1969.

For the most part, the folks at Motown were pleased with the song's success, but that didn't necessarily include Sylvia's old friend Stevie. Songwriters at the label were free to write for others, but some artists became a bit territorial when it came to working with people they really valued. "Stevie got peeved at me a couple of times when I wrote a couple of things with Richard Morris for Martha Reeves. He got mad at me. He had a little attitude problem," she recalled.[9]

Fortunately, Sylvia didn't let Stevie's annoyances slow her down; instead, she teamed up with Morris again and cowrote yet another song for Martha Reeves and the Vandellas called "Honey Chile," which was released in October 1967. The upbeat bop rose to #11 on the Billboard pop chart and #5 on the Billboard R&B chart. The lyrics were inspired by Reeves's Southern roots as well as Sylvia's own roots in Arkansas and Louisiana. It ended up being another Moy family affair, as Sylvia asked her oldest sister, Lazoe, to help her out when she got stuck on the second verse. Reeves loved that Sylvia was incorporating their country roots into the song, since she considered herself a country girl at heart—amid a bunch of city slickers. Reeves and her family were originally from Alabama, and they went back to visit every summer when she was a kid.

"When you listen to me sing, you can hear my Southern accent. 'Honey chile' is what I would call people. Mama would call people 'honey chile.' That was one of the ways she referred to people. I think that is loving and endearing. It's a remarkable greeting. Sylvia took it and talked to her grandmother and found out that [the song's lyrics] 'You're shiftless and you're lazy, just like that hound dog Daisy I had when Grandma raised me, honey chile' was cute [a clever way of saying something]," remembered Reeves. "I liked it. She was actually mocking me, making fun of my Southern accent. It turned out to be a hit. It wasn't number one and I don't know why but it was a real good combination of facts and lyrics. Sylvia was just clever."

Audiences liked "Honey Chile" just as much as Martha did, and Sylvia would go on to win another award from BMI for the song. But though she was credited for writing the lyrics, her name was left out of the producer credits once again, in favor of Morris.

As frustrated as she may have been, Sylvia had no time to dwell—for one of the most challenging years of her life was just around the corner.

# CHAPTER 15

# "I Had a Dream"

Since the early days, Motown had been a prime example of Black excellence, featuring Black talent all the way up to the highest positions in management. Almost a decade after its founding, however, things were starting to change—most noticeably the fact that by 1968, many of Motown's top executives were White. There was Ralph Seltzer, now in charge of the Creative Division (formerly A&R); and the man who assisted him, Harry Balk (Little Willie John's former manager). Over on the money side of things, Ed Pollack ran the financial department, while brothers Harold and Sidney Noveck were the tax attorney and accountant, respectively; Barney Ales, an Italian, led the sales department (and quickly became Gordy's right-hand man); and Michael Roshkind was in charge of public relations. By this time, the company's top songwriting trio, Holland-Dozier-Holland, had officially left the building, but then again, so did the rest of Motown, as the label departed for a larger headquarters to accommodate their growing staff. Administrative dealings for the label had moved over to the Donovan Building, a ten-story gray-brick structure; while the building on West Grand with Studio A, otherwise known as the snake pit, was still used for recording.

Around this time, employees were feeling like this was the beginning of the end, and it really was for some as new leadership started cleaning house. Reportedly, "longtime Motown staffers were fired without being given a reason."[1] It didn't help that Gordy, who had long been considered the father figure at the company, wasn't always aware when folks were being let go, because he began spending less and less time in front of his employees. The good ol' days when people gathered, placed their hands on their hearts, and harmonized to the company's theme song, "Dear Old Motown," were a thing of the past, and the family-like atmosphere that had long defined the label was deteriorating little by little.

With so many new executives heading the main departments, folks started feeling on edge. "People were walking on eggshells around Motown," remembered arranger Paul Riser. "[Sylvia] walked on eggshells, too. She knew things that we didn't know. She brought certain information to people that she cared about. Sylvia was something. She stayed in turmoil because she knew what people were thinking about doing. She had the ability to prophesize and see the future. She stayed in a lot of trouble, too, because of it. She was one of those people that really had the gift where she could see stuff. She would figure out people's situations. I consulted her many times in my life."

The growing paranoia among the ranks wasn't entirely unfounded. Though Gordy always steadfastly denied allegations of mob ties, the rumors continued. In a 1970 issue of *Rock* magazine, an article titled "The Motown Mob" discussed how top administrators were referenced as "Motown's Mafia management." The publication claimed top administrators were "afraid that employees [would] carry information to Gordy or the police." To counter this, they allegedly "established a 'security department'—that department taps phones, photographs everyone entering and leaving the building, and sometimes follows visitors for miles when they leave."[2] The same article alleged that Gordy was "once beaten" so badly, supposedly by "mafia toughs," that he was left with a broken arm and cracked ribs; while Raynoma Gordy Singleton recalled at a different time how another songwriter, Ron Miller, had his own run-in.[3] "'Ray, if I don't get five thousand dollars right away, the mob is going to break my legs,'" she was allegedly told by the former pizza delivery guy who turned into a songwriter and would become best known for penning Stevie Wonder's song "For Once in My Life." "Ron was a gambler always about to get his legs broken. Gambling almost came with the Motown badge."[4] Living on the edge was something that songwriter Ivy Jo Hunter seemed to validate, regarding the rumors of the "mafia" mentality at Motown. "If I wrote a book about Motown, I would go to jail or get killed or something cause Motown ain't nowhere what people think it was. There was so much larceny and shit going on in there. It was nothing to idolize." Ralph Seltzer continued to arouse distrust among the employees. Behind Seltzer's back, employees called him "alka seltzer." After hearing this insulting nickname being tossed around as he strolled by an employee's office, he once stuck his head inside the room to say, "The name is Ralph," before stomping off.

Some felt he was a large contributing factor to the breakdown in the family atmosphere at Motown and was to blame for big changes that hurt individuals' earnings. For example, Seltzer instituted a change where producers would be charged 25 percent of the cost of the recording sessions they supervised. "Normally the artist is charged for the session against his or her royalties, but in Seltzer's account, the producers were to be docked their percentage in addition to what the artist was paying," Raynoma Gordy Singleton later explained. "The upshot was that the company made back one hundred twenty-five percent of its recording costs."[5]

Substandard royalty rates at Motown had long been a problem for employees, especially in comparison to other record labels. Riser recalled how Motown wasn't a union company in the early sixties and how folks were paid less than the union rate per song; Riser himself remembers making only $25 per song. Tensions were rising by the day and employees were getting ready to take action, with intrepid songwriter Ivy Jo Hunter leading the charge.

Initial meetings of producers and songwriters with Seltzer and Gordy hadn't borne any fruit as "numerous employees were looking for higher wages, new deals or more advantageous positions."[6] The small select group included folks like Hunter, Shorty Long, and Morris Broadnax. Since Stevie's mentor, Clarence Paul, had already started having regular gatherings that were "closer to a local union meeting" at his house, Sylvia decided this would be the location to plan their next moves in strategizing ways to have their demands for better pay met.[7] However, on the day of the meeting, those in attendance got wind of something suspicious taking place outside. "That meeting ended prematurely when it was reported that there were two men in a car out front writing down the names of those in the house," remembered Gordy Singleton.[8]

"Berry kept certain people in [Motown] to control the masses, control the patients in the asylum. Berry knew there was some wrong going on, but as long as the product kept coming, he didn't make a big fuss," alleged Riser. "He could have changed a lot of that. He knew what was going on with Sylvia. It was affecting his writers. There were three thousand or four thousand writers signed to Motown at one time. It was that many."

To her credit, Sylvia did not cower from any potential intimidation. According to Riser, "She had real spirit!" and could tell when the different administrators around her were lying through their teeth. She would also pass certain information on to other writers, based on what was really happening behind the scenes. "She had a bunch of writers that she was talking to about a strike because of their rights," said Riser. "She told them they should have had more there at the company. She made a lot of enemies up in there. She got in trouble for that. She told me how her life was being threatened. It was some of those top administrators."

When pressed about who was putting pressure on Sylvia, Riser continued, "It was the key people around Berry, but I wouldn't say him. The writers were the nuts and bolts of that company. They had the songs. She had an affinity for her writer friends. She was going through what they were going through, but they didn't realize they were going through it. She was trying to make others aware of what they were doing around there and what they needed to do to get their propers. She was politically involved. It was a lot of politics there."

As much as she was determined to fight for herself and her colleagues and what she felt they were due, the stress she was incurring on a daily basis at work started to take its toll—literally. The stress manifested in exacerbating complications with her preexisting ulcer, and after a nervous breakdown forced her into the hospital, she knew she'd finally reached her limit.

---

After leaving the hospital, Sylvia returned to her family home, using music as therapy to aid in her recovery much as her brother had done after his return from Vietnam. She even started including her siblings more and more in her work. One time, when Sylvia was holding a contest with family members to help title one of her songs, Sylvia's second-youngest sister, Francetta, took home the prize. "I remember this one song she was working on," recalled Francetta. "She said, 'If anybody can come up with the title, I'll give you $50.' I got that one. I came up with 'I'm More Than Happy (I'm Satisfied).' That was a title for a Stevie Wonder song."

Another one of her more personal songs was about to make its way to the recording studio, too. "Forget Me Not," the song she'd co-written with Richard Morris after her brother was drafted, was now in the hands of Martha Reeves, who, as it turned out, had a special connection of her own. Though the song was initially inspired by Sylvia's brother Melvin, Reeves's brother, also named Melvin, had fought in the Vietnam War, too. Unfortunately, he hadn't made it back stateside. Martha and the Vandellas released their heart-filled rendition of the track in April 1968. Though "Forget Me Not" didn't make many waves upon its release in America, the song did manage to hit #11 on the charts in Great Britain and retained its staying power. "I can hardly do a show in England and Europe without doing this song. I sat with a crowd of maybe two thousand people crying and singing 'Forget Me Not' with the bagpipe sound in it," explained Reeves. "Sylvia was very clever. She wrote that song and it touched everybody's heart who ever went to war or had a loved one who lost their life or spent their time fighting."

The world around Sylvia was rife with unrest. In addition to grappling with the longer implications of the Vietnam War and the lingering impact of the violent riots across the country, African Americans were compelled to keep fighting for basic civil rights and respect at every turn. Motown had been embroiled in that very battle for equality since as early as 1963, the same year the Reverend Dr. Martin Luther King Jr. launched his March on Washington for Jobs and Freedom at the Lincoln Memorial and delivered his iconic "I Have a Dream" speech, galvanizing approximately 250,000 people in attendance. Gordy had the foresight to record the speech and made history as the first record label to ever issue an album of King's Detroit speech, titled *The Great March to Freedom*. King received a $400 advance for the record, which sold for a wholesale price of $1.80 per unit. The label then earned a royalty of forty cents per copy, while King deferred on his personal royalties in favor of pushing the proceeds toward his organization, the Southern Christian Leadership Conference (SCLC). Gordy, inspired by King's efforts, donated an additional $500 to SCLC and allowed his artists to appear at fundraisers, helping to garner more attention for the cause.

In an especially cruel twist of fate, Dr. King's new friends at Motown were forced to mourn his loss alongside the rest of the world after he was assassinated on April 4, 1968—coincidentally, the same day that Sylvia's song "Forget Me Not" was released.

Love and loss were all too familiar to Sylvia, who channeled her feelings into the lyrics of her songs. During this trying time, it was only natural that she would grow closer to her similarly minded friend, singer, songwriter, and musician Frederick Long, whom everyone knew as Shorty Long. Even though his feet could barely touch the pedals, the four-foot-eleven Birmingham native had the power to work a piano to the brink, and much like Stevie, his performances electrified anyone who had the privilege of watching him play live. "Shorty Long and I got really close," said Sylvia. "He was loud and just crazy. In fact, sometimes he'd remind me of that little guy on *Taxi* [Danny DeVito]. I mean Shorty was a mess, a real comedian."[9]

Shorty had a lot of freedom at Motown; aside from singer and songwriter Smokey Robinson, he was the only other person at the label who was allowed to produce his own work. So naturally, when Sylvia and Shorty began to work closely together, everyone took notice. On the surface, they appeared to have been polar opposites. He was a loud man and a gambler who earned a reputation as Motown's "royalty day poker champion," and he always kept a bottle of liquor close at hand, usually in his coat pocket. Sylvia was much more laid-back, with cigarettes readily available. But ultimately, they balanced each other out, and she appreciated Shorty's musicianship and artistry, as he was adept at playing the piano, organ, drums, trumpet, guitar, hand clapper, and harmonica.

The two first met back in 1964. Shorty had already been at the label for years, waiting on the back burner, but around the time Sylvia arrived, he stepped into the national spotlight with a slow blues groove called "Devil with the Blue Dress." Cowritten with Mickey Stevenson, the song was released on the Soul label, an imprint of Motown, where Shorty was a founding artist alongside other performers like Jimmy Ruffin, Gladys Knight and the Pips, and Junior Walker and the All Stars. Flash forward to 1968, and his debut album, *Here Comes the Judge*, was finally being released. Not only was Sylvia happy to see her friend get his long-overdue recognition, but she was elated for herself since they'd cowritten two tunes for the record: "Don't Mess with My Weekend" and "Here Comes Fat Albert."

Both Sylvia and Shorty were serious about having time to themselves because when it came to Motown, making music seemed to be a 24-7 job. But when it came to Saturday and Sunday, Sylvia and Shorty never took private time for granted. That's how they came up with the funky groove "Don't Mess with My Weekend." The playful lyrics represented a perfect blend of her lyrical prowess and his sense of humor.

She even managed to sneak into the lyrics a reference to a previous song of his—"Function at the Junction"—which he found particularly clever.

The other song that the two collaborated on was called "Here Comes Fat Albert," cowritten with Motown singer and songwriter Edwin Starr. The tune was inspired by actor and comedian Bill Cosby's beloved childhood friend, Albert Robertson, whom everyone called Fat Albert. Along with the rest of the world, Sylvia and Shorty first heard Cosby mention and discuss Fat Albert in the comedy routine "Buck, Buck" on his live Grammy Award–winning best comedy album, *Revenge*, which had been released the previous year, in 1967. The lively lyrics mainly poked fun at Albert's voracious appetite ("Mr. Ice Cream man, you better go lock your truck!"), but they also wove in his famous catchphrase, "Hey hey hey." The Fat Albert character continued to enchant audiences, resulting in the creation of a popular TV cartoon about him.

It was only natural that Sylvia and Shorty paid homage to Bill Cosby's friend. After all, Cosby's first musical comedy album featured a parody dedicated to his own grandfather, called "Little Ole Man (Uptight, Everything's Alright)," which came out two years after the debut of the original rendition. Sylvia, Stevie, and Hank Cosby—no relation to Bill—received their proper liner credit for Bill's version, which landed at #4 on the Billboard Hot 100 chart, to everyone's surprise and delight.

Sylvia reaped many benefits from working with Shorty, mainly due to his ability to blend comedy and soul music in order to tap into new audiences. But Shorty learned just as much from her about sincerity and vulnerability in songwriting. The two joined forces once again to write "And This Is Love," a clever yet mournful tune that examined the intricate ups and downs of a relationship. Memorable lines referenced "the hand that struck through jealousy, and broke the ties between you and me," and "a little heart that would not forgive," drawing striking visuals of a person who was heartsick with love.

Sylvia's emotional writing style seemed to rub off on Shorty, too. After witnessing Dr. King's speech in Detroit, he was so moved that he went home and felt the urge to write. Restless and ready, he called his buddy Sylvia to share thoughts about what he'd just witnessed. She, too, was passionate about advocacy and desired a world free of segregation and racism, and she recognized that Dr. King's death had affected Shorty in a profound way, forcing him to examine his own mortality. "I believe that Shorty had a premonition that he wouldn't be around that long and there was something that he wanted said first," Sylvia confided.[10]

The pair ended up cowriting what would become one of Shorty's favorite songs, a soulful prophetic tune about a world with peace and harmony titled "I Had a Dream." If she collaborated with someone, Shorty included, Sylvia usually had a bit of freedom, but for this particular song, he was insistent about the sound and lyrics coming out "a certain way."[11] While finishing up the song, Sylvia noticed that it was almost like her friend had been hypnotized by the piece, and then, at a certain point, the feeling overcame her as well. "He had the melody and kept playing it over and over on the piano, and I immediately felt something from it. I finally tapped into what he had in mind and told Shorty I understood what he wanted, but he'd have to 'leave me alone to work on it. Don't call me all the time like you normally do to see if it's finished,'" she recalled telling him. "I stayed up all of one night just working on it. I just stayed with that track and came up with the vocal melody and the lyrics. Shorty heard it and said, 'That's it. That's got to be said.'"[12]

Something was indeed raging inside Shorty, and Sylvia wasn't the only one who noticed how emotional and reactive her friend had become. Singer Louvain Demps recalled that one day, when her group was doing background vocals for him, he'd gotten especially short-tempered with everyone. Even the slightest thing seemed to set him off. At one point, he got so angry that he eventually stormed out of the session, though he later returned and apologized to everyone.

Whether it was professional, personal, societal, or a mix of all three, it was clear that the pressure around Shorty was getting the best of him. In order to relax, the former DJ enjoyed fishing out on his boat. He'd often invite his Motown colleagues, including Sylvia, to join him. For whatever reason, she never felt inclined to take her songwriting buddy up on his offer, and the following year, she'd lose the chance forever.

## CHAPTER 16

# The Hits Keep Coming

Though Sylvia worked with a number of other people by the late sixties, the songs she worked on with Stevie continued to stand out—like the funky, upbeat, and peculiarly titled tune "Shoo-Be-Doo-Be-Doo-Don-Day." Also cowritten with Hank Cosby, this groove was *catchy*—a mix of rock and roll, gospel, soul, blues, country and hillbilly, all infused with a Southern flavor. Sylvia said Stevie's thought process for it was that "this song's message was like a little scat. It says something and then it doesn't and yet it says a lot."[1] As silly as the name might've sounded to an outside observer, Stevie was insistent on keeping it, and he wasn't pleased when the label renamed it "Shoo-Be-Doo-Be-Doo-*Da*-Day" instead of his original title.

Though lighthearted in name, the song gave Stevie a chance to show off his maturing musicality and experimentation with new instruments, like the Hohner Clavinet. Though the Clavinet looked a lot like a keyboard, it produced a much different sound, more closely resembling an electric guitar. Up to that point, no one had really used the Clavinet in studio recordings, and so when Stevie brought one into "Shoo-Be-Doo-Be-Doo-Da-Day," he became one of the first singers to use the Clavinet in a popular song.[2]

When asked about it later, songwriter Ivy Jo Hunter believed that one of the reasons the song—and their partnership—ended up working so well was that Sylvia trusted Stevie's instincts. "The sounds, the things he could hear, you couldn't hear," said Hunter. "He had everybody and their momma trying to play Clavinet though it had been around for years. Wouldn't nobody even think about it. He came out and played and everybody wanted to do it. They have been following him ever since."

From both a commercial and a critical standpoint, the song would turn out to be a smash hit. Sylvia even won the songwriting award for the tune at the BMI Awards in the R&B category the following year. Though this category had already been in existence, this was the first year that the organization was hosting a specific dinner and awards show just for R&B writers. Detroit mayor Jerome Cavanagh even attended the ceremony and praised Motown as "the second most famous export of the city."[3] In addition to winning an award for "Shoo-Be-Doo-Be-Doo-Da-Day," Sylvia took home two more song awards—one for Stevie's hit "I Was Made to Love Her" and another for the Martha Reeves and the Vandellas tune "Honey Chile"—as well as the coveted Songwriter of the Year award.

Sylvia was proud to win the prestigious songwriting award, which she shared with her female colleague from Motown, Valerie Simpson, who'd cowritten songs like Diana Ross and the Supremes' "Ain't No Mountain High Enough," along with Marvin Gaye and Tammi Terrell's duets "Ain't Nothing Like the Real Thing" and "Your Precious Love." She was especially proud to win in front of the big-league execs who'd turned her down earlier in her career. "Later, when I started appearing at Broadcast Music, Inc.'s banquets, those New York people [who turned down her demos as a budding songwriter] looked pretty embarrassed," Sylvia admitted, satisfied.[4] If this moment wasn't enough, at another industry function, she couldn't believe her eyes when she actually saw the same person who told her she'd never be a songwriter "easing up to Berry Gordy," inquiring about whether he could buy her songwriting contract.[5]

Success was such sweet vindication.

Though Sylvia was happy to be recognized by her peers, she wasn't content to rest on her laurels. And at the end of January 1969, a song she'd finished with Stevie the year before would soar to the top right before her eyes.

This particular tune was one that Stevie had been carrying around in his trusty tape bag, which was filled with unused melodies, for years. He'd started writing it back in 1966, when he was a student at the Michigan School for the Blind, where he trained in classical music and learned music composition and chord structure. During his senior year, he had an hour-long piano period where he spent most of his time writing songs, which ended up including the starting chords of a song that would one day become "My Cherie Amour."

The song's journey to completion was not nearly as smooth as it sounded when Stevie performed it in front of crowds later on. When Gordy first heard Stevie perform a bit of the song, he thought that it had "a little potential"—according to Stevie's tutor, Ted Hull—but he still said it needed some work. Enter Sylvia and Hank Cosby.

During that time in Stevie's life, Sylvia noticed that her young protégé's hormones—like those of most boys his age—were raging, and he was constantly thinking about girls and romance. He'd recently broken up with his girlfriend, and most of his suggestions for the initial title centered around this young lady's name. "Stevie would attach a girl's name to just about every musical idea he had. I said, 'Oh, Stevie, I'm sick of it. I'm not going to call it 'Oh, Marsha.' He said, 'What are you going to call it then?' 'I don't know,' I said. 'I'll surprise you.'"[6] Inspired by her own French lessons back in high school, Sylvia decided to change the name to something a little more grown-up-sounding, a little more exotic. When she suggested "My Cherie Amour," a term of endearment and devotion, Stevie was thrilled.

Unfortunately, Stevie's excitement about the song wasn't felt universally across Motown, and so the song was temporarily shelved. After the song was initially recorded, Gordy was concerned that it might remind people too much of another recent release by the Beatles called "Michelle." Frustrated by the decision, Stevie was relieved when someone decided to sneak it into a quality control meeting two years later. This time, Gordy didn't object—he enjoyed what he heard—but the execs were still not sure that "My Cherie Amour" had what it took to be a hit all on its own, and so it was featured instead as the B-side of "I Don't Know Why."[7]

The song eventually surpassed everyone's expectations—but it almost didn't happen. "I Don't Know Why" didn't end up being quite the hit everyone had been hoping for, but one particular DJ saw potential with "My Cherie Amour" and began playing the B-side. "Some disc jockey turned (the record) over," recalled Sylvia. "And then they started turning it over all over the world."[8] As the song grew in popularity, the record was reissued with "My Cherie Amour" on the A-side and soon climbed all the way up to #4 on the pop charts. However, there was a bittersweet edge to the song's success; even though Sylvia both wrote and produced the song, only Hank Cosby was credited with its production.

Nonetheless, whenever she reflected on her discography later in her career, Sylvia always remembered "My Cherie Amour" with fondness and pride. "Although it wasn't the biggest immediately, 'My Cherie Amour' has turned into a standard and will live longer than I ever will."[9]

In many ways, the song's long lead time resembled Stevie's own career trajectory; here was a kid who'd been written off as a child star, but he grew into his voice and his talent, rode the wave, and trusted the process. "I always basically flowed with things, and I've always felt I had something to offer, something to give," Stevie later explained. "But I didn't try to burden anybody with the fact that I felt that way. I more so just wanted it to happen. And that's why it took from 1966 to 1969 for 'My Cherie Amour' to come out."[10]

The song had a life beyond Stevie's recording, too. The same year it was released, it was covered by his maternal cousins, the Jackson 5, and singer Tony Bennett, renowned for his jazz and pop standards. A year later, in 1970, Smokey Robinson and the Miracles couldn't resist and came out with a rendition of their own. Even Sylvia's peers were impressed with the originality of the song. As songwriter Ivy Jo Hunter expressed, "Writers look at other writers for the uniqueness of their approach to music. 'Uptight' and 'My Cherie Amour,' these were things I never would have thought of. That's how you judge a person's creativity. When it's something you wish you had written."

When asked about it later, Robinson even confessed that "My Cherie Amour" was one of his favorite tunes. He deeply understood just how hard it was to be a good songwriter. It was a talent that could only be nurtured, not instilled. Either a person had the ability or they didn't. "It's a gift from God. So if you have it, you have it and if you don't, you don't. When I first met Berry, I had one hundred songs, and he developed me as a songwriter because my songs were not professional. But as far as just being able to do it, it's like a gift," he explained.

With "My Cherie Amour," Robinson felt that Sylvia had risen to the ranks of Motown's best, alongside Holland-Dozier-Holland and himself. "It was just a great song. I just love great songs. It has a beautiful melody, and it was a big hit for Stevie. A lot of people recorded it. I just love that song."

As high as everyone felt after the surprising success of "My Cherie Amour," they were about to sink lower than they'd ever thought possible. In April 1969, just five days after Sylvia took home handfuls of trophies for her songwriting skills, Motown suffered a devastating blow when drummer Benny Benjamin, considered by many to be the thumping heartbeat of the Motown sound, died at the young age of forty-three, following years of heroin addiction and alcohol abuse. The grief felt by all at the label was palpable. Stevie, who'd been close with the drummer ever since his jam-fest audition as an eleven-year-old, cried so much that he couldn't finish the tribute song he'd attempted to perform at his funeral.[11] Benjamin's faith in Stevie had never wavered, even when others at Motown doubted that the teen could turn his career around. Also, Benjamin had been the drummer on "Uptight," the first hit song that forever changed Sylvia's and Stevie's lives.

And just when things didn't seem as if they could get any worse, two months later, another tragedy struck the Motown family. Sylvia's close friend Shorty Long died tragically in a boating accident in June. Sylvia was heartbroken about both deaths, but she took Shorty's demise especially hard. As his writing partner, Sylvia was troubled by Shorty's death because he seemed to have sensed that it was coming. After collaborating on "I Had a Dream," the next song Shorty wanted Sylvia to help him with was a piece called "Give Me My Flowers While I'm Living." Sylvia was steadfast and refused to touch the last song he gave her, even while he was still around. "I said, 'No, I'm not working on that.' I changed that one around…[and then] before I could finish it, he died," she said.[12]

Though Shorty seemed to anticipate his untimely end, no one could've ever imagined just how tragic it would be. While working on his second album, Shorty had taken his friend Oscar Williams out for a day of fishing on the Detroit River. Reports stated that the wash from a passing freighter swamped Shorty's small vessel, and the boat capsized just off Sandwich Island, after which the two men drowned. Shorty was just twenty-nine years old.

Strangely enough, Angel, one of Sylvia's younger sisters, recalled that "he wanted Sylvia to go out this particular day on his boat with him…Sylvia refused. Mama used to always say, 'You can't drink that much water.' Sylvia never went with him." Coincidentally, Louvain Demps had also been invited by Shorty to go fishing on the boat along with her young son, but, like Sylvia, she also declined.

Five months after his death, Motown released Shorty's final album, *The Prime of Shorty Long*, in November 1969. "I Had a Dream," which was featured on the project, ended up being the last single he'd ever release. Recognizing the tune's importance to him, his family had the title engraved on his tombstone in Birmingham, Alabama. Shorty also was one of the only other artists at Motown—besides Stevie—who played the harmonica, so at Shorty's funeral, Stevie played the instrument in honor of his friend, and when he was finished, he placed it on top of Shorty's casket.

As 1969 drew to a close, Stevie and Sylvia started working on a song that the two felt had great promise. Released six months later, in June 1970, it was the first song that Stevie produced on his own, a catchy pop tune called "Signed, Sealed, Delivered (I'm Yours)." Though Stevie received recognition for the production, Sylvia was once again frustrated to see her name left off the writing credits. On the B-side was "I'm More Than Happy (I'm Satisfied)," a song cowritten by Sylvia with a title inspired by her little sister Francetta. The full album, titled *Signed, Sealed & Delivered*, also featured another gem written by Sylvia called "Never Had a Dream Come True," which later earned her a BMI award.

Though Sylvia's name was left off the credits, as the producer had the power to decide who did and didn't get acknowledged, a compelling observation made by some centers around the intriguing similarities between some songs that point to Sylvia's possible involvement. For example, music scholar James E. Perone made an interesting comparison in his 2006 book between the Temptations' 1966 hit "Ain't Too Proud to Beg" and Stevie's "Signed, Sealed, Delivered (I'm Yours)." While many could rightfully argue this might be purely coincidental and doesn't prove much of anything, this scholar's research findings drew a startling connection between two different songs with the same unknown common denominator: Sylvia. This also demonstrates how powerful songwriters find a way to mark their tunes through lyrics and life experiences that circle back to them even if others try to remove them from their own story. Case in point is that things seem to be leading back to Sylvia in an oddly delightful way.

Perone noted how the lyrics of "Signed, Sealed, Delivered (I'm Yours)" are sung from the point of view of a man who has ditched his lover only to return and ask for forgiveness, much like "Ain't Too Proud to Beg." According to Perone, there is a genuine "utter contriteness of the character who sings the song" in both cases.[13] "It's almost like the singer has a particular character and a particular viewpoint…I mean, it's almost like they could be two songs coming from the same character, almost like if you had a musical theater piece and you had a character that was expressed in two different songs, the same basic point of view," he explained in a 2023 interview. "It's somebody that's been rejected yet he'll do anything to get back with the former lover. And [then] there's 'Signed, Sealed, Delivered (I'm Yours),' where I'm like a parcel that's being delivered to you and just take me."

As Sylvia's family well knew, "[she] marked her songs, by including in the lyrics the titles of other songs that she wrote, so there wouldn't be any question that they were her songs. Thus, it's no surprise to us that you will find the words 'I'm wondering' in this song," said her sister Celeste, referencing the title of another 1967 song Sylvia wrote for Stevie called "I'm Wondering." "Other than this we do not know why she was not credited for this song, but we know that she often had to give interest in songs she wrote to the artist and others at Motown/Jobete to get her songs approved for release." Though she didn't love sharing credits with people who hadn't had a hand in the song whatsoever, "she really didn't mind giving a percentage of her copyright credit to the artist, because the artist's performance contributed to the success of the song," explained Celeste.

According to her family, whenever Sylvia was asked about "Signed, Sealed, Delivered (I'm Yours)" or even "Ain't Too Proud to Beg" in the decades that followed, a wave of grief would cover her face. She'd shake her head in disappointment, close her eyes, and put up her hands to signal the questioner to stop. "We are not sure why Sylvia was so disgusted and unwilling to discuss or answer our questions about these songs," said Celeste. "We often questioned her about these songs because the lyrics and melody sounded so much like her style of writing. We believe she was disgusted because she cowrote and possibly completely wrote these lyrics but did not receive the copyright credits she deserved."

"Signed, Sealed, Delivered (I'm Yours)" earned Stevie two Grammy Award nominations, one for Best R&B Song and the other for Best

R&B Vocal Performance Male. However, during the thirteenth annual ceremony, which took place in 1971, Stevie lost the first award to "Patches" by Clarence Carter, and the second to B. B. King for his performance of "The Thrill Is Gone."

The song ended up being one of the last collaborations between Stevie and Sylvia; as this album ushered in a new era of his work, Stevie decided it was time to start writing and producing his own songs. Cutting ties with Sylvia was "hurtful," but she knew he had to spread his wings—and that meant writing new material with his wife, singer Syreeta Wright, and later on, with background vocalist Yvonne Wright (no relationship).

Though Sylvia continued to be a driving force of success behind the scenes at Motown, her name was relegated to the shadows, even when other contemporary songwriters like Holland-Dozier-Holland, Norman Whitfield and Barrett Strong, or Smokey Robinson were openly lauded. "I can't say that in any short account of what was going on at Motown that her name comes up," bemoaned Perone. "It's like she was a lost figure, yet she received a lot of awards and that sort of thing. In terms of the popular press, you only see the male writers and producers."

Even her peers, like songwriter Barrett Strong, could not understand why Sylvia did not receive the recognition that she rightfully deserved. "She was one of the greatest, if not the greatest songwriters, not just at Motown but in the world of music. Women nowadays need to learn about and read up on her. She shaped history."

## CHAPTER 17

# Staying Home

Well into her sixth year at Motown by this time, Sylvia's work was now capturing the attention of artists from different record labels who wanted to put their own spin on her songs.

One of the most powerful renditions came from a female group signed to A&M Records called Sisters Love, who performed Sylvia's song "And This Is Love." The American R&B and funk ensemble featured former members of Ray Charles's background singers, the Raelettes, who'd recently quit working with Charles and decided to start their own group. Their version of the song, which begins with an intensely beautiful piano intro, was soaring and dramatic, and eventually became a popular tune in gay clubs, especially for drag queens in the early seventies. This rendition would come to be considered "a real torch song" for this community, as one fan described it on YouTube. Sylvia's sentimental lyrics depict an innocent love affair that soon devolves into an emotional landslide filled with drama, heartache, pain, misery, abuse, and infidelity, and continue to resonate with audiences to this day.

By 1971, the winds of change were coming fast and hard at Motown—and Berry Gordy was growing restless. Gordy's expanding interest in film and television meant that his attention was being increasingly diverted away from Detroit and toward the Golden State. Testing the waters on the West Coast, Gordy formed a new label called MoWest in Los Angeles, featuring an eclectic blend of emerging and veteran artists like Frankie Valli and the Four Seasons, the Crusaders, Thelma Houston, Lesley Gore, and Suzee Ikeda. The Commodores, an R&B music group composed of Tuskegee University students and fronted by lead singer, songwriter, and pianist Lionel Richie, were also signed to the label.

In 1972, Gordy officially moved Motown from its birthplace, the Motor City, to Los Angeles, the City of Angels. He was already hard at work there on his first movie, *Lady Sings the Blues*, which focuses on the troubled jazz singer Billie Holiday—aka Lady Day—with Motown's leading lady, Diana Ross, making her film debut in the starring role.

As imagined, not all artists and employees were thrilled with the news that Motown would be uprooted from its home in the Midwest. After all, most of the artists were born and raised in Detroit, and that's where their families still resided. Some Motown employees and artists said they were totally caught off guard by the announcement. Others felt insulted when they weren't among the handpicked, chosen few asked by Gordy to relocate. Artists like Stevie Wonder, Smokey Robinson, Diana Ross, the Supremes, the Temptations, and the Jackson 5, who were a vital part of Motown's success, were expected to move to the West Coast. However, most of the employees ended up losing their jobs, including many who had been pivotal in helping to build the label from the ground up.

Though Sylvia's contract was coincidentally nearing its end, she was one of the top songwriters and producers who was asked to extend her contract with Motown and relocate to Los Angeles. Still, she was hesitant about the offer, as she "wanted to look into other things happening in the music industry...[have] a little more freedom."[1]

Pressure around her continued to rise and the stakes got higher, even to the point where her family got involved. One day in 1972, a big black Cadillac pulled up in front of the Crowley's Department Store where Sylvia's father was employed as an electrical repairman. An imposing figure, an Italian man dressed in all black and wearing a suit and a hat, headed to the service department where Mr. Moy worked to have a talk with him.

According to Sylvia's sister Ronnie, the stranger told Mr. Moy that their family would "have all the money they want" if Sylvia went through with the move. However, "the man told our father that if she didn't do it, she would not be successful on her own. She won't be able to do anything in Detroit if she remained here. Talk to your daughter and convince her to go." Echoing this moment, sister Angel said, "In fact, she and my father were told that if she didn't make the move, 'she would never work in the music industry again.' Dad told all of us about this, and told Sylvia in our presence that if she doesn't want to go, she doesn't have to go."

Conflicted, Sylvia told her dad that she loved Detroit and didn't know anything about California. She'd only heard about earthquakes and pretentious folks feigning a Hollywood lifestyle—that was the extent of her knowledge. "My sister said, 'I'm going to make it on my own,'" Ronnie recalled.

Though she ultimately decided not to renew her contract with Motown, after careful deliberations, Sylvia made an earnest attempt to move to Los Angeles that year. In the end, she stayed there for only six months. Without her family close by, Sylvia felt adrift in the land of twenty-four-hour neon lights.

Upon her return to the Motor City, Sylvia reflected on the past seven years of her career, seven years that she had devoted to helping Motown succeed. In addition to reviving Stevie's career, she'd worked on fifteen gold and platinum songs, and raked in twenty BMI awards that included distinctions in both R&B and pop. And yet, for all her time at the label, she'd never quite managed to receive all the credit she was due. "I don't think during the entire time I was at Motown, I got my credits as a producer. And that was seven years, 'My Cheri Amour,' 'I Was Made to Love Her,' all those songs. 'My Baby Loves Me,' 'Honey Chile,' all those songs."[2]

Even so, Sylvia appreciated the education and experiences that shaped her into the songwriter she had become. "I had some hard times, but I wouldn't change it for anything. I got my Ph.D. there; it was school. For me, Gordy built an empire with people who would have been neglected elsewhere...I'm very grateful for the experience I had at Motown. I think that the Gordys did something really great."[3]

Though she'd learned a lot in just seven short years, Sylvia knew the time had come—the time for her to close one door so that she could open another.

After coming home to Detroit in 1972, Sylvia realized she needed to shift gears and focus her attention on a new undertaking, and so she founded a nonprofit group called the Center for Creative Communications (which would later be known as Masterworks). Her initial goal was to mentor underprivileged youth and teens by training and supporting them in the field of telecommunications and media arts. Sylvia had been laying the groundwork for the nonprofit since 1968 back in her parents' basement, and she used money from her own pocket earned through royalties to keep the organization running. "I couldn't get my mind off the fact that I had been approached by a lot of youngsters who wanted to get involved in music," she said. "So I started a writing seminar...just meeting with youngsters, answering their questions, and getting into rap sessions...and the seminars just mushroomed into a total thing."[4]

The group's mission later broadened when Sylvia saw an expanding need for their services and worked to assist people of all ages, ranging from preteens to the elderly. Friends and neighbors were encouraged to come by for assistance with songwriting or music and to learn from one another. As word spread further, social service agencies began sending troubled youth with creative abilities to her, and she had volunteer social workers come in to help out. The center was actively changing people's lives for the better. A twelve-year-old boy whose father was a pimp was about to run away from home before he found the healing powers of music through the center. Sylvia saw that he could play the piano and organ, though he'd never taken a lesson, and urged him to cultivate his craft. A sixteen-year-old girl had been having problems with her mother's alcoholic boyfriend, who was also prone to criminal activity. Coming to the center helped the young girl to explore her interest in filmmaking and avoid abuse at home.

Sylvia deeply empathized with the troubles of those who came to the Center for Creative Communications, and she knew that in order to really empower them creatively, she needed to make sure their basic needs were being met. "In order to zero in on a person's creativity, you have to be involved with the total human being," Sylvia said. "You can't express creativity if you have a housing problem or a drug problem or a job problem."[5]

Sylvia's youngest brother, Christopher, said that his parents were incredibly patient, given that Sylvia filled the house with so much nonstop activity and noise. "There were people coming in and out of the house all the time. My parents didn't even let it bother them," he said. "They'd sit in the den, in the back room, and watch *Gunsmoke.* People would be banging on the piano or playing the drums in the basement. They just accepted it."

After a few years, however, Sylvia realized that if the nonprofit was to grow, she needed her own space. To that end, she scaled back considerably on her finances, saved up some money, and left her parents' home in 1973 in pursuit of a place to call her own—and she found that perfect place at 1611 Webb. With 4,024 square feet, the single-family, five-bedroom, two-and-a-half-bath home was built in 1916 and designed by Frank Lloyd Wright, the renowned master of American architecture. Sylvia spared no expense in building her own studio, which she christened Masterpiece Sound Studios, in the basement. The studio, which was fully equipped with the latest audio and visual technology following music industry standards, including a 48-track system, was a gateway to new opportunities.

As a result of the new space, she started up other programs at Masterpiece Sound Studios that had a distinctly different agenda than the nonprofit, though she used the space for both. Sylvia made a concerted effort to teach people about every aspect of the recording process, from engineering and producing to mixing, mastering, and editing. People also studied the business of songwriting and recording, and they were trained to be multi-board-track engineers. "Sylvia gave [people] the use of her house, her time, her piano, her drums, other instruments, gave them confidence, put them in touch with record companies when they were ready," said Dr. Barbara Wilson, Sylvia's mentor and close friend.[6] Before turning thirty, Sylvia had finally learned how to read music, and she passed this knowledge along as well, alongside instruction on how to play different instruments. All in all, students received top-notch training at Sylvia's new studio—and Sylvia took ownership of each and every step of the process. She hired engineers who knew the core foundations, and, if an engineer suggested she get certain equipment, she would do it. "She didn't do [something] just because they said so. She understood why," said arranger Paul Riser. "She was very inquisitive."

Although Sylvia's heart was in the right place, the financial burden of her new undertaking weighed on her. She wasn't really turning a profit because she used her own money from royalties for studio time; it's estimated that in the late sixties, she had spent well over $150,000 to help others.[7] "She was a very giving woman. I think about a lot of the things she did, it was just for the youth in the city of Detroit. She just opened her wallet and her heart to the youth," said Christopher. "She wanted particularly the Black youth to understand where they came from. She wanted them to understand their music background and to understand that jazz belonged to us. The blues belonged to us and if we don't continue to teach it to our younger people, the other people will claim it. She put a lot of money into training young people and exposing them to what belongs to Black people."

Costly lessons early on taught her to become wiser, however, and soon she figured out a work-around that enabled the studio to succeed financially. As more and more professionals heard about the exciting new studio space, they asked if they could rent it out for sessions for their projects. "We rented it out to cut demos and some artists even started cutting masters there," she said.[8]

Sylvia's expertise was so in demand that she quickly reached a point where she invited anywhere from one hundred to five hundred young people each summer to come to Masterpiece Sound Studios, where she taught them about music, film, and the arts.[9] Among the kids who were touched by Sylvia's presence were Detroit-based siblings Mark and Jeff Bass, who were seven and eleven years old, respectively, when they landed their first professional job by recording at Sylvia's Masterpiece Sound Studios. They ended up recording a Greyhound Lines radio ad that required "an urban feel."[10] Sylvia was delighted to be able to help young people like the Bass brothers, who grew up and eventually became the award-winning duo behind Detroit-based rapper Eminem's early career (they even coproduced his 2002 Oscar-winning song, "Lose Yourself").

The studio became so popular that Sylvia couldn't get any sleep with all the traffic coming in and out of the house. Eventually, she moved herself out of 1611 Webb and devoted the entire structure to Masterpiece Sound Studios, allowing more professional musicians the ability to purchase studio time. "It wasn't a little old run-down place," said Louvain Demps, who remained in touch with Sylvia even after their Motown days together and later recorded music herself at Masterpiece Sound Studios. "The equipment and everything was A+. There were three major studios in Detroit that had the best sound to me: United Sound, Hitsville, and Sylvia's studio. When we recorded at her studio, the sound was good."

Sylvia also cast a wider net for opportunities by establishing Sylvia Moy Productions and starting a music publishing company with her family called Muziki Publishing. The establishment of Muziki, which is a Swahili word for music, allowed her to maintain control and ownership over her own work. Though it didn't attract huge artists, that was never really Sylvia's intention; she mostly wanted to create a place for people in her community to create music, including members of her own family. At one point, Sylvia encouraged her mom, Hazel, and her oldest sister, Lazoe, to start writing songs. The two of them teamed up with Ruth Burton to pen the 1971 tune "I Can't Win for Losing," which was then recorded by one of the funkiest groups around, Hot Sauce, a female soul trio on Memphis's Stax Records label. Sylvia, of course, made sure they were properly credited for their contributions.

In addition to writing the actual songs, Sylvia knew how important it was to educate people about the business side of songwriting, publishing, and recording. Therefore, Sylvia's production company stressed to students the importance of copyrights and lead sheets, which are abbreviated forms of notation with important music information used for copyright purposes. Cautious and guarded after missing out on the recognition she deserved for her hard work during her time at Motown, Sylvia wanted to help others avoid the same pitfalls. Some of the participants had even mentioned to her that they'd already had their work stolen after sending tunes to publishers or record companies without first copyrighting it. "We are showing people how to protect their interests," she explained.[11]

During this time, Sylvia made sure to pursue her own creative endeavors simultaneously. At one point, Muziki entered into an exclusive contract with 20th Century Records, where Sylvia also signed on as a singer, songwriter, and producer. Feeling empowered, she wrote and produced more than one hundred original songs through her own publishing program thanks to this venture. Her first single was the result of a full-circle moment as she got back into the studio and recorded her own rendition of "And This Is Love," which was released in 1973. She produced the song and received label credit, while one of her former Motown colleagues, Grammy Award winner Paul Riser, arranged it for her. On the flip side of the record, Sylvia performed a song titled, "Time Is Running Out," which she'd cowritten with her mother, Hazel. As it so happened, Gladys Knight and the Pips also put out a cover of "And This Is Love" the same year, just before Knight and her group left Motown to join a new label, Buddah Records.

Meanwhile, the ever-changing music industry was in flux once more. In August 1973, thanks to the efforts of an eighteen-year-old named Clive Campbell, known by all as DJ Kool Herc, a new genre—called hip-hop—took the Bronx by storm. During a party he hosted in an apartment building, he created exciting "breakbeats" by interweaving snippets of funk songs by James Brown and Booker T. and the M.G.'s while playing two turntables simultaneously.

However, beat-driven and dance-heavy disco still reigned supreme as the defining genre of the seventies, sizzling across the airwaves and heating up the nightlife floors. With artists like Donna Summer, the Bee Gees, Gloria Gaynor, Thelma Houston, Sylvester, and the Village People leading the way, the new disco sound typically featured string sections, synthesizers, and four-on-the-floor beats, along with syncopated bass lines and electronic piano and electric rhythm guitars. The genre was particularly popular in marginalized communities (namely, Black, Latinx, and LGBTQ+) in big club scenes like New York City and Philadelphia, and variations of it popped up over the course of the decade.

As ever, Sylvia was inspired by and interested in exploring new sounds and genres, and the seventies provided new opportunities for her to do just that. In 1974, she was asked to write background music for a New Detroit public service announcement aimed at reintroducing the concept of a coalition. New Detroit was a coalition that had been formed in response to lingering civil unrest after the bloody Detroit riots that took place during July 1967. At the request of then–Michigan governor George Romney and Detroit mayor Jerome Cavanagh, business executive Joseph L. Hudson Jr. convened the specialized group with a mission to investigate a multitude of rooted social and community conditions to see where improvements could be made. New Detroit, according to the organization's history on its website, became "the nation's first coalition to identify what went wrong during the riot, what needed to change and how to make that change happen."[12] Sylvia, a Detroit girl through and through, was happy to contribute something that would encourage other members of her community to unite in such a time of turmoil.

Throughout the mid- to late seventies, Sylvia continued to test the boundaries of what she could do. It was during this time that she became one of the few women, and one of the only African American women, to be asked by United Artists and 20th Century-Fox to score music for their upcoming movies.[13] She also wrote music for TV and stage, and let it be known that she was interested in trying her hand at a musical comedy. All the while, songs from her Motown days started making their way into the public landscape on various TV shows, showing that she'd achieved her goal of writing standards that would endure the test of time. Popular dance and variety shows like Dick Clark's *American Bandstand*, *The Sonny and Cher Show*, and Don Cornelius's *Soul Train* were all the rage in this era, and they often played songs she'd written, like "Uptight," "I Was Made to Love Her," and "My Cherie Amour." When *Soul Train* host Cornelius personally asked Michael Jackson to perform one of his favorite songs, "With a Child's Heart," Sylvia was absolutely delighted; she couldn't have been happier to see the impact her music was having on younger generations.

By the early eighties, just as the days of disco were dying down, a new subgenre called Hi-NRG caught the attention of the masses. Hi-NRG was likened to a more up-tempo form of disco, and it featured intense and soulful R&B-infused powerhouse vocals, which lay over highly energetic tracks that got up to 120–140 beats per minute. It had originally been created by DJs looking for playback by blending various tracks in remixes. The music was so energetic and engaging that some listeners even compared it to another newly emerging genre called electronic dance music (EDM), though Hi-NRG predated it.

Sylvia loved the new Hi-NRG sound and made sure to incorporate it into her ventures with her new record company, Michigan Satellite Records (MSR), which was operated out of Masterpiece Sound Studios. The label signed up hometown favorites like powerful contralto singer Ortheia Barnes, who in turn was the sister of J. J. Barnes, recognized as a Motown songwriter and singer of Northern Soul (a 1960s-born subgenre of dance music that originated in England and was influenced by Black American soul music). Ortheia's undeniable talent had her opening shows for people like Stevie Wonder, Gladys Knight, and Marvin Gaye, and she would later go on to become one of Sylvia's most successful artists.

"The first master I put together was on [Ortheia] and Mildred Scott, recording under the name Cut Glass a song called 'Without Your Love,' which was a big disco hit," Sylvia said of the 1980 Hi-NRG song recorded on 20th Century-Fox Records.[14]

Mastering a song is the last step of audio production preparation, in which the overall sound is enhanced by distinct finishing touches before it heads off to wider distribution. Typically, if the finished recording inspired people to get up and groove, it was considered a hit. But if folks *rushed* the dance floor after hearing just a few notes, it was considered a bona fide smash. When club goers heard the distinctively vivacious violins and pulsating piano in the introduction of "Without Your Love," folks couldn't get to the dance floor fast enough. Hailed by some as one of the greatest early Hi-NRG songs, it also became a major Northern Soul disco hit. According to Motown enthusiast Ian Levine, who was the first resident DJ at Heaven, a London-based legendary and world-famous gay nightclub, and later worked closely with Sylvia, "It was one of the biggest floor fillers at both Heaven in London and The Saint in New York."[15]

As the seventies rolled into the eighties, Sylvia's songs continued to connect with audiences everywhere as they popped up on various TV shows and movie soundtracks. Her work was particularly popular on TV sitcoms like *Growing Pains*, along with *Night Court* and *Quantum Leap*. In 1983, Stevie Wonder made TV history when he hosted and performed on the popular late-night live sketch comedy show *Saturday Night Live* (also called *SNL*). New cast member and comedian Eddie Murphy was already starting to make a name for himself thanks in part to his masterful Stevie impersonations. When Stevie finally showed up to host the show, the opportunity to incorporate Stevie into the running gimmick was too good to pass up. In one skit, Murphy auditions a number of Stevie impersonators—including the real Stevie himself. When Stevie purposely sings off-key in an exaggerated phony voice, Murphy decides that he has to show the newbie how it is done and launches into singing his own version of "My Cherie Amour." Stevie follows his lead and eventually gets the swing of things, his real voice peeking out little by little until it comes through in full by the end. Even after the audience goes wild, Murphy says that he hated Stevie's audition, joking that it still sucked.

For Sylvia, hearing classics she wrote was often a reminder of how well she'd done her job. But she wasn't going to stop when things were just heating up. In 1984, she teamed up once again with her former Motown colleague and arranger, Paul Riser, to write the song "Touched" for label darling Ortheia Barnes. The single was the first to be released from her new MSR label and published through Muziki. As the songwriter, vocal arranger, and composer for Barnes's 1986 album *Person to Person*, she included the track on there as well, and was exhilarated—and somewhat caught off guard—by the song's response. "Billboard got hold of the record which resulted in the phone ringing off the hook," said Sylvia. "I couldn't press the record fast enough. I then issued a single on jazz trumpeter Marcus Belgrave."[16]

Sylvia could never get enough of Ortheia's powerhouse sound and vocal prowess. "I've always liked [Ortheia's] voice. It inspires me to write everytime I hear it," she once said. "Sometimes she will sing a line differently to what I had in mind, but you just have to leave it in. Watching Ortheia live is incredible. It's as though some other spirit works through this lady."[17] This is especially worth noting, as it was around this same time that Sylvia's music started incorporating more gospel into her sound. She later reflected that it had been the loss of a friend that had pushed her in this direction for this particular album.

"In the middle of doing the album, we lost a very close friend involved with the project—Darryl Bush," said Sylvia. "After his death, the album took on a different attitude to what we had planned originally. You notice that side two has a more gospel feel to it. We strictly went with feeling on that."[18]

The *Person to Person* album also featured a song that Sylvia had collaborated on with her big sister, Lazoe, who was struggling in her life. Their tune, "Doin' the Do," was a funky groove that focused on a woman observing a "smooth operator…flashing cash, talking trash, trying to scheme to get your way," in a club, and recounts how she works "hard for my money, chile," and decides to do things her *own* way. Essentially, "doin' the do" was another way of referring to the way in which someone takes care of business on their own terms.

And just as the song spoke about living life on one's own terms, Sylvia resolved—after years of putting her own recording career on the back burner—to return to her first love: singing. In 1989, an opportunity presented itself when she signed to the Hi-NRG Nightmare Records label founded by Ian Levine, a British Northern Soul enthusiast and former DJ. As it so happened, Levine had collected her records since his early teen days, loving both her early work with Stevie all the way up to the master she'd made of "Without Your Love." The first song the two cowrote was a catchy dance tune called "Major Investment." The song contained influences of electronic, funk, and soul, and it gave Sylvia a chance to return to her favorite subject of all: love.

Pleased with the first collaboration, Sylvia and Levine teamed up for another joint venture. The name of Levine's label—Nightmare Records—had originally been inspired by a song performed by Motown's own background female session singers, the Andantes, which was called "(Like a) Nightmare." It was one of the few songs that featured the trio exclusively and was released in 1964 on Motown's new soul imprint, V.I.P. Records, which had launched the same year. Levine wanted to better know Detroit, as well as recognize and record some of the artists who'd been signed to yet neglected at Motown during its heyday. As someone who identified with this on a deeper level, Sylvia was very supportive of his ambitions. "In Detroit, the sound has always been here," she said. "It's part of the pavement, part of the street. But Ian's been a big boost, not only to music here but to the whole city."[19]

As part of this initiative, the two teamed up with her former Motown colleague, songwriter and producer Johnny Bristol, to assemble a group of more than sixty former Motown musicians. Orchestrating this reunion reminded her of just how far she'd come, and she was happy to finally be recognized by some of her peers who may have not necessarily recognized the extent of her efforts back in the day.

"I couldn't get label credits for my work as a producer, but I was one of Motown's first female producers," she insisted. "They say that now, thankfully."[20]

When it came time to record their portions of the project, the musicians headed over to Sylvia's Masterpiece Sound Studios, since by this time, the building that once housed Motown was no longer an operable recording studio. It had instead been turned into a nonprofit museum back in 1985, and it quickly became a popular tourist destination.

To garner publicity for the project, they kicked things off with a big reunion photo shoot in February 1989 and invited everyone who was anyone in the press, from local newspapers and TV stations to national media outlets like ABC, NBC, and CBS. There could be no better setting for the photograph than the place where it all started—2648 West Grand Boulevard—and the Motown alumni stood proudly outside the building where they'd spent such a memorable part of their careers. Esther Gordy Edwards, Berry Gordy's eldest sister who had once served as Motown's senior vice president, was instrumental in turning the building into a museum, and she embraced the returning musicians with a large welcome banner placed just above the Hitsville sign that read "Welcome Motown Alumni."[21] In the historic picture of the group, Raynoma Gordy Singleton, who'd helped lay the groundwork for the company during its infancy, is prominently positioned in the front row, with Sylvia standing directly behind her, and Andantes member Louvain Demps right behind Sylvia. In addition to these three key women, notable reunion attendees (and portrait subjects) also included alumni like Mary Wells, Kim Weston, the Andantes, the Originals, Ivy Jo Hunter, David Ruffin, Marv Johnson, Sammy Ward, the Marvelettes, the Velvelettes, the Vandellas, the Contours, the Elgins, Richard "Popcorn" Wylie, and even a member of the Funk Brothers, Earl Van Dyke.

Most of the artists who showed up hadn't interacted or laid eyes on one another in more than a decade. As a result, the reunion became a genuine event, filled with laughter, excitement, catching up, and, of course, the common denominator that had bonded them all together as a family in the first place: music. The musicians loved getting the opportunity to merge their voices in new unique collaborations, and

Sylvia even joined in on a song, with the collective calling themselves the Motorcity All Stars. Gathered together around the iconic grand piano in Studio A, Martha Reeves led an impromptu group performance of the Temptations' "The Way You Do the Things You Do" that had everyone singing their hearts out with glee. Later on, Levi Stubbs, lead vocalist of the Four Tops, led the assembled group in a performance of the Four Tops classic "I Can't Help Myself (Sugar Pie Honey Bunch)."

So inspired by the reunion, Levine changed the record label's name from Nightmare to Motorcity and brought Sylvia along for the ride. It was there that she wrote for more than one hundred of her former Motown colleagues, many of whom recorded their tracks at her studio in Detroit. On the label, Sylvia also got the chance to record a song she composed called "Major Investment." "When she recorded it herself," according to Gordy Singleton, "she at long last was finally able to take advantage of her artist's contract."[22] Later she recorded her own rendition of "My Cherie Amour."

While record sales for the project weren't quite what was expected, this didn't dampen Sylvia's spirit. All the hoopla about the Motown reunion had increased traffic at her studio, bringing in notable artists such as the Four Tops, the Miracles, and Marilyn McCoo, and, of course, Stevie himself. Sylvia's music got another boost when a special cover of one of her classics, "This Old Heart of Mine," was released just before the end of 1989. British pop and rock star Rod Stewart partnered up with Ronald Isley (who'd recorded the tune in 1966 as the lead singer of the Isley Brothers) and released a new rendition of it. The song was a hit, eclipsing the popularity of Stewart's earlier solo version, which had dropped back in 1975.

Stewart, ever a fan of Sylvia's work, continued to bring attention to her songs by releasing duets with other big stars. In 1990, he joined forces with the Queen of Rock and Roll, Tina Turner herself, for a lively rendition of "It Takes Two," which was performed in a Pepsi commercial and then later released as a single by Warner Bros. The catchy version was so popular that it ended up appearing on Stewart's album *Vagabond Heart* that same year, and then in Tina Turner's greatest hits compilation, *Simply the Best*, the following year, in 1991.

Writing standards with the promise of longevity was always Sylvia Moy's goal as a songwriter. It looks like she certainly achieved it through validation with music industry legends.

## CHAPTER 18

# Making History in the Hall of Fame

Curiosity took charge as Sylvia entered the nineties and started to wade deeper into the uncharted waters of entertainment. She was particularly interested in soundtrack work, and ended up writing the song "I Know the Man's in Love With Me" and producing the soundtrack for the 1991 action film *Steele's Law*, which starred former-football-player-turned-actor Fred Williamson.[1] Other films continued to immortalize her songs by using them in new ways, such as the inclusion of "My Cherie Amour" in the 1992 Roman Polanski–directed erotic romantic thriller *Bitter Moon*.

Sylvia never took any of these opportunities or inclusions for granted, which was part of why she was blown away when Oscar-winning filmmaker Sue Marx approached her in 1993 about writing a campaign theme song for Dennis Archer, who became Detroit's fifty-ninth mayor in 1994. A collaboration with fellow Detroiters Darryl Nichols and Carlos Gunn, "Detroit for All" was a blend of several sounds that defined the eclectic city, ranging from pop and R&B to jazz and gospel. Sylvia was honored and excited to be a part of this. "I was born and raised in this city and love it. I started humming a melody and writing the lyrics right away," she said. "Then I went to the studio, got the performers and got the people to assist me in completing the music and arrangements."[2] Focusing on Detroit-based talent, Sylvia invited her friends and colleagues Ortheia Barnes and Erma Franklin, the sister of Queen of Soul Aretha Franklin, who'd attended Northern High School with Sylvia, to join in and elevate the song to new heights.

As a woman who'd been a key contributor to the music industry across multiple decades, Sylvia now had experience that rendered her a trusted expert, and journalists from various media outlets constantly asked her to chime in about the state of modern music. She was generous with print and radio interviews, especially during Black Music Month every June.

And she certainly didn't hold back. In one particular interview with the *Detroit Free Press* in 1995, Sylvia expressed frustration with the counterproductive and problematic categorization of certain genres, who insisted on distancing and distinguishing themselves from one another. "We have so much segregation. There are R&B people who won't accept jazz and jazz people who won't accept others," she said. "Some gospel stations will play traditional music but won't play contemporary gospel. We've got to open our minds and realize what we have."[3]

Beyond genre divisions, she'd also noticed that Black audiences often closed the door on anything that was considered old (such as the music of Motown), but eagerly opened doors for anything fresh and new. "We have a tendency to throw away everything. We deal with what's happening right now," she observed. "Rap and hip hop came in;

we accept that, but you don't discard all the other music that you have. Because of the popularity of rap, for a while there, you almost couldn't get a deal for a singer."[4]

The world of music that Sylvia had cut her own teeth on was a far cry from what was most popular on the radio now. By the 1990s, rap was *king*. It was just slightly more than two decades old at the time, and record labels were constantly seeking the next big rap act to keep up with the growing demand for what was hot, new, now, and next. Sylvia acknowledged that sometimes artists from different genres felt the desire to perform in Europe in order to survive, because foreign audiences seemed more open to them. Appreciation in other countries was appealing for many, and she observed this even about herself. "Obviously everyone else recognizes what we take for granted," she said, pointing out how university courses in other countries focused on Motown while the United States seemed to lag in this regard. "I found out a while back that they were teaching Motown in Europe. They had a textbook, *Motown: The History*, by Sharon Davis. I got called by someone from there because my name was on page 41."[5] Not only was her name mentioned exactly where the sharp-minded Sylvia recalled, but a close-up photograph of her flashing a winning smile was included on the same page, along with a caption beneath it that hailed her as "one of several unsung Motown heroes."

The days of Motown seemed relegated to the past, indeed. Not only was the building that had housed Motown for many years now being used as a museum, but the label itself endured the unthinkable with new ownership. In 1988, Berry Gordy sold his iconic indie label to MCA Records, which would go on to sell Motown to Polygram Records, which would later merge with Universal Music Group. Observing the label (and ownership of all the music it had produced over the years) transfer hands so many times was unnerving, but Sylvia knew there was nothing she could do.

Instead, she focused on what she could control, and she remained active in finding ways to use her music to inspire, uplift, and enlighten. Her songs continued to pop up again and again across TV shows and films. One of the most notable occurrences was in an episode of *Beverly Hills 90210*, a popular teen drama with hefty ratings that focused on a group of college friends residing in Beverly Hills. The series later became a pop culture phenomenon as it dealt with issues ranging from friendship and relationships to fostering engagement with topical issues such as racism, suicide, drug abuse, and date rape. Music was in the background but drove the moment on the show, with episode twenty-six of season four, titled "Blind Spot," including the song with the perplexing title Stevie named that Sylvia helped him write, "Shoo-Be-Doo-Be-Doo-Da-Day." One of this particular show's storylines in 1994 dealt with the sensitive issue of a fraternity president with a hidden lifestyle who gets blindsided when he is outed by his frat brother for all to see. The other storyline tackled a male character, a self-taught musician, who decides to take private piano lessons and develops a crush on his blind female piano teacher.

In August 1995, Sylvia was honored to be asked to help Detroit-based civil rights icon Rosa Parks, Mother of the Civil Rights Movement, commemorate the fortieth anniversary of the Montgomery Bus Boycott. On the compilation album *Verity Presents a Tribute to Mrs. Rosa Parks*, Sylvia's contribution, "The Quiet Strength of Rosa," sat proudly among a group of songs by renowned national gospel recording artists like Oleta Adams, John P. Kee, Fred Hammond, Sounds of Blackness, Richard Smallwood, Yolanda Adams, Daryl Coley, and Vanessa Bell Armstrong.

Meanwhile, songs she'd written decades before continued to find new life on-screen. "I Was Made to Love Her" was included in the film drama *Dead Presidents*, which came out in October 1995. The movie focused on the struggles of Black teens who'd been deployed in Vietnam once they returned home, and her song was featured in the opening scene, where the young protagonist, who works as a milk boy, talks about his first love with his two friends and coworkers while riding in the back of a milk truck.

Another timeless Sylvia tune was featured in a very different kind of movie called *Mr. Holland's Opus*, which was released two months later, in December. As a one-time aspiring music teacher herself, Sylvia identified on a deeper level with the Oscar-winning performance of Richard Dreyfuss as Glenn Holland, a composer who becomes a committed and popular high school teacher who uses music to transform his students' lives. During one of the movie's many heartwarming scenes, the song "Uptight" sets the tone as Mr. Holland tries to teach an "uptight" student about how to loosen up through dancing, clapping, and tapping on the drum until he finds the beat to ultimately become the bass drummer in the school's marching band.

Though the accolades and awards made Sylvia proud, the thing she loved most about the movie was that it underscored a belief she had long held close to her heart: that music is the best medicine to heal a soul.

In January 1998, the Moy family was hit by a tragedy that knocked the wind out of their lungs: the death of the beloved eighty-one-year-old family patriarch, Melvin. At the time of his passing, Sylvia's parents had been married for sixty-three years, and her mother, Hazel, who'd wed Melvin as a teen, struggled with the idea of carrying on without her companion.

"They were inseparable," said Sylvia's youngest sister, Anita. "When my father died, for a while I thought I was going to lose my mother. She really wanted to follow my father."

Concerned about Hazel, Sylvia moved back into the home her family grew up in to care for her ailing mother and offer her companionship so that she wouldn't be lonely. Though she encouraged her mother to write songs with her as a way of processing her grief, the two of them slowly settled into a pattern that kept them mostly homebound. As she poured so much of her time and energy into assisting her mother, Sylvia loved indulging in Dr Pepper soft drinks while watching game shows on TV like *Jeopardy* or spending time doing crossword puzzles that she filled out using an ink pen.

"She was like my mother," recalled sister Anita. "They liked sitting at home. She loved sports like my mother, who was a sports fanatic. Sylvia loved her Detroit teams. The Pistons. The Lions. The Tigers. Her and my mom did not miss these games. They also liked games with Michigan State and the University of Michigan."

As that year came to a close, Sylvia was surprised to learn that Whitney Houston, aka "the Voice," was planning to use one of Sylvia's songs for her 1998 album, *My Love Is Your Love.* But Houston wasn't alone. Sylvia joined forces with Lauryn Hill for something the industry was putting on albums called a hidden track, considered an extra bonus to surprise listeners. Their funky, up-tempo rendition of "I Was Made to Love Her" changed the title's pronoun from her to him and featured Stevie playing the harmonica. Times were constantly changing, and Sylvia had no objections as new audiences were being introduced to her work.

By the start of the millennium, Sylvia was starting to slow down, but Masterpiece Sound Studios was anything but. Though she remained present and involved in the productions, she was not actively working in the studio on a day-to-day basis as she had been previously. Nevertheless, her studio remained as busy as ever, with musicians, producers, and engineers alike vying for studio rental time to make their own recordings or produce masters for other contemporary artists.

And after decades of hustle, Sylvia was finally in a place in her life where she could take her foot off the gas. Financially, she was well situated, with her enduring music paying off exponentially. And though she didn't always receive the credit for all of the songs she'd worked on at Motown, the royalties she did receive were solid and steady. "The first of March and the first of September (the dates royalty checks are mailed) are very popular days around here," she once said.[6]

Due to the fact that her songs were so timeless, Sylvia was able to rake in royalties, or fees paid for the use of a song, from a variety of sources, including radio, TV, movies, live performances, clubs, commercials, and, eventually, internet radio and music streaming services. From sitcoms like *Cybill*, *Everybody Hates Chris*, and *New Girl*, to comedy dramas like *Early Edition* and *Six Feet Under*, to critically acclaimed political dramas like *The West Wing*, to music-heavy shows like *American Idol* and even *Glee*, Sylvia's songs found new life in all kinds of scripted and unscripted scenarios.

Her songs kept making their way into a variety of movie soundtracks, too, including *It Takes Two*, *I Spy*, *Pirate Radio*, and *Glory Road*. "My Cherie Amour" was undoubtedly one of the most popular of Sylvia's songs, and it was used in a number of different scenes across many genres over the years. One of the most memorable instances can be found in the acclaimed coming-of-age drama from 2000 *Almost Famous*, which follows a high school boy, William Miller, who lands a writing gig with *Rolling Stone* magazine and ends up following a touring rock band. In one of the film's most iconic and emotional scenes, the main female character, Penny Lane, attempts to take her own life by overdosing, and "My Cherie Amour" plays softly in the background as her stomach is pumped and her life is saved, all while she is being watched by the teen who has grown to love her. The song's delicate placement in the scene speaks to the depth of the boy's unconditional love for Penny, while also showcasing the timelessness of Sylvia's lyrics on love and longing.

On the music front, sampling popular soul songs might have gained prominence in the late seventies and eighties, but by the nineties, it was common for songwriters and producers to reach back to the greats by incorporating a portion of a previously recorded tune into a new song, sometimes pulling from multiple sources to create something different. Sampling was a staple in hip-hop, whose songwriters and producers often shined a light on hidden Motown gems to incorporate them into their aggressive beats. Kanye West, who by this time had become one of music's top songwriters and producers, was known for having one of the best ears in the industry as a producer. In 2002, he used Sylvia's song "And This Is Love" to sample a rap tune he produced titled "In Cold Blood," performed by Houston-based rapper Scarface, hailed as one of rap music's top lyricists of all time. The song was given more mileage when Kanye also produced a remix of the same tune that featured rappers 50 Cent and Lloyd Banks. Until this point, Sylvia had little dealing with rap music, but here she was smack-dab in the middle of it. To think that at one point in her career she had to fight to have her name placed on songs, and now she was being credited as a songwriter because her music was sampled by a new generation of musicians. The irony of it all was fascinating to her.

Another testament to the enduring nature of Sylvia's work came when she was notified that she would be inducted into the Songwriters Hall of Fame. The prestigious honor is no easy feat and difficult to earn, because composers and lyricists must have demonstrably shaped the art of songwriting and music worldwide. To qualify, a musician has to have released a substantial catalog of memorable songs; however, they are not eligible for induction until twenty years after the first commercial release of a song that has withstood the test of time. The rigorous process also relies on a selection committee, who evaluates the influence, impact, and creativity of the musician's contributions.[7]

By this time in her life and career, Sylvia had written nearly two hundred songs, and public recognition for her prolific output was long overdue. Sylvia's induction was momentous in and of itself. Out of more than four hundred inductees, Sylvia would be only the second Black woman ever enshrined. Back in 2002, her former Motown colleague, singer and songwriter Valerie Simpson, made history as the first Black woman ever to be inducted into the same Hall of Fame when she accepted an award alongside her husband and songwriting partner, Nickolas Ashford.

Surprisingly, there was a moment when Sylvia actually considered not accepting the honor or attending the event. Her shyness was severe and crippling in ways most never knew, and it had only gotten worse with her age and reclusion from general society. "Sylvia received many invitations to receive awards, but she rarely accepted them and attended," said her sister Celeste. This time around, it took a small army of family and friends to convince her that this recognition represented decades' worth of hard work, sacrifice, and struggles—and she deserved to be honored. After listening intently to their pleas, both in person at her parents' house and on several phone calls, something clicked and she agreed to attend, with the caveat that many of her biggest supporters come with her. As Celeste explicitly stated later on, "Sylvia paid our travel expenses."

At last, the big day had arrived: June 15, 2006. The induction ceremony was to be held at the Marriott Marquis hotel in New York City, and though Sylvia was filled to the brim with nerves, she kept her composure. Right by her side was her firstborn younger brother, Motown songwriter Melvin Moy, who escorted her to and during the event. Sylvia had such a tight lock with her left arm on his right arm as they entered and strolled the red carpet that supposedly he later on teased about losing circulation as she latched on to him for dear life.

Right behind them on the red carpet was Celeste, who'd helped her big sister get ready for the special night. "I took extra jewelry for her to wear because Sylvia was a minimalist when it came to jewelry," she recalled. Celeste chose rhinestone hanging earrings, which Sylvia at first found a bit "too gaudy," along with a pearl-and-rhinestone necklace. The set ended up going perfectly with the exquisite attire she wore that included an off-white satin jacket, adorned with black and gold sequin appliqués, that hung slightly below her waist. Underneath, she wore a floor-length black gown with a crystal belt.

Rounding out "the posse" of closest supporters were Sylvia's two best buddies: Dr. Barbara Wilson, the former singer and retired Detroit public school art teacher who guided Sylvia through much of her life; and Rita Carter Perry, a former Motown creative writer and artist management employee who later became Florida's first female founding publisher of the *Jacksonville Free Press* and named her only daughter after Sylvia.

As she warmed up to the red carpet, Celeste noticed that her sister's "alter ego" kicked in—the same one that had surfaced whenever she'd faced intense stage fright as a singer. Instantly, she was in camera-ready mode, flashing her picture-perfect smile as her red lipstick complemented her authentic, long-flowing auburn hair that still cascaded down her back like when she was younger. Normally quite reserved, Sylvia was as gracious as a social butterfly backstage at the VIP cocktail reception, greeting her fellow inductees, who included Thom Bell (one of the principal architects of the "Philly Soul" sound); Mac Davis (who wrote some of Elvis Presley's biggest hits, such as "Memories," "In the Ghetto," "Don't Cry Daddy," and "A Little Less Conversation"); and

Will Jennings (who was responsible for several award-winning songs for Celine Dion, Eric Clapton, Whitney Houston, and Dionne Warwick). Her former Motown mentor Hank Cosby, who'd died in 2002, was also inducted posthumously.

When it came time to pose inside among the Class of 2006, Sylvia beamed with pride and joy. She also stood out like a sore thumb—as she had many times over her decades in the music industry—because she was the only woman inducted that year.

The gala wouldn't have been complete without the presence of some of Sylvia's favorite colleagues from the Motown days to help her celebrate. The dynamic songwriting duo, husband and wife Nickolas Ashford and Valerie Simpson, were in attendance, as well as Patricia Cosby, Hank's widow, who accepted the honor on his behalf, and Motown's first female songwriter, Janie Bradford, who happened to have been related to Hank Cosby through marriage.

As the ceremony began, it was Sylvia's time to shine. A full-circle moment came when Stevie Wonder surprised Sylvia by walking onstage to induct her and Hank. "I was so lucky to have these two tremendously talented people working as part of my career and my life," Stevie told the packed house. "And they were much more than simply collaborators. They provided inspiration, friendship, and love, and I will always cherish these priceless gifts."

With prerecorded music softly playing in the background, Stevie then sang a live rendition of the timeless classic "My Cherie Amour" to Sylvia. Surprising everyone, she joined him in song, and the two performed together publicly for the first time. After the induction ceremony, Stevie praised Sylvia further for finding "unique ways to take the melodies" he wrote and "put them into a lyric that was incredible, that touched many hearts."[8]

Decades earlier, after releasing his 1976 album *Songs in the Key of Life*, Stevie had readily admitted that "you can still hear [Sylvia's] influence on the words I write today."[9] And as Sylvia basked in the recognition given not just by her peers but by the general public, she realized that he was not the only one who'd been forever changed by her.

## CHAPTER 19

# Winding Down

After receiving one of the most esteemed honors in New York, Sylvia returned home to Detroit, where she was greeted by family members, including her mom, Hazel, who'd been unable to attend. Sylvia's sister Celeste recalled how Sylvia told everyone upon her return that "she was glad she went, enjoyed herself, and was very proud to be inducted." Hazel was beyond proud, too, that her daughter never gave up on her dreams and stuck it out at Motown, in spite of all the obstacles she faced. No doubt she wished that Sylvia's father, Melvin, could see the lovely award with the crystal pointed top that was now displayed on a table at Sylvia's childhood home. "[As far as] the award itself, my mother was more excited than Sylvia," sister Anita said with a smile. "My mother would sit on the couch and it would sit in front of her."

All of the Songwriters Hall of Fame honorees were also gifted with a Gibson guitar of their choice. Sylvia had formally taken guitar lessons earlier in life, so she was delighted to receive the instrument, though when it arrived, it wasn't the guitar she had selected. "They were asked to choose the one they wanted," said Celeste. "I don't know who or why it was switched. I remember and loved the one she selected myself."

As for the award itself, Christopher, Sylvia's youngest brother, remembered that his sister was not nearly as showy about it as their mother was. "Sylvia was an interesting person. She did not display her awards that readily. Maybe one or two were on the wall in the front office. Most were in the closet somewhere. I don't think the awards were as important to her as the process of writing songs. She enjoyed making something from nothing."

The following year, in January 2007, Sylvia's longtime mentor and dear friend Dr. Barbara Wilson, who'd made the journey to the induction ceremony with her, suffered a stroke and died at the age of seventy-eight. Sylvia was paralyzed with grief. From that moment on, most agreed, Sylvia never seemed the same.

"That loss was just unbearable and then the way it happened in front of her," said Anita. "It really all began with that."

After Dr. Wilson's death, Sylvia started pulling away from many of her oldest friends, including Andantes member Louvain Demps. "There was kind of a disconnection between Sylvia and me when [Barbara] passed away," Demps said. "I reached out because I was thinking about her. I called to talk to her, but I spoke with her brother Melvin."

Already a private person by nature, Sylvia became more and more withdrawn. Nothing really seemed to move her much anymore, but that would not stop the long-overdue accolades from rolling her way.

Sylvia never dreamed that she'd live in a world where a Black man would actually one day become president of the United States. Of course, she remembered when Shirley Chisholm began her historic presidential campaign in 1972 as the first Black woman to run through a major party, and she also recalled when the Reverend Jesse L. Jackson threw his hat in the ring twelve years later, but neither of those attempts had succeeded in the end.

And then, two years after she was inducted into the Songwriters Hall of Fame, Senator Barack Obama, a Democrat from Illinois, vied for the highest office in the land against Senator John McCain, a Republican from Arizona. During the Democratic National Convention in Denver on Monday, August 25, 2008, Barack's wife, Michelle, was accompanied by the sweet sounds of "I Was Made to Love Her" as she walked onstage to give the opening-night keynote address—the first major speech she'd ever deliver. Just a few months later, Obama made history on November 16 as the first Black man to ascend to the coveted presidential spot.

At the time, the Obamas hadn't shared anything with the world about the role that Stevie Wonder's music had played in the beginning of their relationship. But they never forgot about the significance of the profound music and lyrics that came to represent the love they'd share.

And so, Sylvia was as surprised as anyone when, in 2009, she received a gift just as timeless and precious as the song she had written. Between sips of Dr Pepper and feverishly working on her crossword puzzle with a ballpoint pen, she was taken aback by the gratitude of the First Lady, who reached out to Sylvia and wanted to thank her for writing such a soul-stirring and inspirational song about the power of love. "I remember the day a special package came that Sylvia had to sign for," recalled Anita. "She opened it and then sat back down to do her crossword puzzle in ink. She said I could look at it. It was a special letter to her and a copy of Michelle Obama's speech to her husband."

That same year, President Barack Obama presented Stevie Wonder with the prestigious Library of Congress Gershwin Prize. During his speech, Obama talked about how had he not been a Stevie fan, Michelle probably would not have dated him or taken any interest in him at all. "We might not have married. The fact that we agreed on Stevie was part of the essence of our courtship," Obama confessed to the audience.[1]

And though it might have been Stevie's soulful voice that captivated their attention, it was Sylvia's words that worked their way into their hearts.

The last time Sylvia was interviewed live on a national TV show was during the episode of *Geraldo* in 1990. And though she continued to grant magazine, newspaper, and radio interviews over the years, as well as speaking to scholars about her role in the development of Motown, the requests slowed to a trickle as time went on and she grew older.

Which was why she was so surprised in 2011 when, out of nowhere, a request for an interview arrived from a reporter named Michelle Wilson. Wilson, an award-winning producer renowned for her Christian storytelling, had decided to embark on a personal side project to get Sylvia the widespread recognition she so deserved. As she later explained, "I believe that God placed on my heart Sylvia Moy."

Unbeknownst to Sylvia during the initial outreach, Michelle had actually met Sylvia as a child at Masterpiece Sound Studios. As it turned out, Michelle's father, James D. Wilson, was a professional photographer who also happened to have been Sylvia's longtime friend and personal photographer for more than a decade. A former professor at Wayne County Community College, James was instrumental in starting the school's photography curriculum. Over the years, James had taken a number of priceless shots of not only Sylvia but also folks like Berry Gordy, Diana Ross, Stevie Wonder, Sammy Davis Jr., Ray Charles, Natalie Cole, Aretha Franklin, and the Reverend Dr. Martin Luther King Jr., to name just a few.

However, even with Michelle's connection through her dad, she had no clue what she was up against when she initially called Sylvia. Knowing she'd need a bit of time to mull things over, Sylvia requested that Michelle call her back. "I didn't know that she was as private as she was," said Michelle. "Sometimes God doesn't show you the bigger picture because he doesn't want you to be intimidated, or he doesn't want you to walk in fear."

When Michelle called back a few days later, Sylvia officially agreed to the interview—and she made sure Michelle knew that it was happening only because of her deep reverence for Michelle's father. "She talked to me because she was, like, blessing my father's memory. It was like, 'I'm doing this because of your father, and I'm doing this because I loved him.'" All in all, the two shared four precious hours together: one of which was a sit-down one-on-one interview at Sylvia's house, and the remaining three were at Sylvia's studio and at Motown.

Normally one to wear a sweatshirt with her hair pulled back and covered by a baseball cap, Sylvia was dressed casually for the first day of filming on August 22, 2011. She was living back at the Moy family home, the one she'd grown up in, and she dedicated much of her time to caring for her ailing mother, Hazel.

"The first day that we talked, she was definitely more reserved. She did lighten up when I had her talk about her childhood," said Michelle, who brought with her some of the many images her father had taken of Sylvia over the years. It ended up being just the spark to ignite a flame. "Here's the thing. She is not a talkative person. The thing that got her to talk was, I believe the wisdom of God was to bring those images so that she could see herself and see the other people. And so, I remember we sat down maybe together on the piano bench, and we filmed her looking through those images of herself and we got her talking about that."

On the following day, at Michelle's gentle urging, Sylvia decided to shake things up a little—and opened the door with flawless makeup, coiffed hair, and beautiful matching jewelry, all courtesy of her younger sister Anita. Though she was just three weeks shy of her seventy-third birthday, Sylvia was as radiant as ever and stunningly pretty in pink, wearing a jacket and blouse matching ensemble with black slacks. Ready to take on the day with Michelle and her film crew, the team started with an interview at Masterpiece Sound Studios and then migrated over to the place where Sylvia's songwriting career all began: the Motown building.

"The brilliance that flowed through her is what she wanted to display," said Michelle of those interviews, which were eventually released publicly three years later on YouTube. "I believe when she was at Motown, she really came alive—and it brought back a lot of great memories for her."

The previous day, Sylvia had tired easily while filming, but visiting her studio and traveling to Motown gave her a new surge of energy. She sat comfortably at the control booth with the mixing board in front of her, reminiscing in the studio she'd built. Adorning the walls behind her nearby were certified plaques from Detroit-based and Motown-signed R&B singer Kem, who gained national attention after recording his 2003 debut album, *Kemistry*, at her studio.

Walking the hallway later at Motown, Sylvia was asked to comment on the Motown Wall of Fame. With her arms folded, she stared intently at the many images of her former colleagues, including pictures of Stevie's spunky cousins, the Jackson 5, and the glamorous Diana Ross, whom she had known since they were kids and for whom Sylvia had done background vocal work in the past on some of the Supremes' big hits. When Michelle's film crew took Sylvia into Studio A, also known as the snake pit, Sylvia pointed out where the musicians usually sat, talked about the instruments they played, and reflected on how the song "Uptight" had saved a floundering Stevie's early career.

"I think that she appreciated me doing her story," Michelle mused once the interviews were completed. "She said, 'I'm grateful that you had this appreciation for my life and what I was able to contribute, especially to the music world.' And we did keep in touch afterward."

The following year, in February 2012, singer Martha Reeves invited a camera crew to follow her over to Sylvia's Masterpiece Sound Studios—only the reason behind it had nothing to do with Sylvia. Reeves had only wanted to record a song about her love for Detroit called "I'm Not Leaving," but she was delighted to be able to see and greet her dear friend. "Thank God I got a chance to see Sylvia in that studio and record a special thing with Crystal Method, ReGENERATION." Sylvia loved the song "I'm Not Leaving" because she identified with it so strongly as a Detroit native.

Meanwhile, Sylvia's songs continued to reach new audiences through movies, this time in a romantic comedy drama called *Silver Linings Playbook*, starring Bradley Cooper and Jennifer Lawrence, which later garnered winning reviews and Oscar acclaim. The song "My Cherie Amour" served a twofold purpose, as the lead character, Pat (played by Cooper), and his estranged wife had turned to the song on their wedding day, but it was also the same one playing when he walked in on his wife being unfaithful with her lover. Unfortunately, the heartwarming tune ends up being a severe trigger for Pat throughout the movie as he learns how to process his grief.

Unfortunately, nothing or no one is forever. That same year, Sylvia was devastated to hear about the death of her oldest sister, Lazoe. From her early days of living in the fast lane in New York as an in-demand fashion model to partying it up with the likes of Jimi Hendrix, Lazoe's past finally caught up with her after decades spent battling various addictions. Watching her older sister's decline was especially hard on Sylvia, who helped out when Lazoe lost a limb to diabetes. Anita, Sylvia's youngest sister, said, "Every so often Sylvia talked to me about not liking to see Lazoe like that. I was also close to Lazoe. We called each other the 'alpha' and the 'omega' because she was at the beginning of the family as the oldest and I am at the end as the youngest."

"Baby sis," as Lazoe used to call Sylvia, had often stepped up over the course of their relationship and helped their parents care for Lazoe's son, Jackie, during her early career. Lazoe was always grateful to her for it, and the two grew closer and closer as they aged. "Sylvia and Lazoe were partners in crime, so to speak," recalled Jackie, who remained extremely close to his nurturing aunt. "They enjoyed doing bad things together. Not really bad things but little things just to enjoy life."

Tragedy for the Moys compounded further when the family matriarch, Hazel, died the same year at the age of ninety-four. Reeling from the deaths of her mother and sister, Sylvia spiraled into an abyss of deep depression. She didn't want to do much of anything except stay at home. The following year, Ortheia Barnes, Sylvia's friend and fellow artist, passed away, too.

"Sylvia had helped Ortheia for more than ten years, doing her albums and music and her bookings. All of a sudden, Sylvia was saying,

'Everyone I know is gone now. I think maybe it's time for me,'" Jackie said. He'd been concerned by the sudden change in her attitude as she reckoned with her own life's inevitable end.

Sylvia's body had started slowing down, her memory fading bit by bit. In interviews, she was more rambling than she'd ever been, but when asked about her songwriting days, she seemed a bit more coherent—as if a light bulb went on, if just for a moment.

"She had gotten to the point where she was tired and was giving up," her sister Anita explained.

In 2016, during Sylvia's birthday month of September, a new NBC TV family drama called *This Is Us* started racking up acclaim from critics and audiences alike. In the twelfth episode of that first season, "Uptight" made its way out into the world yet again as the track was featured in a flashback of the young father, Jack, bonding with his pregnant wife, Rebecca. As he touches her belly, he laughs and says, "Oh! I told you they'd like Stevie!" just as the triplets start kicking to the rhythmic beat of Stevie's words "Baby, everything is alright." Jack kisses Rebecca's belly in delight and sings "out of sight!" right along with Stevie. Sadly, the third baby was stillborn.

More and more, Sylvia was having flashbacks of her own. She'd always considered her songs to be her "children" and drew inspiration from each one. She'd also think about the many teens she'd encountered and how she touched their lives through her nonprofit. But the one who never strayed far from her thoughts was the baby she'd given birth to so many years earlier and never got to raise. Even in her darkest days, she never gave up hope that the two would one day be reunited.

"She would get a look on her face and say, 'I wish I could find my son.' She said that not long before she died, even. I said, 'One day, I *know* you're going to see him. I just got a feeling that you're going to see him,'" her sister Ronnie recalled reassuring her.

Little did either of them know just how soon that reunion would be.

On April 15, 2017—the forty-ninth anniversary of the day that Sylvia made Motown and music history as one of the country's top songwriters of the year—Sylvia finally succumbed to pneumonia and passed away at Detroit's Beaumont Hospital–Dearborn. In a strong coincidence of timing, it was the same day that Stevie Wonder was honored as the inaugural recipient of the first Key of Life Award, presented by the American Society of Composers, Authors and Publishers.[2]

Sylvia's funeral was held on April 22, 2017, at Greater Grace Temple in Detroit. Unable to attend in person as he was set to perform at pro golfer Rory McIlroy's wedding in Ireland on the same day, Stevie sent along a taped recording of his gratitude for the role Sylvia played in his life.

Though he mentioned that he was away, he let everyone know that so much of his spirit, heart, and soul was with them. He described Sylvia as a woman who wanted so much and went out of her way to make things happen. For instance, he recalled the day she had to deliver some tough news when she "came to my mother's home and told us that they were planning to let me go from Motown. My voice changed and they didn't know what they were going to do with me. And she committed to them, that she would work with me and work with the songs, with the abilities that I had. We would come up with something and it would be worth their while to keep me there. *She's* the reason for all of that."

For anyone who'd ever doubted that Motown once considered getting rid of Stevie, he was determined to set the record straight—and give Sylvia her flowers. He explained how anything that happened after "Fingertips" was because of her unwavering faith in his immediate and long-term success. He went on to say, "it was because of her saying, 'Listen, he has so much to give. We can't let him go. Myself and Hank Cosby will work with him. We can come up with some great stuff,' and we did together. 'Uptight' and 'My Cherie Amour.' Sylvia, all the various melodies that I had, she took those melodies and put words to it." Stevie also discussed writing a song about his girlfriend named Marsha, whom he sang about and became the inspiration behind a tune he initially wanted to title "My Marsha," but Sylvia stepped in and her shrewd thinking altered this. He shared how her decision, based on keen insight, "changed the words to 'My Cherie Amour,' making it one of the most classical, legendary songs that I've had in my career."

Stevie ended the message by professing his undying admiration for the gentle woman who'd done so much for him over the years, explaining that he knew she was there with her loved ones in spirit. He ended by summarizing his everlasting feelings for her with the following sentiments: "I love you. Will always love you. I'm just hoping that someday, someday, I'll be so fortunate to go through heaven's doors and meet you and again be able to write songs of love, eternally, for the universe. Forever."[3]

He also took the time to express his condolences to the Moy family directly, reminding them in a letter that we are all just human beings, passing through this thing called life. "You know that we learn at an early age that we are not meant to be here forever," he wrote in the message that Celeste shared at the funeral. "So please, even through the pain of it all, celebrate this wonderful African American woman's life, for she was another example of one of God's greatest creations."

The funeral itself was every bit as regal and distinguished as Sylvia deserved. As people entered the church for the service, they were greeted by large, full-sized photographs that were taken through the years by James D. Wilson. A collection of more of his portraits were also placed on easels at the front of the church altar, surrounding Sylvia's casket, where her body lay peacefully, dressed in a beautiful gold outfit. Wilson's daughter, Michelle, who'd remained in touch with Sylvia after their interview, had provided the grieving Moy family with the pictures. "I was marveling at how people were walking in and looking at those images of her. It was like a gift. That's the best way that I can explain it."

What stood out even more to Michelle was later discovering how much Sylvia had shared financially over the course of her life without ever drawing attention to it. At the service, anyone Sylvia had ever helped monetarily was asked to stand. Few in the packed church remained seated. "I didn't know that she was such a generous person until I went to the funeral," said Michelle. "I thought that was a big deal."

It seemed as if the beauty of Sylvia's heart shone through even to the end, radiating out to her physical form. Longtime friends and colleagues like Martha Reeves and Louvain Demps were amazed to see and hear of how beautiful Sylvia looked in her casket. "People told me how soft her skin looked and how pretty her hair still looked," Demps recalled. "I thought, 'Oh, gosh, that girl's still fine as can be. Now she's probably better.'"

Sylvia also received official commemorations from the Detroit City Council and the State of Michigan during the service. Berry Gordy sent over a lavish floral arrangement of white roses with a white ribbon with gold writing that stood prominently beside the head of the casket. Unable to attend in person, he'd written a message to be passed along by a family member who attended.

"At this moment we are all sharing a tremendous loss," Gordy's grandniece Robin Terry, head of the Motown Museum, read aloud. In addition to Sylvia's early work with Stevie, Gordy acknowledged how

"Sylvia went on to do many other great things at Motown, gaining the respect of fellow songwriters and opening the door for other women."[4]

In addition to testimonies shared in person at the funeral, Sylvia's memory was honored with gracious public tributes from media outlets across the country. Sony/ATV issued the following statement to *Billboard*: "We are extremely sad to hear about the death of Sylvia Moy, whose songwriting played an important part in Motown's history, including its influence on Stevie Wonder's career. Her songwriting versatility is also evident in songs including 'It Takes Two' and 'This Old Heart of Mine.' She additionally broke down barriers as one of Motown's first-ever female producers. Her classic songs will live on forever."

But perhaps the most meaningful public statement of all came from none other than Stevie Wonder himself. In a letter to *Rolling Stone*, Wonder acknowledged that it was Sylvia who had laid the groundwork for him as a lyricist.

"How do you stop loving the ones you loved for a lifetime? You don't," Stevie wrote. He praised her songwriting skills, which he admitted made him a better lyricist, and he shared how her influence remained as he progressed in his career. "Sylvia Moy has made it possible to enrich my world of songs with some of the greatest lyrics. But not only that, she, through her participation and our co-writing those songs, helped me become a far better writer of lyrics." Stevie continued by stating how even in later years, he often anticipated a reunion. "I longed for us to collaborate again, yet who am I to fight with the Most High in His decision to make her one of His angels of song for eternity? Maybe someday in eternity, at its given time and space, we will write together again.

"I love you, Sylvia."[5]

# EPILOGUE

In continuing to recap Sylvia's journey, the same year of her transition, she was given yet another honor by being posthumously inducted into the National Rhythm & Blues Hall of Fame. This was a treasured memory for her family as they dealt with life without their beloved big sister.

Sylvia's physical presence would be no more, but the songs she helped bring to life remain. The longevity and enduring nature of her music earned her BMI Million-Air Awards, which are given to songwriters whose works achieve the rare feat of surpassing one million broadcast performances on radio. The million-performance stats indicated where the song was performance-wise. As of 2023, Sylvia had earned BMI Million-Air Certificates for the following: "I Was Made to Love Her" at three million; "It Takes Two" at two million; "My Cherie Amour" at seven million; "This Old Heart of Mine" at seven million; and "Uptight" at four million.

Those songs have resonated not only with audiences but with her contemporaries. Throughout the years, other artists have gone on to record Sylvia's music because of its perpetual nature and ability to transcend genres with pop, rock, soul, and jazz. Her discography has allowed a new crop of people in widespread music demographics to unearth her music through covers by folks as far back as Tom Jones, Barry Manilow, Dusty Springfield, and Tony Bennett to recent times with Boyz II Men and Joss Stone. Artists such as Grammy Award–winning performers John Legend and Alicia Keys, both acclaimed for their sophisticated techniques in producing elegant and refined arrangements as singers, pianists, and songwriters, have expressed Stevie Wonder's influence on their musical proficiency. No doubt that Sylvia's polished orchestration of his classics contribute to providing inspiration for many others through the thought-provoking lyrics and stirring instrumentations.

The likelihood is feasible because Sylvia believed in the influence and importance of writing standards, which she strived to accomplish by creating songs that could be relevant across generations. She'd tell her family members that even if a person went to a dentist's office or heard the music being played as classical or jazz music, that constituted a standard. And standards meant that her songs would outlive her, as "they'd still be playing when I'm not here," as Sylvia's siblings recalled her always saying. In looking back on Sylvia's legacy, this type of work ethic wasn't surprising to singer Martha Reeves, who knew from first-hand experience working alongside Sylvia. "She was always about the art of writing music, but because of her strong personality and ability to write beautiful lyrics, she stood firm," said Reeves. "Sylvia was very sure that everything she did was top-notch."

During a milestone Motown anniversary tribute, *Motown 60: A Grammy Celebration*, one of the most touching moments came from a performance by Stevie at the Microsoft Theater in Los Angeles. As a headliner at the April 2019 event, he delivered a passionate nationally televised performance of his 1971 classic "Never Dreamed You'd Leave in Summer." High above him onstage were large photographs of some of the people who were instrumental in shaping his early career at the label. There were Clarence Paul and Hank Cosby, who both began working with him at the tender age of eleven as soon as he stepped foot inside Motown. But one image illuminated radiantly. Positioned prominently in the middle, centered between Clarence and Hank was a picture of the person always holding her own, Sylvia.

With all the things she cultivated at Motown, for her to have been the first woman contracted in-house to simultaneously, consistently, and consecutively write songs *and* produce alongside her male counterparts during the label's peak in the sixties, and not be distinguished for it at the time, is deplorable. Throughout nearly five decades, more than fifty books have been written about Motown that include subjects ranging from its history to memoirs and biographies by its artists. Ethnomusicologists and historians have conducted scholarly research and produced works about the iconic label and its cultural and social impact. Many of the historical accounts include only a mere mention of Sylvia Moy's name. Other accounts have short profiles of her ties to Stevie Wonder tunes. Then there were a few authors who actually interviewed her to share bits and pieces about her life and thoughts about labelmates or about the company itself. But all the while, the greatest story was right before them in Sylvia's gentle whisper, waiting to be seen and heard, patiently hoping to take flight.

In an industry that has historically and perpetually thrived on exploitation and thievery, Sylvia *bravely* spent time relentlessly pushing back against both—even risking her life—to teach others, by her example, to fight for what was rightfully theirs. She unapologetically talked the talk, and she boldly walked the walk. Unlike so many others before her in the music industry who died broke, she did not leave this world penniless. As a matter of fact, Sylvia left her family armed with wealth and knowledge on protecting her legacy. Growing up they witnessed how diligent Sylvia was in working to educate and inform others about safeguarding their work from being taken and exploited. She stayed vigilant so that others would not have to endure what she did.

Appropriately so, the younger sisters and brothers Sylvia once took care of, in turn, are now doing the same for her. Work continues to be done on her behalf through them and nephew Jackie, with the studio she built being preserved and her legacy upheld through the Estate of Sylvia Moy LLC d/b/a Masterpiece Sound Studios, comanaged by Celeste and brother Christopher. In 2022, Sylvia's family launched a Song Cover Contest by Masterpiece Sound Studios where seven of ten songs chosen by participants were cowritten by Sylvia. Actor Omar Gooding hosted the event, which was cosponsored by Sony Music Publishing. Detroit artists Drey Skonie and the Klouds ultimately took home the top prize in April 2023 with their rendition of "I Was Made to Love Her" at the Motor City Casino's Sound Board theater. In addition to Audrey J. Ashby, senior vice president of Business Affairs and Catalog at Sony/ATV, some of Sylvia's Motown colleagues from Detroit and Los Angeles showed their support and attended the event, including Janie Bradford, Claudette Robinson, Paul Riser, Patricia Cosby, Gloria Jones, Brenda Holloway, and McKinley Jackson. Brenda Wilson, the daughter of singer Jackie Wilson, who during his lifetime did a few electrifying renditions of Sylvia's songs when he joined forces with the legendary jazz bandleader Count Basie, was there to witness the special evening as well. Two years later, in June, she was posthumously inducted into the Women Songwriters Hall of Fame.

As Sylvia's music continues to be played, performed, and celebrated by fans and musicians alike as the soundtrack of their lives, all the world can now attest to the fact that this woman's work made her one of Motown's *greatest* songwriters—and producers.

Through it all, Sylvia Rose Moy was blessed to live a purpose-driven life. Her gift was to touch people in words and songs. She truly believed, deeply within the fibers of her soul, just as she did while performing in church during her early life, that if she could help somebody, then her living would not be in vain. It wasn't.

# Acknowledgments

Many thanks to my wonderful Hachette publishing family, who allowed *It's No Wonder* to see the light because they believed in Sylvia's radiant life and story. This includes the following people: Ben Schafer, you came in during a critical time as *It's No Wonder* was being ushered toward production. But after I learned that you were an early supporter of the book in-house back to the time of acquisition after thoroughly enjoying the proposal, this was immensely comforting and made me smile. I'm so glad that I was placed in the best possible hands. Excellence on every level from two folks with Midwest roots! Brant Rumble, your excitement about this book since it was signed assured me that we are a mighty force behind an anointed project! Carrie Napolitano, what can I say? From the first day I met you and read your passionate plea to take on *It's No Wonder*, I knew you "got it" and you got Sylvia. You were the editor ordained for me. As a scholar known for educating others, I was schooled by you in maneuvering this story by digging deeper while fervently making sure that Sylvia always remained the "beating heart" at every turn. I couldn't have asked for a better person by my side to the finish line.

Joseph Perry, Esq., you were the perfect literary agent for me to see this project through. From the moment I reached out to you, we aligned and you patiently went to work. At first, there were more lows than highs. I'd always tell you, "We're gonna keep the faith. It's all going to work out. One day we'll share our test as a testimonial!" Your respect for me and this project has not gone unnoticed. You witnessed the journey and now we'll share the glory! That's faith.

You're only as good as the team around you. John S. Kendall, Esq., we've been riding this wave together for more than two decades and it's always been chess, never checkers. Thank you to others for providing additional guidance: Denise Gibbon of Above the Dotted Line and Michael Gross of The Authors Guild.

Here's a recognition to the Motown family, who came through in sharing powerful testimonials about their "quiet" colleague. It is because of you, utilizing your voices to amplify her story through observations, that you've allowed the world to know who Sylvia was. It's a blessing that so many who worked directly with her were here to eloquently share encounters as if they happened yesterday. Acknowledging the following: Mickey Stevenson, Smokey Robinson, Eddie Holland, Janie Bradford, Martha Reeves, Paul Riser, Louvain Demps, Cornelius Grant, Patricia Cosby, Ivy Jo Hunter, and Barrett Strong. Kim Weston, you are not forgotten. I appreciate your willingness to try to contribute information. The conversations we had about Sylvia, and you singing some of the songs she wrote for you, was a magnificent gift between us. Berry Gordy, if there was no Motown, there'd be no Sylvia Moy. Thank you for being an open door to real, raw talent and excellence.

So many others helped me along this journey, including Dr. Jim Perone, Dr. Charles Sykes, and the late Raynoma Gordy Singleton, for helping to speak in Sylvia's name and honor. Your astute examinations and revelations in interviews and in books allowed me to support her work as a producer and crediting songwriting claims that might have otherwise been impossible. Thanks for your assistance to the following along the way: Harry Weinger, Jodie Thomas and Raette Johnson (BMI), S'Von, Linda Stewart, Dr. Rollo Dilworth, and Rhoda Stamell.

Family is forever, so I am thanking my siblings (Eddie Jr., Cheryl, Rachel, and Dana) and nieces (Amenta and Alauna). Floyda Norrisa Pearson, we've been in tandem since high school and you've always been an anchor for me. You've been the early sounding board on all of my projects. This was no exception, from being an early proponent, to getting goosebumps learning about it, to cheering me on about the subject and gifting me with a thought-provoking moniker. My sister, you're my rock. Dr. Reginald Jackson, thanks for the good laughs that have always settled me since our days earning our doctorates. To my devoted friends in Sisters Coming Together (Nicolle, Jennifer, Natasha, Debbie, Ericka, Tracey) and Third Friday Club (Eric, Nicolle, Randall, Reggie, Darren, Senalda), your unconditional love and support are ever-present and priceless. To my former colleagues in English and professional writing at the University of Illinois Chicago along with former students, your unwavering support was the wind beneath my wings. I appreciate you sharing the ride. To my former *Ebony* and *Jet* magazine colleagues, we've learned how to succeed against the odds. And still we rise. Always and forever!

Finally, thank you to the Moy family for their cooperation in assisting with this book.

Last but not least, Sylvia Rose Moy, honey chile, your spirit woke me up faithfully each night for several years. When I needed an answer or where to locate something, miraculously, you always pointed me in the right direction as if I summoned St. Anthony, the patron saint of lost things. There it was. I'm convinced that you, my Virgo sister, were letting me know you were always by my side, especially in the wee hours. As I wrote feverishly, I felt you guiding my hand. I was always humbled that you chose me to magnify your voice and to channel your energy so that the world will forever know you. There seemed to have been so much taken from you in your life, both professionally and personally. Sylvia, it feels good for me to be able to give you back something that no one will ever take again—your credit, your recognition, and your rightful place in music history. I graciously thank you for opening doors, for clearing paths, and for moving mountains from the beginning of this journey until the end of it. You are in control. And this is love. Shine, Sylvia! Shine!

# Bibliography

Abrams, Al. *Hype & Soul! Behind the Scenes of Motown: The Official Archives of the Legendary Hitsville Spin Doctor*. Temple Street Publishing, 2011.

Adams, Sam. "Stevie Wonder and the Obamas: A Love Story." December 21, 2016. Slate.com.

Alterman, Loraine. "Stevie Wonder." *Detroit Free Press*, March 17, 1967, Teen Beat.

Arseneau, Guy. "Long Playing: Rose Marie McCoy Is Churning Out the Tunes at 92." NJ.com/inside-jersey. September 2014, pp. 84, 86.

Ashford, Jack, and Charlene Ashford. *Motown: The View from the Bottom*. Bank House Books, 2003.

Barton, Laura. "Simply Brill: The Women Who Shaped Rock 'N' Roll." September 3, 2009. TheGuardian.com.

Benjaminson, Peter. *The Story of Motown*. Grove Press, 2018 (ebook Barnacle/LA).

Betts, Graham. *Motown Encyclopedia*. "Tears of a Clown—Smokey Robinson & the Miracles (single)." AC Publishing, 2014.

"BMI Awards to 58 R&B Writers." *Billboard*, April 26, 1969.

"BMI Mourns the Loss of Legendary Motown Songwriter Sylvia Moy." April 17, 2017. BMI.com.

Bowles, Dennis. "Dr. Beans Bowles 'Finger Tips': The Untold Story." Sho-nuff Productions, 2005.

Boyd, Herb. "Sylvia Moy, a Breakthrough Songwriter and Producer at Motown Records." *New York Amsterdam News*, May 18, 2017.

Brackett, David. "The Politics and Practice of 'Crossover' in American Popular Music, 1963 to 1965." *Musical Quarterly* 78, no. 4 (Winter 1994): 774–93.

"Brain 'Rewires' Itself to Enhance Other Senses in Blind People," Mass Eye and Ear, Mass General Brigham, March 22, 2017, Masseyeandear.org/news/press-releases/2017/03/brain-rewires-senses-blind.

Breskin, David. "Waiting on the Man: Stevie Comes Down from the Mountaintop." *Musician*, no. 64 (February 1984): 56.

"Brill Building/Aldon Music/1650 Broadway." strathdee.wordpress.com/2015/05/2017/brill-building-aldon-music-1650-broadway/.

Brown, Jeremy K. *Stevie Wonder: Musician.* Infobase Publishing, 2010.

Buford, Larry. "Sylvia Moy: Motown's First Female Record Producer." April 20, 2017. EUR.com.

Cain, Pete. "The Motown Mob." *Rock*, July 6, 1970.

Carlson, Kathryn Blaze. "Your Baby Is Dead: Mothers Say Their Supposedly Still-born Babies Were Stolen from Them." March 23, 2012. NationalPost.com.

Carson, David. "Grit Noise and Revolution: The Birth of Detroit Rock 'N' Roll." University of Michigan Press, 2006.

Caucusclubdetroit.com. History in Detroit.

Chesterton, George. "The Blessed Stevie Wonder: The Blessing Is All Ours." May 13, 2021. GQ-magazine.co.uk.

Collins, Patricia H. *Black Feminist Thought: Knowledge, Consciousness, and the Politics of Empowerment.* Routledge, 1990.

Cosgrove, Stuart. *Detroit 67: The Year That Changed Soul.* Bk. 1 of *The Soul Trilogy*. Polygon, 2016.

Dahl, Bill. *Motown: The Golden Years*. Krause Publications, 2001.

Davis, Sharon. *Stevie Wonder: Rhythms of Wonder*. Robson Books, 2006.

DetroitHistorical.org. Conant Gardens Historic District.

Douglas, Mike. Stevie Wonder performance and interview. "I Was Made to Love Her." 1967.

Douglas, Mike. Stevie Wonder performance and interview. "Uptight." 1966.

Dozier, Lamont. *How Sweet It Is: A Songwriter's Reflections on Music, Motown, and the Mystery of the Muse*. BMG, 2019.

Evans, Farrell. "The 1967 Riots: When Outrage over Racial Injustice Boiled Over." History.com, June 17, 2021.

Fitzgerald, Jon. "Motown Crossover Hits 1963–1966 and the Creative Process." *Popular Music* 14, no. 1 (1995).

"Friday Night with Jonathan Ross: Stevie Wonder." Interview by Jonathan Ross. Series 15, episode 2, September 12, 2008.

Gaar, Gillian G. *She's a Rebel: The History of Women in Rock & Roll*. 2nd ed. Seal Press, 1992.

Gabriel, Larry. "The World Beyond Pop: Black Roots Music." *Detroit Free Press*, June 28, 1995.

Gallant, Trudy. "Motown Revue Reunion." American Black Journal, 1989. https://abj.matrix.msu.edu/videofull.php/id=198-733-519/.

Garofalo, Reebee. "Culture Versus Commerce: The Marketing of Black Popular Music." In *The Black Public Sphere: A Public Culture Book*, edited by the Black Public Sphere Collective. University of Chicago Press, 1995.

Gentray, Mae Whitlock. "Stevie Wonder: A Musical Giant." *Ebony Jr!*, March 1977.

George, Nelson. *The Rise and Fall of Motown Sound: Where Did Our Love Go?* University of Illinois Press, 1985.

Gordy, Berry. *To Be Loved: The Music, the Magic, the Memories of Motown*. Rosetta Books, 2013.

Hall, Russell. "Smokey Robinson: The Master of Motown." *Performing Songwriter* 7, no. 42 (December 1999).

Hamilton, Andrew. "Shorty Long Biography." AllMusic.com.

Heard Maclin, Frances. *I Remember Motown: When We Were Just Family*. Yorkshire Publishing, 2010.

Holland, Brian, and Eddie Holland. *Come and Get These Memories: The Genius of Holland-Dozier-Holland Motown's Incomparable Songwriters*. Blackstone, 2020.

Hughes, Timothy S. "Groove and Flow: Six Analytical Essays on the Music of Stevie Wonder." PhD diss., University of Washington, 2003.

Hull, Ted, and Paula Stahel. *The Wonder Years: My Life & Times with Stevie Wonder*. Ted Hull, 2002.

Jancelewicz, Chris. "The 'Whitewashing' of Black Music: A Dark Chapter in Rock History." *Global News*, July 10, 2023.

Jarnow, Jesse. "Stevie Wonder." In *Icons of R&B and Soul: An Encyclopedia of the Artists Who Revolutionized Rhythm*, edited by Bob Gulla. Greenwood Publishing, 2008.

Jones, Laurence. "Sylvia's Work: Sister Soul Songwriting Standing in the Shadows of Motown, 1964–1975." *DJLarsupreme* (blog), June 21, 2017.

Kreps, Daniel. "Stevie Wonder Pays Tribute to Motown Songwriter Sylvia Moy." *Rolling Stone*, April 18, 2017.

Kreps, Daniel. "Sylvia Moy, Motown Songwriter and Stevie Wonder Collaborator." *Rolling Stone*, April 17, 2017.

Levine, Ian. Cut Glass Featuring Ortheia Barnes. "Without Your Love." YouTube, March 27, 2007.

Lodder, Steve. *A Musical Guide to the Classic Albums*. Backbeat Books, 2005.

Love, Dennis, and Stacy Brown. *Blind Faith: The Miraculous Journey of Lula Hardaway, Stevie Wonder's Mother*. Simon & Schuster, 2002.

Lundy, Zeth. *Songs in the Key of Life*. Bloomsbury, 2007.

Lynskey, Dorian. "How We Made Motown." *Guardian*, March 22, 2016. Theguardian.com.

Marble, Steve. "Sylvia Moy, Motown Songwriter Who Wrote Hits for Stevie Wonder." *Los Angeles Times*, April 18, 2017.

McCann, Ian. "Motown and Martin Luther King Jr.'s 'I Have a Dream Speech.'" January 16, 2023. Udiscovermusic.com.

McCollum, Brian. "Detroit's 100 Greatest Song: Counting Down 33 to 30." *Detroit Free Press*, June 19, 2016.

McCollum, Brian. "Motown Greats Pay Tribute to Sylvia Moy at Funeral." *Detroit Free Press*, April 23, 2017. Freep.com.

McCollum, Brian. "Sylvia Moy, Motown Producer and Stevie Wonder Collaborator, Dies at 78." *Detroit Free Press*, April 17, 2017.

MacNeil, Robert. *MacNeil/Lehrer NewsHour*, February 7, 1990. PBS.

MacNeil, Robert. *MacNeil/Lehrer NewsHour*, July 3, 1991. PBS.

Mitchell, Gail. "Motown Icon Valerie Simpson Talks 'Girls with Impact,' Songwriter Advice & New Projects." *Billboard*, March 8, 2023. Billboard.com.

Momodu, Samuel. "Detroit Walk to Freedom (1963)." April 4, 2022. Blackpast.Org.

Moss, Rob. "The Ivy Jo Hunter Story." October 29, 2013. Soul Source UK.

"Names and Faces: Briefly." *Detroit Free Press*, August 17, 1991.

"New Detroit: A Racial Justice Organization." https://www.newdetroit.org/our-history/.

"Obituaries." *Telegraph*, April 20, 2017. Telegraph.co.uk.

"On the Influence of the Great Migration of the 1920s–50s." *Detroit Free Press*, May 31, 1999.

"On Top of It." *Detroit Free Press*, March 2, 1990.

Pack, Richard. "Sylvia Moy: From Motown to MSR." *Soul Survivor* (Winter 1986–87).

"Penobscot Building." Detroit Historical Society. Detroithistoricalsociety.org.

Perone, James E. *The Sound of Stevie Wonder: His Words and Music*. Praeger Publishing, 2006.

Posner, Gerald. *Motown: Music, Money, Sex, and Power*. Random House, 2005.

"Race Riot of 1943." Detroit Historical Society. Detroithistoricalsociety.org.

"Remembering Sylvia Moy and Her Contributions to R&B." *All Things Considered*, December 29, 2017. NPR.org.

Ribowsky, Mark. *Signed, Sealed, and Delivered: The Soulful Journey of Stevie Wonder*. John Wiley & Sons, Inc, 2010.

Risen, James. "Motor City Records Is Trying to Bring a Piece of the Motown Sound to Its Birthplace in Detroit." *Los Angeles Times*, March 16, 1990.

Ritz, David. *Divided Soul: The Life of Marvin Gaye*. Da Capo Press, 1991.

Rivera, Geraldo. "The Women of Motown." *Geraldo*, October 19, 1990.

Robinson, Charlotte. "It's a House Full of Creativity: Lack of Funds Cloud Future." *Detroit Free Press*, August 23, 1974.

Robinson, Lisa. "It Happened in Hitsville." *Vanity Fair*, December 13, 2008. VanityFair.com.

Robson-Scott, Markie. "Hitsville: The Making of Motown–A Thrilling Celebration of the Record Label's Heyday." October 1, 2019. Theartsdesk.com.

Sandomir, Richard. "Sylvia Moy, Motown Songwriter Who Worked with Stevie Wonder." *New York Times*, April 18, 2017.

Sharley, Jean. "Little Stevie Wonder and His Growing Pains." *Detroit Free Press*, December 5, 1965.

Shaw, Arnold. *The World of Soul: Black America's Contribution to the Pop Music Scene*. Cowles Book Company, 1970.

Singleton, Raynoma G. *The Untold Story: Berry, Me, and Motown*. Contemporary Books, 1990.

Slutsky, Allan "Dr. Licks." "Sidemen: Benny Benjamin." 2019. RockHall.com.

Smith, Stacy L., Katherine Pieper, Karla Hernandez et al. *Inclusion in the Recording Studio? Gender & Race/Ethnicity of Artists, Songwriters & Producers Across 1,200 Popular Songs from 2012 to 2023*. January 2024. USC Annenberg Inclusion Initiative sponsored by Spotify.

Songwriters Hall of Fame. www.songhall.org.

"Songwriter with Motown Who Salvaged Stevie Wonder's Flagging Career with the Joyous Uptight." *Daily Telegraph*, April 21, 2017.

Squires, Catherine. *African Americans and the Media*. Polity Press, 2009.

Stevenson, William M. "Motown's First A&R Man. William Mickey Stevenson." Stevenson International Entertainment, 2015.

"Stevie Wonder to Accept Inaugural 'Key of Life' Award and Will Be Featured Keynote at 2017 ASCAP 'I Create Music' EXPO, April 13–15 in Los Angeles." March 16, 2017. ASCAP.com.

"Stevie Wonder's Tribute to Sylvia Moy at Her Funeral in Detroit." April 22, 2017. SoundCloud. https://soundcloud.com/detroitfreepress/stevie-wonder-tribute-to-sylvia-moy.

Swenson, John. *Stevie Wonder*. Harper & Row, 1986.

Sykes, Charles E. Motown Collection. Indiana University Archives of African American Music and Culture.

"Sylvia Moy." (United Kingdom) *Times*, April 22, 2017.

"Sylvia Moy." Interview by Charles E. Sykes. Filmed August 5, 1994, at Motown Museum in Detroit.

"Sylvia Moy: 15 Gold Records to Her Name and She's Only 28." *Detroit Free Press*, July 22, 1973.

Tee, Ralph. *Who's Who in Soul Music*. Weidenfeld and Nicolson, 1991.

Teegardin, Carol. "Song for the City: Musicians Tell How the Inaugural Theme Was Born." *Detroit Free Press*, December 18, 1993.

Waller, Don. *The Inside Story of America's Most Popular Music: The Motown Story*. Scribner, 1985.

Walling, Richard. "The Music Endures; the Payoff Does, Too." *USA Today*, June 11, 1998.

Wang, Oliver. "The Strange Sound of Motown's Early Hollywood Years." July 14, 2011.

Werner, Craig. "'Heaven Help Us All': Stevie Wonder, Michael Jackson, and the Meaning(s) of Motown in the Age of Obama." *Michigan Quarterly Review* 49, no. 4 (2010): 467.

Werner, Craig. *Higher Ground: Stevie Wonder, Aretha Franklin, Curtis Mayfield, and the Rise and Fall of American Soul.* Crown Archetype, 2007.

Werner, Craig. "Stevie Wonder: Singing in the Key of Life." Goldmine. October 8, 1999.

*What's Good with Stretch and Bobbito.* "Stevie Wonder." August 30, 2017. NPR.org.

Whitall, Susan. "'Little Stevie Wonder' Fearless: Blindness Doesn't Slow Detroit's Music Legend." *Detroit Free Press*, December 5, 1999.

White, Adam. *Motown: The Sound of Young America.* Thames & Hudson, 2016.

White, Adam. "Sylvia and Stevie: Inspiration and Influence." April 9, 2017. Westgrandblog.com.

Williams, Tenley, and James S. Brady. *Stevie Wonder.* Infobase Publishing, 2002.

Williams, Tenley, and James S. Brady. *Stevie Wonder: Overcoming Adversity.* Chelsea House Publishers, 2002.

Wilson, Michelle. *Motown's Sylvia Moy First Female Producer's Humble Beginnings.* June 1, 2014. Filmed August 2011 at Masterpiece Sound Studios and Motown.

Winkler, Gabriele, and Nina Degele. "Intersectionality as Multi-Level Analysis: Dealing with Social Inequality." *European Journal of Women's Studies* 18, no. 1 (2011): 51–66.

Winn, Ashley. "Songwriting Pioneer Sylvia Moy's Legacy Continues at Her Detroit Recording Studio." February 8, 2021.

Wright, Vickie et al. *Motown from the Background: The Authorized Biography of the Andantes.* Bank House Books, 2007.

Yenigun, Sami. "Stevie Wonder Reflects on Motown, God and Prince." August 30, 2017. NPR.

# Interviews

Celeste Moy, personal interview with the author, November 12, 2021.

Louvain Demps, personal interview with the author, November 22, 2021.

Merril Baronica "Ronnie" Moy Thompson Ward, personal interview with the author, December 2, 2022.

Merril Baronica "Ronnie" Moy Thompson Ward, personal interview with the author, December 3, 2022.

Merril Baronica "Ronnie" Moy Thompson Ward, personal interview with the author, January 23, 2022.

Patricia "Pat" S. Cosby, personal interview with the author, February 5, 2022.

Janie Bradford, personal interview with the author, February 8, 2022.

Patricia "Pat" S. Cosby, personal interview with the author, February 11, 2022.

Melvin Pernell Moy, personal interview with the author, February 12, 2022.

Christopher Moy, personal interview with the author, February 12, 2022.

Angelica "Angel" Moy Adams, personal interview with the author, February 19, 2022.

Ivy Jo Hunter, personal interview with the author, March 5, 2022.

Jackie Vernon Boyd, personal interview with the author, March 17, 2022.

William "Mickey" Stevenson, personal interview with the author, March 24, 2022.

William "Smokey" Robinson, personal interview with the author, March 24, 2022.

Paul Riser Sr., personal interview with the author, April 27, 2022.

Paul Riser Sr., personal interview with the author, April 29, 2022.

Barrett Strong, personal interview with the author, April 29, 2022.

Martha Reeves, personal interview with the author, May 2, 2022.

Cornelius Grant, personal interview with the author, May 20, 2022.

Anita Moy, personal interview with the author, June 18, 2022.

Louvain Demps, personal interview with the author, June 22, 2022.

Francetta Moy-Johnson, personal interview with the author, June 22, 2022.

Michelle B. Wilson, personal interview with the author, June 30, 2022.

Eddie Holland, personal interview with the author, May 12, 2023.

Dr. James Perone, personal interview with the author, May 26, 2023.

Dr. Charles Sykes, personal interview with the author, May 26, 2023.

Merril Baronica "Ronnie" Moy Thompson Ward, personal interview with the author, May 30, 2023.

Celeste Moy, email message to the author, February 5, 2024.

Celeste Moy, email message to the author, February 19, 2024.

Celeste Moy, email message to the author, April 29, 2024.

# Notes

**Introduction**

1. *Geraldo*, "The Women of Motown," October 19, 1990.

2. Stacy L. Smith et al., *Inclusion in the Recording Studio? Gender & Race/Ethnicity of Artists, Songwriters & Producers Across 1,200 Popular Songs from 2012 to 2023* (USC Annenberg Inclusion Initiative sponsored by Spotify, January 2024).

3. Smith et al., *Inclusion in the Recording Studio?*

**Chapter 1: "I Was Made to Love Her"**

1. "Sylvia Moy: 15 Gold Records to Her Name and She's Only 28," *Detroit Free Press*, July 22, 1973, 124.

2. Adam White, "Sylvia and Stevie: Inspiration and Influence," April 9, 2017, adampwhite.com.

3. "On the Influence of the Great Migration of the 1920s–50s," *Detroit Free Press*, May 31, 1999.

**Chapter 2: Banging on Pots and Pans**

1. "Sylvia Moy: 15 Gold Records to Her Name and She's Only 28." *Detroit Free Press*, July 22, 1973, 125.

2. Vickie Wright et al., *Motown from the Background* (Bank House Books, 2007), 185.

3. "Race Riot of 1943," Detroit Historical Society, Detroit Historical Society.org.

**Chapter 3: "I Ain't Too Proud to Beg"**

1. Kathryn Blaze Carlson, "Your Baby Is Dead: Mothers Say Their Supposedly Stillborn Babies Were Stolen from Them," March 23, 2012, NationalPost.com.

2. Carlson, "Your Baby Is Dead."

**Chapter 4: Coming to the Stage**

1. Wright et al., *Motown from the Background,* 121.

2. "Brill Building/Aldon Music/1650 Broadway," https://strathdee.wordpress.com/2015/05/27/brill-building-aldon-music-1650-broadway/.

3. Michelle Wilson, "Motown's Sylvia Moy First Female Producer's Humble Beginnings," June 1, 2014, filmed August 2011 at Masterpiece Sound Studios in Detroit, https://youtube/9T4TwM6PWIM.

4. Charles E. Sykes, Motown Collection, Indiana University Archives of African American Music and Culture.

**Chapter 5: Hitsville U.S.A. and the Motown Sound**

1. Berry Gordy, *To Be Loved: The Music, the Magic, the Memories of Motown* (Rosetta Books, Kindle, 2013), 137.

2. Gordy, *To Be Loved,* 152.

3. Lisa Robinson, "It Happened in Hitsville," *Vanity Fair,* December 13, 2008, VanityFair.com.

4. Gordy, *To Be Loved,* 165.

5. William M. Stevenson, "Motown's First A&R Man. William Mickey Stevenson" (Stevenson International Entertainment, 2015), 65.

6. John Swenson, *Stevie Wonder* (Harper & Row, 1986), 49.

7. Steve Lodder, *A Musical Guide to the Classical Albums* (Backbeat Books, 2005), 22.

8. Stevenson, "Motown's First A&R Man," 81.

9. Gordy, *To Be Loved,* 166.

10. David Carson, *Grit Noise and Revolution: The Birth of Detroit Rock 'N' Roll* (University of Michigan Press, 2006), 34.

11. Swenson, *Stevie Wonder,* 42.

12. Robinson, "It Happened in Hitsville."

13. Russell Hall, "Smokey Robinson: The Master of Motown," *Performing Songwriter* 7, no. 42 (December 1999).

14. "Trade Debates Black Terminology: Does 'African-American' Strike a Musical Note?" *Billboard* 101, no 8 (February 25, 1989): 1, 82.

15. David Brackett, "The Politics and Practice of 'Crossover' in American Popular Music, 1963 to 1965," *Musical Quarterly* 78, no. 4 (Winter 1994): 774.

16. "Trade Debates Black Terminology," 1, 82.

17 Gordy, *To Be Loved,* 215.

18. Gordy, *To Be Loved,* 198.

19. Gordy, *To Be Loved,* 222.

**Chapter 6: Change of Plans**

1. "Penobscot Building," Detroit Historical Society, Detroit Historical Society.org.

2. Charles E. Sykes, Motown Collection, Indiana University Archives of African American Music and Culture.

3. "Obituaries," *Telegraph*, April 20, 2017, telegraph.co.uk.

4. "Obituaries," *Telegraph*.

5. Peter Benjaminson, *The Story of Motown* (Barnacle Book, 2018), 75.

6. Brian McCollum, "Sylvia Moy, Motown Producer and Stevie Wonder Collaborator, Dies at 78," *Detroit Free Press*, April 17, 2017.

7. Sykes, Motown Collection.

8. Richard Pack, "Sylvia Moy: From Motown to MSR," *Soul Survivor* (Winter 1986–87), 22.

9. Pack, "Sylvia Moy," 20.

10. Wright et al., *Motown from the Background*, 123–24.

11. Sykes, Motown Collection.

12. Sykes, Motown Collection.

**Chapter 7: And Then Came You**

1. Stevenson, "Motown's First A&R Man," 77.

2. Gillian G. Gaar, *She's a Rebel: The History of Women in Rock & Roll*, 2nd ed. (Seal Press, 1992), 51.

3. "Sylvia Moy: 15 Gold Records to Her Name and She's Only 28," 125.

4. Sykes, Motown Collection.

5. Pack, "Sylvia Moy," 20.

6. Pack, "Sylvia Moy," 20.

7. Bill Dahl, *Motown: The Golden Years* (Krause Publications, 2001).

**Chapter 8: Little Stevie**

1. Ted Hull and Paula Stahel, *The Wonder Years: My Life & Times with Stevie Wonder* (Ted Hull, 2002), 18.

2. "Friday Night with Jonathan Ross: Stevie Wonder," interview by Jonathan Ross, series 15, episode 2, September 12, 2008.

3. Gordy, *To Be Loved*, 195.

4. Dennis Love and Stacy Brown, *Blind Faith: The Miraculous Journey of Lula Hardaway, Stevie Wonder's Mother* (Simon & Schuster, 2002), 161.

5. Sharon Davis, *Stevie Wonder: Rhythms of Wonder* (Robson Books, 2006), 32.

6. Mark Ribowsky, *Signed, Sealed, and Delivered: The Soulful Journey of Stevie Wonder* (John Wiley, 2010), 1666.

7. Tenley Williams and James S. Brady, *Stevie Wonder: Overcoming Adversity* (Chelsea House Publishers, 2020), 28.

**Chapter 9: No One-Hit Wonder**

1. Swenson, *Stevie Wonder*, 35.

2. Gordy, *To Be Loved*, 226–27.

3. Swenson, *Stevie Wonder*, 31.

4. Swenson, *Stevie Wonder*, 35.

5. Swenson, *Stevie Wonder*, 35.

6. Loraine Alterman, "Stevie Wonder," *Detroit Free Press*, March 17, 1967, Teen Beat, 44.

7. Hull and Stahel, *Wonder Years*, 16.

8. Jean Sharley, "Little Stevie Wonder and His Growing Pains," *Detroit Free Press*, December 5, 1965.

9. Williams and Brady, *Stevie Wonder: Overcoming Adversity*, 28.

10. Davis, *Stevie Wonder*, 38.

11. Davis, *Stevie Wonder*, 47.

12. Sykes, Motown Collection.

13. Swenson, *Stevie Wonder*, 39.

14. Hull and Stahel, *Wonder Years*, 72.

**Chapter 10: Trying Times**

1. Sharley, "Little Stevie Wonder."

2. Hull and Stahel, *Wonder Years*, 45.

3. Lodder, *Musical Guide*, 34.

4. George Chesterton, "The Blessed Stevie Wonder: The Blessing Is All Ours," May 13, 2021, GQ-magazine.co.uk.

5. Hull and Stahel, *Wonder Years*, 65.

6. Gordy, *To Be Loved*, 324–25.

7. Hull and Stahel, *Wonder Years*, 65.

8. Love and Brown, *Blind Faith*, 204.

9. Swenson, *Stevie Wonder*, 47–48.

10. Williams and Brady, *Stevie Wonder*, 30.

11. Love and Brown, *Blind Faith*, 206.

12. Davis, *Stevie Wonder*, 39.

13. David Breskin, "Waiting on the Man: Stevie Comes Down from the Mountaintop," *Musician*, no. 64 (February 1984): 56.

14. Sykes, Motown Collection.

15. Raynoma Gordy Singleton, *The Untold Story: Berry, Me, and Motown* (Contemporary Books, 1990), 184.

16. Wilson, "Motown's Sylvia Moy."

17. Sykes, Motown Collection.

18. Singleton, *Untold Story*, 184.

19. Wright et al., *Motown from the Background*, 122.

20. Gail Mitchell, "Motown Icon Valerie Simpson Talks 'Girls with Impact,' Songwriter Advice & New Projects," *Billboard*, March 8, 2023, Billboard.com.

21. Wright et al., *Motown from the Background*, 122.

22. Sykes, Motown Collection.

23. Sykes, Motown Collection.

24. "Sylvia Moy," (United Kingdom) *Times*, April 22, 2017, 81.

25. Sykes, Motown Collection.

26. Singleton, *Untold Story*, 184.

**Chapter 11: "Uptight"**

1. "Stevie Wonder's Tribute to Sylvia Moy at Her Funeral in Detroit," April 22, 2017 (Stream Stevie Wonder's tribute to Sylvia Moy at her funeral in Detroit by *Detroit Free Press*; listen online for free on SoundCloud).
2. Craig Werner, "Stevie Wonder: Singing in the Key of Life," Goldmine, October 8, 1999.
3. Sykes, Motown Collection.
4. Wright et al., *Motown from the Background*, 122.
5. Alterman, "Stevie Wonder."
6. Lodder, *Musical Guide*, 40.
7. Ribowsky, *Signed, Sealed, and Delivered*, 2449.
8. Dahl, *Motown*, 5038.
9. Hull and Stahel, *Wonder Years*, 63.
10. Breskin, "Waiting on the Man," 56.
11. Gordy, *To Be Loved*, 291.
12. Sykes, Motown Collection.
13. Singleton, *Untold Story*, 185.
14. Sykes, Motown Collection.
15. Sykes, Motown Collection.
16. Wright et al., *Motown from the Background*, 123.
17. Singleton, *Untold Story*, 185.

**Chapter 12: Credit, That's What I Want**

1. Gordy, *To Be Loved*, 288.
2. James E. Perone, *The Sound of Stevie Wonder: His Words and Music* (Praeger Publishing, 2006), 20–21.
3. Perone, *Sound of Stevie Wonder*, 20–21.
4. Brian McCollum, "Sylvia Moy, Motown Pioneer and Stevie Wonder Collaborator, Dies at 78," *Detroit Free Press*, April 17, 2017.
5. Breskin, "Waiting on the Man," 56.
6. Dahl, *Motown*.
7. Swenson, *Stevie Wonder*, 53.
8. Swenson, *Stevie Wonder*, 62.
9. Davis, *Stevie Wonder*, 57.
10. Susan Whitall, "'Little Stevie Wonder' Fearless: Blindness Doesn't Slow Detroit's Music Legend," *Detroit Free Press*, December 5, 1999, 9.
11. Pack, "Sylvia Moy," 22.
12. Pack, "Sylvia Moy," 22.

**Chapter 13: Writing to Win**

1. Pack, "Sylvia Moy," 20.
2. Sylvia Moy: 15 Gold Records to Her Name and She's Only 28," 125.

3. Sykes, Motown Collection.

4. Wright et al., *Motown from the Background*, 122.

5. Wright et al., *Motown from the Background*, 121.

6. Stuart Cosgrove, *Detroit 67: The Year That Changed Soul*, bk. 1 of *The Soul Trilogy* (Polygon, 2016), 35.

7. Stevenson, "Motown's First A&R Man," 173.

8. David Ritz, *Divided Soul: The Life of Marvin Gaye* (Da Capo Press, 1991), 61.

9. Rob Moss, "The Ivy Jo Hunter Story," October 29, 2013, Soul Source UK.

10. Gordy, *To Be Loved*, 312–13.

11. Singleton, *Untold Story*, 170.

12. Gordy, *To Be Loved*, 312–13.

13. Gallant, Trudy. "Motown Revue Reunion," American Black Journal, 1989, https://abj.matrix.msu.edu/videofull.php/id=198-733-519/.

14. Hull and Stahel, *Wonder Years*, 159.

15. Singleton, *Untold Story*, 173.

16. Gordy, *To Be Loved*, 313.

17. Stevenson, "Motown's First A&R Man," 178.

**Chapter 14: Signature Style**

1. Pack, "Sylvia Moy," 22.

2. Graham Betts, "Tears of a Clown–Smokey Robinson & the Miracles (single)," in *Motown Encyclopedia* (AC Publishing, 2014), 1083.

3. Singleton, *Untold Story*, 172.

4. "Sylvia Moy," *Times*.

5. Stevie Wonder on *The Mike Douglas Show*, 1967.

6. Pack, "Sylvia Moy," 22.

7. Wright et al., *Motown from the Background*, 123.

8. Farrell Evans. "The 1967 Riots: When Outrage over Racial Injustice Boiled Over." History.com, June 17, 2021.

9. Pack, "Sylvia Moy," 22.

**Chapter 15: "I Had a Dream"**

1. Pete Cain, "The Motown Mob," *Rock*, July 6, 1970.

2. Gerald Posner, *Motown: Music, Money, Sex, and Power* (Random House, 2005), 200; Cain, "Motown Mob," 32.

3. Cain, "Motown Mob," 32.

4. Singleton, *Untold Story*, 183.

5. Singleton, *Untold Story*, 173.

6. Cosgrove, *Detroit 67*, 205.

7. Cosgrove, *Detroit 67*, 205.

8. Singleton, *Untold Story*, 173.

9. Pack, "Sylvia Moy," 20.

10. Pack, "Sylvia Moy," 20.
11. Pack, "Sylvia Moy," 20.
12. Pack, "Sylvia Moy," 20.

**Chapter 16: The Hits Keep Coming**

1. Davis, *Stevie Wonder*, 52.
2. Zeth Lundy, *Songs in the Key of Life* (Bloomsbury, 2007), 77.
3. "BMI Award to 58 R&B Writers," *Billboard*, April 26, 1969.
4. "Sylvia Moy: 15 Gold Records to Her Name and She's Only 28."
5. "Obituaries," *Telegraph*, April 20, 2017, telegraph.co.uk.
6. Pack, "Sylvia Moy," 21.
7. McCollum, "Sylvia Moy."
8. Brian McCollum, "Detroit's 100 Greatest Songs: Counting Down 33 to 30," *Detroit Free Press*, June 19, 2016, E6.
9. Pack, "Sylvia Moy," 21.
10. Breskin, "Waiting on the Man," 56.
11. Allan "Dr. Licks" Slutsky, "Sidemen: Benny Benjamin," November 2019, RockHall.com.
12. Pack, "Sylvia Moy," 20.
13. Perone, *Sound of Stevie Wonder*, 20–21.

**Chapter 17: Staying Home**

1. Gallant, "Motown Revue Reunion."
2. Sykes, Motown Collection.
3. Pack, "Sylvia Moy," 22.
4. *Detroit Free Press*, November 10, 1974, 170.
5. Charlotte Robinson, "It's a House Full of Creativity: Lack of Funds Cloud Future," *Detroit Free Press*, August 23, 1974.
6. "Sylvia Moy: 15 Gold Records to Her Name and She's Only 28," 124.
7. Robinson, "Motown Revue," 25.
8. Pack, "Sylvia Moy," 22.
9. Robert MacNeil, *MacNeil/Lehrer NewsHour*, July 3, 1991, PBS.
10. Brian McCollum, "8 Mile Style: Eminem Producers Built on Rapper's Raw Potential," *Detroit Free Press*, August 11, 2002, 58.
11. Robinson, "Motown Revue," 23.
12. "New Detroit: A Racial Justice Organization," https://www.newdetroit.org/our-history/.
13. "Sylvia Moy: 15 Gold Records to Her Name and She's Only 28," 125.
14. Pack, "Sylvia Moy," 22.
15. Ian Levine, Cut Glass Featuring Ortheia Barnes, "Without Your Love," YouTube, March 27, 2007.
16. Pack, "Sylvia Moy," 22.
17. Pack, "Sylvia Moy," 22.

18. Pack, "Sylvia Moy," 22.

19. James Risen, "Motor City Records Is Trying to Bring a Piece of the Motown Sound to Its Birthplace in Detroit," *Los Angeles Times*, March 16, 1990, Entertainment.

20. Robert MacNeil, *MacNeil/Lehrer NewsHour*, February 7, 1990, PBS.

21. Singleton, *Untold Story*, 324.

22. Singleton, *Untold Story*, 325.

**Chapter 18: Making History in the Hall of Fame**

1. "Names and Faces: Briefly," *Detroit Free Press*, August 17, 1991, 2.

2. Carol Teegardin, "Song for the City: Musicians Tell How the Inaugural Theme Was Born," *Detroit Free Press*, December 18, 1993, 3.

3. Larry Gabriel, "The World Beyond Pop: Black Roots Music," *Detroit Free Press*, June 28, 1995, 53.

4. Gabriel, "World Beyond Pop," 53.

5. Gabriel, "World Beyond Pop," 53.

6. Richard Walling, "The Music Endures; the Payoff Does, Too," *USA Today*, June 11, 1998.

7. Songwriters Hall of Fame, https://www.songhall.org.

8. "Obituaries," *Telegraph*, April 20, 2017, 2, telegraph.co.uk.

9. White, "Sylvia and Stevie."

**Chapter 19: Winding Down**

1. Sam Adams, "Stevie Wonder and the Obamas: A Love Story," December 21, 2016, Slate .com, https://slate.com/culture/2016/12/stevie-wonder-and-the-obamas-a-love-story.html.

2 "Stevie Wonder to Accept Inaugural 'Key of Life' Award and Will Be Featured Keynote at 2017 ASCAP 'I Create Music' EXPO, April 13–15 in Los Angeles," March 16, 2017, ASCAP .com.

3. "Stevie Wonder's Tribute to Sylvia Moy at Her Funeral in Detroit," April 22, 2017 (Stream Stevie Wonder's tribute to Sylvia Moy at her funeral in Detroit by *Detroit Free Press*; listen online for free on SoundCloud).

4. Brian McCollum, "Motown Greats Pay Tribute to Sylvia Moy at Funeral," *Detroit Free Press*, April 23, 2017, Freep.com.

5. Daniel Kreps, "Stevie Wonder Pays Tribute to Motown Songwriter Sylvia Moy," *Rolling Stone*, April 18, 2017, RollingStone.com.

# Index